Appalachian Trail Guide to

SHENANDOAH NATIONAL PARK
with side trails

1991
Tenth Edition

THE POTOMAC APPALACHIAN TRAIL CLUB
118 Park St., S.E.
Vienna, Virginia 22180

Tenth Edition
Edited
by
Jean Golightly

Photos by Nick Williams

Printing History

The area covered in this Guide was originally part of a more comprehensive publication known as *Guide to Paths in the Blue Ridge*. The first version was issued in 1931, and referred to Virginia only. In a second edition in 1934, the area covered was extended to include Pennsylvania and Maryland; supplements were issued in 1935 and 1937. The third edition was published in 1941 and the fourth in 1950. In 1959, the comprehensive guidebook was divided into three sections, one of which covered the area represented by this Guide. Subsequent editions were published in 1967, 1973, 1977 and 1986.

L.C. No. 86-61071
ISBN 0-915746-42-5

In a Guide this size it is inevitable that errors, both typographical and factual, will occur. Please report any you find to the editor, in care of PATC Headquarters, so that they may be corrected in future editions.

In Memory

This book is dedicated to the mem
Denton, active member of Potomac
Club from 1960-1991 and editor of t
1967-1989. Molly knew Shenandoah
well as most of us know our own ba
with husband Jim, hiked all of the
about them from first hand experien
the years have been greatly appreci
community.

Acknowledgments

The current revision of this guidebook has been made possible through the cooperation of many folks, both in the Potomac Appalachian Trail Club and in Shenandoah National Park. A special thanks to George Walters, Nick Williams and Larry Linebrink of PATC for their assistance in reviewing the *AT* portions, and Steve Bair, Laurie Shannon and Shawn Green of Shenandoah National Park for their help with the side trails. Many thanks, also, to the numerous trail overseers who brought corrections to my attention and who work diligently year round to keep the trails in good condition.

A special thanks to Lee Collyer and Bill Grant for their help with the nitty gritty and their patient instruction to a novice computer operator; also to Mary Holmes for her help with proof-reading.

Jean Golightly, Editor 1991

ABBREVIATIONS

AT	Appalachian Trail
mi.	mile or miles
PATC	Potomac Appalachian Trail Club
SNP	Shenandoah National Park
SDMP	Skyline Drive milepost
USGS	United States Geological Survey
SR	secondary road

USE OF MILEAGE NUMBERS

In the section titled "Side Trails", wherever two series of mileages are given (example: 0.0-9.2), the lefthand figures are the mileages in the direction as described, the figures to the right are the mileages in the reverse direction.

TABLE OF CONTENTS

Appalachian Trail Data: US 522 to Rockfish Gap

USE OF GUIDE AND TRAIL

This guide is one of a series of guidebooks covering the entire Appalachian Trail (*AT*) from Maine to Georgia. The Potomac Appalachian Trail Club is responsible for preparing this guide, Volume 7 in the series, and also Volume 6 covering the area extending north from Shenandoah National Park to the Maryland-Pennsylvania border.

Format of Guidebook

Shenandoah National Park falls naturally into three districts, northern, central and southern, each defined by a major road crossing of the Blue Ridge and an entrance station to Skyline Drive. The Trail data are divided into 9 sections, demarcated by Blue Ridge gaps and numbered from north to south. The Northern District includes Sections 1 and 2, the Central District includes Sections 3,4 and 5 and the Southern District includes Sections 6,7,8 and 9. Within each section, the Trail Description is given first from north to south, followed by the same information given from south to north.

For each section, both general information and detailed Trail data are provided:

- The general information includes a brief description of the overall route and notes features of particular scenic or historic interest; it lists side trails, trail approaches, accommodations (huts and cabins), and appropriate PATC or USGS maps.

- The detailed data are designated for on-the-Trail use by hikers. They briefly describe the beginning and end of each Trail section, outline geographical features and mileages which would be useful in following it, and note precise location of accommodations (huts and cabins), water and side trails.

The Trails

This guide provides information on 107.1 miles of the Appalachian Trail and over 500 miles of side trails of various types. Of the total *AT* mileage, 94.9 is within the Park and 11.8 is outside (3.8 miles at the northern end and 8.0 miles at the southern end).

Trail Markings

At key points along the *AT* and side trails the Park Service has erected concrete posts which provide trail information. The data are stamped on metal bands ringing the posts.

The Appalachian Trail itself is marked by white paint blazes, each about 2" by 6". A double blaze (two blazes, one placed above the other) is placed as a warning sign. It may indicate an obscure turn or a change in direction which otherwise might not be noticed.

Blue-blazed side trails may be used for foot travel only. Most are maintained by the Potomac Appalachian Trail Club.

Yellow-blazed trails are for use of both horses and foot travelers. Most are maintained by Shenandoah National Park crews with some assigned to horse riding groups. Most Park fire roads are yellow-blazed. Horses are limited to trails, including fire roads, that are yellow-blazed.

Park Service stroller trails and nature trails, usually short in length, are marked with appropriate signs and are easily followed.

Trail Use

Those using the *AT* or side trails should, of course, be very careful not to damage property or to litter. Park regulations forbid the use of any motorized vehicle on trails. Fire and camping regulations are listed in detail. Cutting of any standing tree, dead or alive, is prohibited. Flowers should not be picked. All forms of wildlife are protected and firearms are prohibited.

Some of the side trails have their lower ends outside the Park on private land. Owners can and sometimes do close them to hikers - usually after some unfortunate event. It is, therefore, *extremely important that private property rights be respected.* If you are unsure about current status of boundary access on private land, check with SNP.

Trail Maps

Three detailed maps of trails in the Shenandoah National Park are available in the Park, from Potomac Appalachian Trail Club and from various outdoor shops. It is recommended that they be used in conjunction with this guide. The maps correspond to the three major divisions of the Park, Northern District, Central District, and Southern District, and are numbered respectively 9, 10, and 11. The maps have been prepared by the Maps Committee of the Potomac Appalachian Trail Club and are based on U.S. Geological Survey quadrangles.

Appropriate USGS quadrangles may be purchased by mail from: USGS Map Sales, Box 25286, Denver, CO 80225. Walk-in sales are available from USGS offices in Reston, Va. (12201 Sunrise Valley Drive) and Washington D.C. (18th and E Sts. N.W., Room 2650).

Park Regulations-General

1. Dogs are not permitted in the Park except on leash. They are prohibited on certain trails which are posted by appropriate signs.

2. No open wood or charcoal fires may be kindled except in fireplaces provided at trailside shelters and those provided in established picnic grounds and campgrounds.

3. No lighted cigarette, cigar, pipe heel, match or other burning material shall be thrown from any vehicle or saddle horse, or dropped into any grass, leaves, twigs, tree mold or other combustible or inflammable material. Smoking within the Park may be prohibited or limited

by the superintendent when, in his judgment, a current fire hazard makes such action expedient.

4. The use of fireworks or firecrackers in the Park is prohibited.

Camping Regulations

1. Permits are required for backcountry camping. See next section.

2. At public campgrounds the regular fireplaces constructed for the convenience of visitors must be used. Firewood is sold at the waysides during the summer travel season.

3. No person, party or organization shall be permitted to camp in any public camping area in the Park for more than 14 days in any calendar year.

4. The installation of permanent camping facilities by visitors is prohibited. The digging or leveling of the ground in any campsite is prohibited.

5. Campers shall not leave their camps unattended for more than 24 hours without special permission from superintendent, obtained in advance. Camping equipment left unattended in any public camping area for more than 24 hours is subject to removal by order of the superintendent, the expense of such removal to be paid by the person or persons leaving such equipment.

6. The superintendent may, with the approval of the Director of the National Park Service, establish hours during which quiet must be maintained at any camp, and prohibit the running of motors at or near a camp during such hours.

7. At all campsites, food or similar organic material must be either: (1) completely sealed in a vehicle or camping unit that is constructed of solid, nonpliable material; or (2) suspended at least ten (10) feet above the ground and four (4) feet horizontally from any post, tree trunk or branch. This restriction does not apply to food that is in the process of being transported, being eaten or being prepared for eating.

Backcountry Camping Regulations

Definition of Terms

For purposes of clarification, at Shenandoah National Park "backcountry camping" is defined as any use of portable shelter or sleeping equipment in the backcountry. "Backcountry" is defined as those areas of the Park which are more than 250 yards from a paved road, and more than one-half mile from any Park facilities other than trails, unpaved roads and trail shelters.

Permit Required

No person or group of persons traveling together may camp without a valid backcountry camping permit. The issuance of this permit may be denied when such action is necessary to protect Park resources or Park visitors, or to regulate levels of visitor use in legislatively-designated wilderness areas. Permits are available without charge at Park headquarters, all entrance stations, all visitor centers and at the self-service backcountry permit booth on the Appalachian Trail at its northern entrance to the Park. Requests for permits by mail must be accompanied by the camper's name, address, number in party and the location and date of each overnight camp.

Group Size

No person may camp in or with a group of more than nine (9) other persons.

Location of Camp

No person or group may backcountry camp:

(1) within 250 yards of, or in view from, any paved Park road or the Park boundary;

(2) within one-half mile of, or in view from, any automobile campground, lodge, restaurant, visitor center, picnic area, ranger station, administrative or maintenance area, or other Park development or facility except a trail, an unpaved road or a trail shelter;

(3) on, or in view from, any trail or unpaved road, or within sight of any sign which has been posted by Park authorities to designate a no camping area;

(4) within view of another camping party or trail shelter;

(5) within 25 feet of any stream.

Duration of Stay

No person shall backcountry camp more than two (2) consecutive nights at a single location. The term "location" shall mean that particular campsite and the surrounding area within a two hundred fifty (250) yard radius of that campsite.

Fires

No open wood or charcoal fires may be kindled in backcountry areas except in fireplaces provided at trailside shelters. The use of small gasoline, propane or solid fuel camping stoves is recommended.

Fires must not be left unattended.

Water

Although the Park may have sources of clean, potable water, any water source can become polluted. Most water sources along the trails (with the exception of public campgrounds) are unprotected and consequently very susceptible to contamination. All water should be purified, preferably by boiling or filtering with a portable water filtering system.

Avoid contaminating the water supply and the surrounding area. Dishes, clothes and hands should never be washed in the water supply. Water should be drawn from the supply and washing done elsewhere.

Dogs

Dogs must be on a leash at all times. Dogs are prohibited on certain trails which are posted by appropriate signs.

Bears

At all campsites, food or similar organic material must be suspended at least 10 feet above the ground and 4 feet horizontally from any post, tree trunk or branch. This restriction does not apply to food that is in the process of being transported, being eaten or being prepared.

Sanitation

No disposing of refuse in other than refuse receptacles. Burnable trash may only be burned at fireplaces located at huts, shelters or public campgrounds. Park regulations prohibit glass containers in the backcountry.

No bathing or washing of food, clothing, dishes, or other property at public water outlets, fixtures or pools, except at those designated for such purpose.

No polluting or contaminating of Park area waters - springs, streams, etc.

In developed areas, no disposal of human body waste, except at designated locations or in fixtures provided for that purpose.

In non-developed areas, no disposal of human body waste within 10 yards of any stream, trail, unpaved road or Park facility. Fecal matter must be placed in a hole and covered with at least 3" of soil.

Other

The cutting of green boughs for beds is prohibited.

The digging or leveling of the ground in any campsite without a ranger's permission is prohibited.

Any article likely to frighten horses shall not be hung near a road or trail used by horses.

Hunting or possession of fire-arms is prohibited. No camp may be established in the Park and used as a base for hunting outside the Park.

Saddle, pack or draft animals shall not be kept in or near any camping area.

Clothing and Equipment

Hikers should keep in mind that temperatures are often much lower along the Blue Ridge crest than at low elevations, especially in winter. Snow accumulates sooner and lasts much longer in the Park than it does in the Washington area. In addition, when hiking along exposed ridges in windy weather, one must consider the wind chill factor as well as the actual temperature.

Long pants offer considerable protection from snakes, poison ivy and nettles. In rainy weather water repellant jackets or ponchos are advisable and it is wise to have a set of dry clothes to change into.

Good shoes or boots are important if one is hiking very far. Special attention should be given to obtaining comfortable shoes with non-slip soles and heels.

The amount of equipment needed will, naturally, vary with the length of hike. But, in general, it is good advice to carry at least a compass, a first aid kit, a whistle and a small canteen (or a large canteen in hot weather).

Do not depend on springs for water during hot, dry weather. Carry enough water for your needs. Back-country users are encouraged to purify all unprotected surface water.

Distress Signals

An emergency call for distress consists of three short calls, audible or visible, repeated at regular intervals. A whistle is particularly good for audible signals. Visible signals may include a light flashed with a mirror in daytime or flashlight at night. (Do this only in a genuine emergency).

Anyone recognizing such a signal should acknowledge it by a signal of two calls - if possible by the same method of signaling. Then, obviously, he should go to the distressed and determine the nature of the emergency. If more competent aid is needed, he should try to arrange it.

Emergencies

Report emergencies to a ranger or to any uniformed personnel at Front Royal Entrance Station, Dickey Ridge Visitor Center, Piney River Ranger Station, Park Headquarters, Big Meadows, Swift Run Gap Entrance Station, Simmons Gap Ranger Station or Rockfish Gap Entrance Station; or call emergency number at 999-2227.

First Aid along the Trail
by Robert Ohler, M.D., and the Appalachian Trail
Conference

Hikers encounter a wide variety of terrain and climatic conditions along the Appalachian Trail. Prepare for the possibility of injuries. Some of the more common Trail-related medical problems are briefly discussed below.

Preparation is key to a safe trip. If possible, every hiker should take the free courses in advanced first aid and cardiopulmonary-resuscitation (CPR) techniques offered in most communities by the American Red Cross.

Even without this training, you can be prepared for accidents. Emergency situations can develop. Analyses of serious accidents have shown that a substantial number originate at home, in the planning stage of the trip.

Think about communications. Have you informed your relatives and friends about your expedition: locations, schedule, and time of return? Has all of your equipment been carefully checked? Considering the season and altitude, have you provided for water, food, and shelter?

While hiking, set your own comfortable pace. If you are injured or lost or a storm strikes, stop. Remember, your brain is your most important survival tool. Inattention can start a chain of events leading to disaster.

If an accident occurs, treat the injury first. If outside help is needed, at least one person should stay with the injured hiker. Two people should go for help and carry with them notes on the exact location of the accident, what has been done to aid the injured, and what help is needed.

The injured will need encouragement, assurances of help, and confidence in your competence. Treat him gently. Keep him supine, warm, and quiet. Protect him from the weather with insulation below and above him. Examine him carefully, noting all possible injuries.

General Emergencies

Back or neck injuries: Immobilize the victim's entire body, where he lies. Protect head and neck from movement if the neck is injured, and treat as a fracture. Transportation must be on a rigid frame, such as a litter or a door. The spinal cord could be severed by inexpert handling. This type of injury must be handled by a large group of experienced personnel. Obtain outside help.

Bleeding: Stop the flow of blood by using a method appropriate to the amount and type of bleeding. Exerting pressure over the wound with the fingers, with or without a dressing, may be sufficient. Minor arterial bleeding can be controlled with local pressure and bandaging. Major arterial bleeding might require compressing an artery against a bone to stop the flow of blood. Elevate the arm or legs above the heart. To stop bleeding from an artery in the leg, place a hand in the groin and press toward the inside of the leg. Stop arterial bleeding from an arm by placing a hand between the armpit and elbow and pressing toward the inside of the arm.

Apply a tourniquet only if you are unable to control severe bleeding by pressure and elevation. Warning: This method should be used only when the limb will be lost anyway. Once applied, a tourniquet should only be removed by medical personnel equipped to stop the bleeding by other means and to restore lost blood. The tourniquet should be located between the wound and the heart. If there is a traumatic amputation (loss of hand, leg, or foot), place the tourniquet two inches above the amputation.

Blisters: Good boot fit, without points of irritation or pressure, should be proven before a hike. Always keep feet dry while hiking. Prevent blisters by responding early to any discomfort. Place adhesive tape or moleskin over areas of developing redness or soreness. If irritation can be relieved, allow blister fluid to be reabsorbed. If a blister forms and continued irritation makes draining it necessary, wash the area with soap and water and prick the edge of the blister with a needle that has been sterilized by the flame of a match. Bandage with a sterile gauze pad and moleskin.

Dislocation of a leg or arm joint is extremely painful. Do not try to put it back in place. Immobilize the entire limb with splints in the position it is found.

Exhaustion is caused by inadequate food consumption, dehydration and salt deficiency, overexertion, or all three. The victim may lose motivation, slow down, gasp for air, complain of weakness, dizziness, nausea, or headache. Treat by feeding, especially carbohydrates. Slowly replace lost water (normal fluid intake should be two to four quarts per day). Give salt dissolved in water (one teaspoon per cup). In the case of overexertion, rest is essential.

Fractures of legs, ankles, or arms must be splinted before moving the victim. After treating wounds, use any available material that will offer firm support, such as tree branches or boards. Pad each side of the arm or leg with soft material, supporting and immobilizing the joints above and below the injury. Bind the splints together with strips of cloth.

Shock should be expected after all injuries. It is a potentially fatal depression of bodily functions that is made more critical with improper handling, cold, fatigue, and anxiety. Relieve the pain as quickly as possible. Do not administer aspirin if severe bleeding is present; Tylenol or other nonaspirin pain relievers are safe.

Look for nausea, paleness, trembling, sweating, or thirst. Lay the hiker flat on his back, and raise his feet slightly, or position him, if he can be safely moved, so his head is down the slope. Protect him from the wind, and keep him as warm as possible. A campfire will help.

Sprains: Look or feel for soreness or swelling. Bandage and treat as a fracture. Cool and raise joint.

Wounds (except eye wounds) should be cleaned with soap and water. If possible, apply a clean dressing to protect the wound from further contamination.

Chilling and Freezing Emergencies

Every hiker should be familiar with the symptoms, treatment, and methods of preventing the common and sometimes fatal condition of *hypothermia*. Wind chill and/or body wetness, particularly aggravated by fatigue and hunger, can rapidly drain body heat to dangerously low levels. This often occurs at temperatures well above freezing. Shivering, lethargy, mental slowing, and confusion are early symptoms of hypothermia, which can begin without the victim's realizing it and, if untreated, can lead to death.

Always keep dry, spare clothing and a water-repellent windbreaker in your pack, and wear a hat in chilling weather. Wet clothing loses much of its insulating value, although wet wool is warmer than other wet fabrics. Always, when in chilling conditions, suspect the onset of hypothermia.

To treat this potentially fatal condition, immediately seek shelter and warm the entire body, preferably by placing it in a sleeping bag and administering warm liquids. The addition of another person's body heat may aid in warming.

A sign of *frostbite* is grayish or waxy, yellow-white spots on the skin. The frozen area will be numb. To thaw, warm the frozen part by direct contact with bare flesh. When first frozen, a cheek, nose, or chin can often be thawed by covering with a hand taken from a warm glove. Superficially frostbitten hands sometimes can be thawed by placing them under armpits, on the stomach, or between the thighs. With a partner, feet can be treated similarly. Do not rub frozen flesh.

Frozen layers of deeper tissue beneath the skin are characterized by a solid, "woody" feeling and an inability to move the flesh over bony prominences. Tissue loss is minimized by rapid rewarming of the area in water slightly below 105 degrees Fahrenheit (measure accurately with a thermometer).

Thawing of a frozen foot should not be attempted until the patient has been evacuated to a place where rapid, controlled thawing can take place. Walking on a frozen foot is entirely possible and does not cause increased damage. Walking after thawing is impossible.

Never rewarm over a stove or fire. This "cooks" flesh and results in extensive loss of tissue.

Treatment of a deep freezing injury after rewarming must be done in a hospital.

Heat Emergencies

Exposure to extremely high temperatures, high humidity, and direct sunlight can cause health problems.

Heat cramps are usually caused by strenuous activity in high heat and humidity, when sweating depletes salt levels in blood and tissues. Symptoms are intermittent cramps in legs and abdominal wall and painful spasms of muscles. Pupils of eyes may dilate with each spasm. The skin becomes cold and clammy. Treat with rest and salt dissolved in water (one teaspoon of salt per glass).

Heat exhaustion, caused by physical exercise during prolonged exposure to heat, is a breakdown of the body's heat-regulating system. The circulatory system is disrupted, reducing the supply of blood to vital organs such as the brain, heart, and lungs. The victim can have heat cramps and sweat heavily. Skin is moist and cold with face flushed, then pale. Pulse can be unsteady and blood pressure low. He may vomit and be delirious. Place the victim in shade, flat on his back, with feet 8-12 inches higher than head. Give him sips of salt water - half a glass every 15 minutes - for about an hour. Loosen his clothes. Apply cold cloths.

Heat stroke and *sun stroke* are caused by the failure of the heat-regulating system to cool the body by sweating. They are emergency, life-threatening conditions. Body temperature can rise to 106 degrees or higher. Symptoms include weakness, nausea, headache, heat cramps, exhaustion, body temperature rising rapidly, pounding pulse, and high blood pressure. The victim may be delirious or comatose. Sweating will stop before heat stroke becomes apparent. Armpits may be dry and skin flushed and pink, then turning ashen or purple in later stages. Move victim to cool place immediately. Cool the body in any way possible (*e.g.*, sponging). Body temperature must be regulated artificially from outside of the body until the heat-regulating system can be rebalanced. Be careful not to overchill once temperature goes below 102 degrees.

Heat weakness: Symptoms are fatigue, headache, mental and physical inefficiency, heavy sweating, high pulse rate, and general weakness. Drink plenty of water, find as cool a spot as possible, keep quiet, and replenish salt loss.

Sunburn causes redness of the skin, discoloration, swelling, and pain. It occurs rapidly and can be severe at higher elevations. It can be prevented by applying a commercial sun screen; zinc oxide is the most effective. Treat by protecting from further exposure and covering the area with ointment and a dressing. Give the victim large amounts of fluids.

Artificial Respiration

Artificial respiration might be required when an obstruction constricts the air passages or after respiratory failure caused by air being depleted of oxygen, such as after electrocution, by drowning, or because of toxic gases in the air. Quick action is necessary if the victim's lips, fingernail beds, or tongue have become blue, if he is unconscious, or if the pupils of his eyes become enlarged. If food or a foreign body is lodged in the air passage and coughing is ineffective, try to remove it with the fingers. If the foreign body is inaccessible, grasp the victim from behind, and with one hand hold the opposite wrist just below the breastbone. Squeeze rapidly and firmly, expelling air forcibly from the lungs to expel the foreign body. Repeat this maneuver two to three times, if necessary.

If breathing stops, administer artificial respiration, as air can be forced around the obstruction into the lungs. The mouth-to-mouth, or mouth-to-nose, method of forcing air into the victim's lungs should be used. The preferred method is:

1. Clear the victim's mouth of any obstructions.
2. Place one hand under the victim's neck and lift.
3. Place heel of other hand on the forehead, and tilt head backwards. (Maintain this position during procedure.) Use thumb and index finger to pinch nostrils.
4. Open your mouth, and make a seal with it over victim's mouth. If the victim is a small child, cover both the nose and the mouth.
5. Breathe deeply, and blow out about every five seconds, or 12 breaths a minute.
6. Watch victim's chest for expansion.
7. Listen for exhalation.

Lyme Disease

Lyme disease is contracted from bites of certain infected ticks. Hikers should be aware of the symptoms and monitor themselves and their partners for signs of the disease. When treated early, Lyme disease usually can be cured with antibiotics.

Inspect yourself for ticks and tick bites at the end of each day. The four types of ticks known to spread Lyme disease are smaller than the dog tick, about the size of a pin head, and not easily seen. They are often called "deer ticks" because they feed during one stage of their life cycle on deer, a host for the disease.

The early signs of a tick bite infected with Lyme disease are a red spot with a white center that enlarges and spreads, severe fatigue, chills, headaches, muscle aches, fever, malaise, and a stiff neck. However, one-quarter of all people with an infected tick bite show none of the early symptoms.

Later effects of the disease, which may not appear for months or years, are severe fatigue, dizziness, shortness of breath, cardiac irregularities, memory and concentration problems, facial paralysis, meningitis, shooting pains in the arms and legs, and other symptoms resembling multiple sclerosis, brain tumors, stroke, alcoholism, mental depression, Alzheimer's disease, and anorexia nervosa.

Some doctors are not yet well-informed about the disease and can misdiagnose the symptoms. It may be necessary to contact a university medical center or other research center if you suspect you have been bitten by an infected tick. It is not believed people can build a lasting immunity to Lyme disease. For that reason, a hiker who has contracted and been treated for the disease should still take precautions.

Lightning Strikes

Although the odds of being struck by lightning are low, 200 to 400 people a year are killed by lightning in the United States. Respect the force of lightning, and seek shelter during a storm.

Do not start a hike if thunderstorms are likely. If caught in a storm, immediately find shelter. Hard-roofed automobiles or large buildings are best; tents and convertible automobiles offer no protection. When indoors, stay away from windows, open doors, fireplaces, and large metal objects. Do not hold a potential lightning rod, such as a fishing pole. Avoid tall structures, such as ski lifts, flagpoles, powerline towers, and the tallest trees or hilltops. If you cannot enter a building or car, take shelter in a stand of smaller trees. Avoid clearings. If caught in the open, crouch down, or roll into a ball. If you are in water, get out. Spread out groups, so that everyone is not struck by a single bolt. If a person is struck by lightning or splashed by a charge hitting a nearby object, the victim will probably be thrown, perhaps a great distance. Clothes can be burned or torn. Metal objects (such as belt buckles) may be hot, and shoes blown off. The victim often has severe muscle contractions (which can cause breathing difficulties), confusion, and temporary blindness or deafness. In more severe cases, the victim may have feathered or sunburst patterns of burns over the skin or ruptured eardrums. He may lose consciousness or breath irregularly. Occasionally, victims stop breathing and suffer cardiac arrest.

If someone is struck by lightning, perform artificial respiration and CPR until emergency technicians arrive or you can transport the injured to a hospital. Lightning victims may be unable to breathe independently for 15 to 30 minutes but can recover quickly once they can breathe on their own. Do not give up early; a seemingly lifeless individual can be saved if you breathe for him promptly after the strike.

Assume that the victim was thrown a great distance; protect the spine, treat other injuries, then transport him to the hospital.

Snakebites

Hikers on the Appalachian Trail may encounter copperheads or timber rattlesnakes on their journey. These are pit vipers, characterized by triangular heads, vertical elliptical pupils, two or less hinged fangs on the front part of the jaw (fangs are replaced every six to ten weeks), heat-sensory facial pits on the sides of the head, and a single row of scales on the underbelly by the tail.

The best way to avoid being bitten by poisonous snakes is to avoid their known habitats and reaching into dark areas (use a walking stick to move suspicious objects). Wear protective clothing, especially on feet and lower legs. Do not hike alone or at night in snake territory; always have a flashlight and walking stick. Do not handle snakes. A dead snake can bite and envenomate you with a reflex action for 20 to 60 minutes.

Not all snakebites result in envenomation, even if the snake is poisonous. The signs of envenomation are one or more fang marks in addition to rows of teeth marks, burning pain, and swelling at the bite (swelling usually begins within five to ten minutes of envenomation and can become very severe). Lips, face, and scalp may tingle and become numb 30 to 60 minutes after the bite. (If these symptoms are immediate and the victim is frightened and excited, then they are most likely due to hyperventilation). Thirty to 90 minutes after the bite, the victim's eyes and mouth may twitch, and he may have a rubbery or metallic taste in his mouth. He may sweat, experience weakness, nausea and vomiting, or faint one to two hours after the bite. Bruising at the bite usually begins within two to three hours, and large blood blisters may develop within six to ten hours. The victim may have difficulty breathing, have bloody urine, vomit blood, and may collapse six to 12 hours after the bite.

If someone you are with has been bitten by a snake, act quickly. *The definitive treatment for snake-venom poisoning is the proper administration of antivenom. Get the victim to a hospital immediately.*

Keep the victim calm. Increased activity can spread the venom and the illness. Retreat out of snake's striking range, but try to identify it. If you cannot do this easily, kill the snake with a blow to the head, and take it to the medical facility so the authorities can identify it and estimate the amount of antivenom necessary. (Remember to carry the snake in a container so that the jaws' reflex action cannot harm someone else.) Check for signs of envenomation.

Immediately transport the victim to the nearest hospital. If possible, splint the body part that was bitten, to avoid unnecessary motion. If a limb was bitten, keep it at a level below the heart. ***Do not apply ice directly to the wound***. If it will take longer than two hours to reach medical help, and the bite is on an arm or leg, place a 2"x 2", 1/4"- thick cloth pad over the bite and firmly wrap the limb (ideally with an elastic wrap) directly over the bite and six inches on either side, taking care to check for adequate circulation to the fingers and toes. This wrap may slow the spread of venom.

First-Aid Kit

The following kit is suggested for those who have had no first-aid or other medical training. It costs about $15, weighs about a pound, and occupies about a 3" x 6" x 9" space.

Eight 4" x 4" gauze pads	One 3" Ace bandage
Four 3" x 4" gauze pads	Twenty salt tablets
Five 2" bandages	One 3" x 4" moleskin
Ten 1" bandages	Three safety pins
Six alcohol prep pads	One small scissors
Ten large butterfly closures	One tweezers
One triangular bandage (40")	Personal medications
Two 3" rolls of gauze	as necessary
Twenty tablets of aspirin-free	One 15' roll of 2"
pain killer	adhesive tape

References
Red Cross first-aid manuals.

Mountaineering First Aid : A Guide to Accident Response and First Aid, The Mountaineers, Seattle, 1985.

Emergency Survival Handbook, by the American Safety League, 1985. A pocket-sized book and survival kit with easy instructions.

Medicine For the Outdoors: A Guide to Emergency Medical Procedures and First Aid, by Paul S. Auerbach, M.D., Little Brown & Co., Boston, 1986.

THE APPALACHIAN TRAIL

The Appalachian Trail (*AT*) is a continuous, marked footpath extending 2,144 miles from Katahdin, a granite monolith in the central Maine wilderness, south to Springer Mountain in Georgia along the crest of the Appalachian mountain range.

The Trail traverses mostly public land in 14 states. Virginia has the longest section, with 536 miles, while West Virginia has the shortest, almost 26 miles along the Virginia-West Virginia boundary and a short swing into Harpers Ferry at the Maryland border. The highest elevation along the Trail is 6,643 feet at Clingmans Dome in the Great Smoky Mountains. The Trail is only slightly above sea level near its crossing of the Hudson River in New York.

Trail History

Credit for establishing the Trail belongs to three leaders and countless volunteers. The first proposal for the Trail to appear in print was an article by regional planner Benton MacKaye of Shirley, Massachusetts, entitled,"An Appalachian Trail, a Project in Regional Planning," in the October 1921 issue of the *Journal of the American Institute of Architects*. He envisioned a footpath along the Appalachian ridge line where urban people could retreat to nature.

MacKaye's challenge kindled considerable interest, but at the time most of the outdoor organizations that could participate in constructing such a trail were east of the Hudson River. Four existing trail systems could be incorporated into an Appalachian Trail. The Appalachian Mountain Club (AMC) maintained an excellent series of trails in New England, but most ran north-south; the Trail could not cross New Hampshire until the chain of huts built and operated by the AMC permitted an east-west alignment. In Vermont, the southern 100 miles of the Long Trail, then being developed in the Green Mountains, were connected to the White Mountains by the trails of the Dartmouth Outing Club.

In 1923, a number of area hiking clubs that had formed the New York-New Jersey Trail Conference opened the first new section of the *AT*, in the Harriman-Bear Mountain section of Palisades Interstate Park.

The Appalachian Trail Conference (ATC) was formed in 1925 to stimulate greater interest in MacKaye's idea and coordinate the clubs' work in choosing and building the route. The Conference remains a nonprofit educational organization of individuals and clubs of volunteers dedicated to maintaining, managing, and protecting the Appalachian Trail.

Although interest in the Trail spread to Pennsylvania and New England, little further work was done until 1926, when retired Judge Arthur Perkins of Hartford, Connecticut, began persuading groups to locate and cut the footpath through the wilderness. His enthusiasm provided the momentum that carried the Trail idea forward.

The southern states had had few trails and even fewer clubs. The "skyline" route followed by the *AT* in the South was developed largely within the new national forests. A number of clubs were formed in various parts of the southern Appalachians to take responsibility for the Trail there.

Perkins interested Myron H. Avery in the Trail. Avery, who served as chairman of the Conference from 1931 to 1952, enlisted the aid and coordinated the work of hundreds of volunteers who completed the Trail by August 14, 1937, when a Civilian Conservation Corps crew opened the last section (on the ridge between Spaulding and Sugarloaf mountains in Maine). At the eighth meeting of the ATC, in June 1937, Conference member Edward B. Ballard successfully proposed a plan for an "Appalachian Trailway" that would set apart an area on each side of the Trail, dedicated to the interests of those who travel on foot.

Steps taken to effect this long-range protection program culminated first in an October 15, 1938, agreement between the National Park Service and the U.S. Forest Service for the promotion of an Appalachian Trailway, through the relevant national parks and forests, extending one mile on each side of the Trail. Within this zone, no new parallel roads would be built or any other incompatible development allowed. Timber cutting would not be permitted within 200 feet of the Trail. Similar agreements, creating a zone one-quarter mile in width, were signed with most states through which the Trail passes.

After World War II, the encroachments of highways, housing developments, and summer resorts caused many relocations, and the problem of maintaining the Trail's wilderness character became more severe.

In 1968, Congress established a national system of trails and designated the Appalachian Trail and the Pacific Crest Trail as the initial components. The National Trails System Act directs the secretary of the interior, in consultation with the secretary of agriculture, to administer the Appalachian Trail primarily as a footpath and protect the Trail against incompatible activities and the use of motorized vehicles. Provision was also made for acquiring rights-of-way for the Trail, both inside and outside the boundaries of federally administered areas.

In 1970, supplemental agreements under the act — among the National Park Service, the U.S. Forest Service, and the Appalachian Trail Conference — established the specific responsibilities of these organizations for initial mapping, selection of rights-of-way, relocations, maintenance, development, acquisition of land, and protection of a permanent Trail. Agreements also were signed between the park service and the various states, encouraging them to acquire and protect a right-of-way for the Trail outside federal land.

Slow progress of federal efforts and lack of initiative by some states led Congress to strengthen the National Trails System Act. President Jimmy Carter signed the amendment, known as The Appalachian Trail Bill, on March 21, 1978.

The new legislation emphasized the need for protecting the Trail, including acquiring a corridor, and authorized $90 million for that purpose. With less than 150 miles unprotected by 1988, this project is expected to be completed in the early 1990s.

In 1984, the Interior Department formally delegated the responsibility of managing the *AT* corridor lands outside established parks and forests to the Appalachian Trail Conference. The Conference and its clubs retain primary responsibility for maintaining the footpath, too.

The Conference publishes information on constructing and maintaining hiking trails, official *AT* guides, and general information on hiking and trail use.

The Conference is governed by a volunteer Board of Managers, consisting of a chair, three vice chairs, a treasurer, a secretary, a corresponding secretary, and 18 members, six from each of the three regions of ATC: New England, mid-Atlantic, and southern.

The Conference membership consists of organizations that maintain the Trail or contribute to the Trail project and individuals. ATC membership provides a subscription to *Appalachian Trailway News*, published five times a year, and 15-percent discounts on publications. The Conference also issues two newsletters, *The Register*, for Trail maintainers, and *Trail Lands*, for contributors to its land-trust program, the Trust for Appalachian Trail Lands. Annual membership dues range from $18 to $30, with life memberships available for $500 (individual) or $750 (couple).

Membership forms and a complete list of publications are available from the Appalachian Trail Conference, P.O. Box 807, Harpers Ferry, W. Va. 25425; (304) 535-6331. The office is open 9am to 5pm (Eastern Time), Monday through Friday, and 9pm to 4pm on weekends from mid-May through October.

Potomac Appalachian Trail Club

The Potomac Appalachian Trail Club, founded in November 1927, is one of the 32 organizations which maintains the Appalachian Trail under the Conference. It is also the third largest in number of members (over 2500) being surpassed only by the Appalachian Mountain Club in Boston and the Green Mountain Club in Vermont, both older organizations.

Altogether, the PATC is responsible for the maintenance of about 230 miles of the Appalachian Trail and over 500 miles of other trails. The *AT* is largely divided between the area reported in this guide and the portion north of the Park, described in *Appalachian Trail Guide: Maryland and Northern Virginia with Side Trails.* In addition, PATC maintains side trails in George Washington National Forest and is currently developing an extended side trail known as the "Big Blue". See chapter on "Side Trails". As noted earlier, PATC also maintains a network of shelters and cabins.

The Club issues a number of publications prepared by members. These include the maps and guides cited previously as well as two periodicals which are sent to members: a monthly newsletter, *Potomac Appalachian,* and an occasional special issue in magazine form. A complete list of publications, with prices, may be obtained from PATC Headquarters, 118 Park St., S.E., Vienna, VA 22180.

The Club has an active Mountaineering Section which offers assistance and training in rock climbing techniques, as well as more difficult climbing opportunities for the advanced climber. Information on their weekly activities is contained in UPROPE, a monthly publication of the Section, available from PATC Headquarters.

The Ski Touring Section conducts workshops for beginners, participates in work trips to improve ski trails in local areas and organizes ski trips to local and distant ski areas. These, as well as other activities, are described in UPSLOPE, the Section's monthly newsletter.

The Shenandoah Mountain Rescue Group is dedicated to wilderness search and rescue and to outdoor safety education. The group meets twice a month at PATC Headquarters and conducts frequent training workshops in the field.

THE SHENANDOAH NATIONAL PARK

Shenandoah National Park extends for 80 miles along the Blue Ridge Mountains between Front Royal on the north and Waynesboro on the south. It encompasses over 300 square miles with 60 peaks ranging in elevation from 3,000 to 4,000 feet.

The Park is divided into three main districts by two US highways. The Northern District extends from Front Royal south to US 211 in Thornton Gap, the Central District from Thornton Gap to US 33 in Swift Run Gap, and the Southern District from Swift Run Gap to Jarman Gap.

Skyline Drive extends the full length of the Park. It runs 105.4 miles from Front Royal to Rockfish Gap, with entrance stations at Front Royal, Thornton Gap, Swift Run Gap and Rockfish Gap. Parking overlooks are provided at 75 points along the Drive. A single-entry fee is charged for those not carrying Golden Eagle or Golden Age passes.

History of the Park

Shenandoah National Park was established through a remarkable combination of efforts at the federal, state, and local level. In 1923 the National Park Service recommended the establishment of a park in the Appalachian Range. The following year Congress passed a bill setting up a Southern Appalachian National Park Commission. A site in the Blue Ridge Mountains was recommended and a bill introduced in Congress providing for the acquisition of land. It was signed by President Coolidge in February 1925.

The next problem was the familiar one of financing. No federal funds were available. A Shenandoah Park Association was formed to raise money. In the course of nine months, $1,249,000 was raised from private sources. The Virginia Assembly, at the request of then Governor Harry F. Byrd, voted an additional $1 million. Congress passed a bill in May 1926 to establish the Park when title to the lands had passed to the federal government.

Land purchases were begun by the state in 1926 and went on for eight years. Some land was not given up willingly. Altogether, 3870 private tracts were acquired. Approximately 400 families still living in the Park had to settle elsewhere. The Park was formally established with the deeding of the land -176,430 acres- to the federal government in December 1935. President Roosevelt dedicated the Park at Big Meadows on July 3, 1936.

The Civilian Conservation Corps moved in in 1933 and soon a thousand individuals were at work on fire protection and recreation developments. To provide other facilities, the Interior Department conceived the idea of awarding the entire Park to one concessioner; the first bid was received in March 1936.

The retreat on the Rapidan River which Herbert Hoover used while president of the United States was donated to the federal government by him at the close of his term in office. The property, known today as Camp Hoover, is now within the Shenandoah Park and is administered by the Park Service.

A skyline drive was visualized at the outset as one of the major attractions. Construction was started in July 1931. The central section was completed in September 1934. The northern section was opened in October 1926 and the southern section in 1939. Construction costs were paid out of federal funds. They are reported to have averaged $47,000 per square mile, or nearly 45 million dollars for the total length.

Clearing the original Appalachian Trail route in the Park was done by the Potomac Appalachian Trail Club in the late 1920s and early 1930s. The northern section was opened in 1929-30. Many sections subsequently had to be relocated with the construction of Skyline Drive and hence were built by the Park - more specifically the CCC - from 1933 to 1937.

The Park has not grown greatly in size since establishment - it presently contains 195,000 acres - for a number of legal and financial reasons. But the boundaries are subject to change as the Park exchanges property. Southeast of the Park boundaries in the Central District, a number of Virginia wildlife areas have been established.

Since 1965 the number of hikers and backcountry hikers has been increasing exponentially, or so it seems. Shelter areas, where camping was allowed on a first come, first served basis, had so deteriorated from overuse that the Park Service discontinued their use for camping and removed some of them entirely. More recently six shelters have been designated "huts" and these six may be used by long distance Appalachian Trail backpackers with a valid backcountry camping permit. To prevent overuse or improper use, huts are monitored by volunteer hutkeepers supplied by the Potomac Appalachian Trail Club during the seasons of heavy use.

In 1976 a federal wilderness act established a number of wilderness areas in Shenandoah Park, covering about 80,000 of the total 195,000 acres of Park land. In the wilderness areas roads have been demoted to trails, a few trails have been eliminated, and the remaining ones may have less maintenance than formerly - with a narrower path, occasional blockage from downed trees, elimination of bridges over streams, etc. - but should be properly blazed.

For additional history on the Park the following books are sold by the Shenandoah Natural History Association at Shenandoah National Park visitor centers. Some are also available from PATC Headquarters. Books published by PATC include *Shenandoah Heritage, Shenandoah Vestiges* and *Shenandoah Secrets*, all by Carolyn and Jack Reeder, *Lost Trails and Forgotten People* by Tom Floyd, and *The Dean Mountain Story* by Gloria Dean. Other books of interest are *Skyland, the Heart of Shenandoah National Park* by George Freeman Pollock, *Earth-Man Story* and *Herbert Hoover's Hide-away,* both by Darwin Lambert, and *Guide to Skyline Drive and Shenandoah National Park* by Henry Heatwole.

Other books on the Park include *Geology of the She-nandoah National Park* by Thomas M. Gathright II, *Trees of Shenandoah National Park* and *Ferns and Fern Allies of Shenandoah National Park,* both by Peter M. Mazzeo.

Natural History of the Park

The area presently composing the Park was once farmed and heavily lumbered. From the middle 1700s to the late 1800s the area was fairly prosperous. In the mid-1800s there was a flurry of interest in mining. But late in the 19th century economic decline began to set in; the demand for handicraft products of the hills dropped off and, early in the 20th century, blight killed most of the chestnut trees. Families began to move elsewhere and population dwindled.

With the decline of farming and lumbering, the forest began to take over. This process was further accelerated with the establishment of the Park. Today nearly all of the land is wooded.

Geology of Shenandoah National Park

Once upon a time (pre-Cambrian time), perhaps 800 million years ago, the area that is now the Shenandoah Park was a relatively level land with hills no higher than a thousand feet above the valleys. The underlying rock was granite or other igneous rock, with only a shallow soil on the hilltops and slopes, but with a deeper accumulation of eroded material in the low areas. Then came the only known major period of volcanic activity for this area. Lava welled up through cracks in the earth's crust and spread out rather evenly over the land, first filling the valleys but finally drowning the hilltops. There was not just a single flow but a series of at least seven for a total thickness of 1500 ft. (Eroded material which accumulated between the flows helps mark the divisions.) Finally, the volcanic action ceased and normal erosion again caused soil and gravel to accumulate.

Geologists today believe that mountain building has almost always been caused by collisions of continental plates. There is evidence that the Atlantic Ocean has opened and closed, perhaps several times, since the creation of the earth. One important era of mountain building occurred about 420 million years ago during a collision between North America and Europe. Although the mountains formed by this collision have been eroded away, traces of their existence still remain. The super-continent of Euro-America existed for a long time. During the period from about 325 to 300 million years ago there is evidence that the sea-level was high and that much of Euro-America was covered by shallow seas with some land along the present eastern coast of North America above sea level, while the present Appalachian region was part of an inland sea. Rains eroded these eastern highlands and the streams and rivers which originated in them dumped tremendous amounts of sand, then clay, then more sand into the shallow inland sea, covering deeply the older volcanic soil and the lava beds and igneous rock below. As the seas widened and deepened, sea animals (invertebrates only) flourished and their skeletons accumulated on the sea bottom as limey muds atop the earlier sands and clays. Pressure of the top layers caused the lower layers of sediment to harden the sand into sandstone, the clay into shale and the limey muds into limestone. Apparently, at some point during this geologic period, the land of the Blue Ridge rose above sea level whereas that farther west remained below sea level for many more years, receiving thick deposits of sand, clay and lime.

Then, about 250 million years ago, there was a tremendous continental collision as Africa moved in and rammed the continent of Euro-America. The destruction of ocean between Africa and Euro-America and the disappearing ocean floor created volcanic mountains on the Africa side. On the Euro-American side the edge of the continent was rumpled and uplifted, forming mountains. In some places the African plate was shoved over the North American plate. The tremendous pressure, coming from the southeast in our area, caused the earth's crust to fold, like a rug, into long parallel ridges. The mountain chain so formed extended from Poland and Germany (Harz Mountains) west through Belgium, France and southern England, then on to Newfoundland and thence southwest to Birmingham, Ala. As the pressure continued the folds became higher and steeper and rocks which had been laid down in horizontal beds were tilted vertically in places.

In some places the deeply buried basaltic (lava) and granitic rocks were shoved westward over upturned layers of sandstone, shale and even limestone. The Blue Ridge Thrust Fault can be traced from Alabama to Roanoke and probably as far north as Pennsylvania. The present Blue Ridge mountains were then the lower western edge of a huge anticlinorium which formed a mountain range possibly 5 miles high, although erosion may have kept pace with the lifting of the land, in which case this early mountain range was never so high. Besides the folding of the earth's crust here, the same tremendous pressures caused much of the rock, both igneous and sedimentary, to be altered - the basalt into greenstone, the sandstone into quartzite, and the shales, at some localities, into slate.

The supercontinent, made up of Euro-America and Africa and called by geologists *Pangaea,* broke up around 190 million years ago when the Atlantic reopened between North America and Africa (leaving remnants of the African continent along a southeastern strip of North America). Separation of North American from Europe was not completed for another 100 million years.

By the beginning of Cretaceous time, 130 million years ago, the period of mountain building was over and erosion had leveled much of the land, leaving low hills here and there. River drainage was now to the east, into the Atlantic Ocean. Sometime in Early Cretaceous time the land was gently tilted, with the Appalachian region lifted as the coastal areas were lowered. This gave the formerly lazily flowing rivers renewed vigor, so they were able to cut through the hard rocks of the Blue Ridge. However, as time went on, the headwaters of many of the rivers and streams west of the present Blue Ridge were captured by the biggest rivers, the Potomac, the James and the Roanoke. The gaps the beheaded rivers had cut ceased to deepen and rose as the land rose. They make today's wind gaps. Thornton Gap may have originally been cut by the Thornton River. Manassas Gap, just north of the Park, is one of the deepest of the wind gaps.

Looking at our mountains in the Shenandoah Park of today we can see reminders of their history. Most of the Blue Ridge crest in Shenandoah National Park is capped by the hard, erosion-resistant greenstone. Although altered from the original basalt this rock still retains many of its original characteristics. One can find amygdules, filled gas bubbles, in almost every greenstone outcrop. In many places columnar jointing, characteristic of basalt, is still quite evident. It can be seen very strikingly at the southeastern viewpoint on Compton Mtn. (One must get down below the rocks to see this display.) It can also be seen on cliffs above the AT about 0.15mi. north of Hawksbill Gap and again about 200 ft. south of Little Stony Man Parking Area. Evidence of the multiple layers of lava laid down can be seen along the AT below Franklin Cliffs and Crescent Rocks. In both places the AT follows a shelf "between layers" as shown by the vertical cliffs above and below the Trail. One of the ancient granite hills that was drowned by the lava flows can be seen along the walls of Whiteoak Canyon. The stepwise series of falls in this canyon also indicate the multiple lava flows.

In some places along the Blue Ridge crest in the Park the greenstone has been completely eroded away and it is the "base rock" that outcrops. One such place is Marys

Rock where the outcrop is the igneous rock, granodiorite. Radiogenic age measurements indicate that this rock is 1,100,000,000 years old! Some of the peaks on the eastern side of the main ridge consist primarily of granite. Old Rag Mountain is one of these. Numerous greenstone dikes are present on Old Rag. Here the greenstone is eroding faster than the surrounding granite, leaving narrow passageways, with vertical sides and surprisingly regular "steps" made by erosion of the columnar-structured dike material.

To the west of the main crest are the remnants of two lower paralleling ridges, both of sandstone-quartzite. These ridges took shape as the limestones west of them, the shale between them, and the conglomerate between the sandstone and greenstone of the main crest eroded much faster than they did. The remnants of these sandstone ridges show today as peaks on the side ridges that run from the Blue Ridge crest westward. On these side ridges the peak farthest from the main crest is composed of a type of sandstone-quartzite known as the Antietam formation. This sandstone is easily recognized as it is characterized by fine straight parallel tubes that cross the bedding at right angles; these tubes are the fossil burrows of sea worms - skolithos - filled with sand. (Because of its appearance this rock has been called pipe-rock.) Estimated age of the wormhole fossils is 500,000,000 years. Peaks underlain by the old Antietam sandstone include Rockytop (the highest and farthest out peak, 2,556 ft., of the Rockytop ridge), Lewis Peak, Austin Mtn., Turk Mtn. and Brown Mtn. in the Southern District of the Park. Those in the Central and Northern Districts are not as obvious to the hiker. In some places the greenstone and base rock were shoved west covering completely the sandstone and shale deposits and even some of the limestone. This is true at the very northern end of the Park and explains the location of Skyline Caverns, a limestone cave, located under the western slopes of the Blue Ridge.

Park Fauna

The favorite mammal of the Park is the white-tailed deer. This creature of the woods seems to sense that it is protected in the Park so shows little fear of humans. Since 1935 when this area was restocked with 15 deer, they have so multiplied that today there is a stable population of several thousand deer in the Park. They are most often seen in the early morning and at dusk.

The black bear has returned to the Park in good numbers, though it is not as plentiful here as in the Great Smokies. Black bears weigh up to 400 or more pounds. Treat them with great caution. So that bears may continue to be enjoyed as free wild creatures in the SNP do all you can to discourage their developing a dependence on man and his garbage.

Other mammals of the Park include the gray fox, raccoon, opossum and bobcat. Some persons have even claimed sightings of puma and mountain lion. Striped skunks, weasels, gray, flying and red squirrels, chipmunks, woodchucks and a number of small rodents all make the Park their home.

Trout fishing is permitted in season but a license is required. A 5-day license may be purchased for use in the Park. Check Park regulations. The Staunton River and the Rapidan River are "fish-for-fun" streams with year round season. Here only artificial lures with one barbless hook may be used and all fish caught must be returned to the water.

Among the birds breeding in the Park upland are the pileated woodpecker, the wood thrush, veery, chestnut-sided warbler, blackburnian warbler, Canada warbler, scarlet tanager, rose-breasted grosbeak, dark-eyed junco, eastern wood peewee, white-breasted nuthatch, robin, rufous-sided towhee and red-eyed vireo. Turkey and black vultures, ruffed grouse, wild turkey and the common raven are frequently seen from Skyline Drive and the AT. Red-tailed hawks are found throughout the year, broad-winged hawks in spring, summer and fall.

A Christmas bird count is conducted annually in SNP. The count is sponsored by the Shenandoah Natural History Association in conjunction with the National Audubon Society.

Snakes are occasionally seen, black rat snakes probably being the most common. There are two poisonous snakes in the Park, the copperhead and the timber rattler. These pit vipers are generally much shorter than the black snakes but thicker. The rattlers vary considerably in color and banding but can be recognized by their triangular-shaped heads and (usually) tell-tale rattles.

Of all the insects, the pesky gnat is the most annoying to hikers and campers. Mosquitoes are rarely encountered. An insect beauty often seen in the Park is the luna moth. In autumn one may discover a mountaintop covered with tiny red ladybugs, getting ready to hibernate. The Allegheny Mound ant lives in large colonies within huge, often two foot high, ant hills. The tent caterpillar and fall webworm often cover whole trees with their heavy webs, the black cherry being a particular favorite of the tent caterpillar.

The gypsy moth is becoming established in the Park and may cause areas of intense defoliation. Campers should inspect their camping equipment before leaving the Park to be certain that the gypsy moth has not attached itself in some form.

Three arachnids are a nuisance to the hiker. The common tick is often a carrier of Rocky Mountain spotted fever; the tiny deer tick is a carrier of Lyme disease, recently spreading to this area. Hikers should always check their bodies and clothes for ticks at a hike's end before these varmints have had a chance to bury their heads under the skin. A very tiny mite, the chigger or "red bug" of the deep south, can be an annoyance here. These tiny pests may form small red welts on legs or arms but their favorite place for locating on the human body seems to be along waistlines. The bite of a pinhead chigger can be as bad as that from a mosquito a hundred times its size.

Park Flora

If one looks at a botanical map of the United States, one will notice a long finger of the hemlock-hardwood forests typical of the Great Lakes Region and the northeastern United States extending down the Appalachian mountains as far as Georgia. The boreal forests of Canada also extend southward, not as a long finger, but as isolated islands along the very highest peaks and ridges of the southern Appalachians. One of these "islands" is located in the Skyland-Big Meadows area of Shenandoah National Park.

At low elevations in the Park we find flowers and trees typical of the south's Piedmont area. Above 2,500 ft. we begin to find many plants more common to the northeast United States. Finally, at elevations above 3,500 ft. we may find Canadian Zone plants. How did such northern plants find their way to these scattered spots? Probably they are relics of the ice age when the country was colder than it is now. Balsam fir, red spruce, speckled alder, gray dogwood, round-leaved dogwood, quaking aspen, fly honeysuckle, and gray birch are native only in the Skyland to Big Meadows stretch of the Park. About six small stands of native white (or paper) birch exist in the Park. Other typically northern trees that are natives here include the American mountain-ash, black ash, and the mountain and striped maples. Small flowers of the Canadian Zone found in the Park include the "common" wood sorrel (Oxalis), which is not common here at all but can be found in the Limberlost area, and the three-toothed cinquefoil (Potentilla) which may be found along a few very high rock outcrops such as the Hawksbill summit and Bettys Rock. Bunchberry or dwarf cornel (Cornus) grows in the Southern District of the Park - the only place in Virginia where it is found.

At the other extreme we find a few plants that are near the northern-most limit of their range. Trees in this category include the short-leaf pine, umbrella magnolia and the Carolina willow. The Catawba rhododendron is found only in the southern third of the Park and only in a few spots even there. Though beautiful it does not make the mass displays in the Park that it does just a short distance farther south.

The predominant trees of the Park are the oaks and hickories. The American chestnut was once the queen of the area but this important tree was destroyed by the chestnut blight before the establishment of the Park. The forests of the Park are by no means virgin, except in a few ravines. Man long ago axed or set fire to the trees for use as lumber or tanbark, or to clear the land for homesteads and farms. Virgin timber, chiefly hemlock, can be found in the deep gorges, especially in the Limberlost, Whiteoak Canyon and Cedar Run Canyon. In areas only recently going back to woods from farm-lands one will find black locust, hawthorn, sumac, Virginia pine and white pine, trees typical of a "pioneer" forest.

Over 1200 species of flowering plants have been recorded as growing in the Park. It is not unusual to find the Park's first flowers of spring blooming in low, wet areas as early as late February. This is the skunk cabbage (*Symplocarpus*). Hepatica, red maple (*Acer*), coltsfoot (*Tussilago*) and spice-bush (*Lindera*) soon join it, often blooming in early March after a week of warm weather. By early April the shadbush or service berry (*Amelanchier*) will be in bloom and bloodroot (*Sanguinaria*), rue-anemone (*Anemonella*), cut-leaved toothwort (*Centaria*), and violets of many species line the trails at low elevations. Look for Dutchman's britches (*Dicentra*) and dogtooth violets (*Erythronium*) in low areas, golden ragwort (*Senecio*) along stream banks and trails, and bright yellow marsh marigold (*Veratrum*) in swampy areas. As April progresses the same sequence of blooms will be found at higher and higher elevations.

In late April, redbud (*Ceris*) and flowering dogwood (*Cornus*) decorate the woods at lower to mid elevations.

Star chickweed *(Stellaria),* may apple *(Podophyllum),* wood betony *(Pedicularis),* golden corydalis and a host of other flowers adorn the Park. Early May is blossoming time for the two species of pink azalea or pink honeysuckle, the pinxter-flower at lower to mid altitudes and the roseshell azalea at the mid to higher altitudes, *i.e.,* along the *AT* and Skyline Drive. These showy plants are particularly plentiful in the Central District of the Park, as are white (or pink) trillium. Wild geranium and sweet Cicily *(Osmorhiza),* with its lacy white flowers and aniselike odor, are common along the *AT*; observant hikers may see Jack-in-the-pulpit *(Ariasaema),* pink and yellow lady's slippers *(Cypripedium)* and showy orchises as well. In late May the Catawba rhododendron displays its showy purple-pink flowers along the Riprap Trail and near the Skyline Drive at Turk Gap.

June is the month for mountain laurel *(Kalmia)* to show off its beauty. Two interesting members of the lily family, fly-poison *(Amianthium)* and turkeybeard *(Xerophyllum),* bloom at this time. The former is very common along the *AT* whereas the latter, which prefers sandy soil, is found growing along the sandstone ridges west of the main Blue Ridge crest in the Southern District of the Park. On the roadbanks feathery wands of goatsbeard *(Aruncus)* and tall plumes of black cohosh *(Cimicifuga)* are much in evidence. In July the turkscap lily *(Lilium)* is quite common along the Drive. Many umbelliferae, including the huge cow-parsnip *(Heracleum)* will be found in bloom. By August, members of the compositae predominate - black-eyed Susans, sunflowers, coreopsis, Joe-Pye-weed, knapweed and goldenrods. Asters continue to bloom until late in the fall.

Ripening berries help color the September woods; beautiful clusters of vivid mountain-ash berries peek out between the rocks along the rocky crest of the Blue Ridge. The cardinal-flower *(Lobelia)* and great lobelia brighten stream banks. Brightest fall foliage often appears in early October when the dogwoods, sour gum, sumac and woodbine put on their leaf display. The peak of autumn brilliance is usually mid-October. By late in the month the entire Park turns to gold as the oaks and hickories blend their yellows, deep reds and browns. Last flower of the year, the witchhazel, will be found in bloom from late September to early December.

Winters in the park are unpredictable. There may be periods of balmy springlike weather, followed by a week of severe cold, with Park temperatures hovering around zero. Some years there is much snow, other years almost none. One big ice storm can turn the ridges into fairyland; but such a storm can also do indescribable damage to the trees of the Park, especially those growing in exposed locations.

Among the plants of the Park one should mention a few immigrants from Europe and Asia that have made themselves very much at home here. Japanese honeysuckle (Lonicera) is so thick in some of the low elevation areas of the Park that it has made an almost impenetrable jungle. Dyers woad (Isatis) has a special liking for Skyline Drive and grows profusely along the roadbanks. Viper's bugloss (Echium), the common ox-eye daisy, chicory, mulleins, Queen Anne's lace, and bull thistle are thick along the roadsides during the summer months. Deep in the woods one may walk into thick patches of the shiny-leaved periwinkle (Vinca), often a sign of an old family cemetery site. Daylilies (Hemerocallis) also persist near former homesites and the plants have continued to flourish though they seldom bloom in the deep shade. The princess tree (Paulownia), often mistaken for a catalpa, and the fast growing tree of heaven (Ailanthus) are also immigrants. Wineberry, a type of raspberry, is found at certain spots in the Southern District.

Two very common plant pests should be mentioned. One of these is poison ivy, which is common in brushy areas and among exposed rocks. It is similar in appearance to woodbine (Virginia creeper) except that each leaf contains three leaflets rather than five. Another very annoying plant is the wood nettle *(Laportea)* which is densely covered with stinging hairs. Nettles are particularly troublesome on side trails of the Park which often get only one time a year maintenance. Best protection from nettles, ivy, greenbriers and berry bushes is long pants. The juice from the fleshy stems of jewelweed *(Impatiens)* may help to relieve the stinging sensation of nettle and the itching of poison ivy. It is often found growing near these pests.

HEIGHTS OF WATERFALLS IN SHENANDOAH NATIONAL PARK

(This chart is reproduced, with permission, from the Shenandoah National Park's PARK GUIDE, copyrighted in 1968.)

Waterfall	Ht. ft.	District	Stream
Big Falls	93	North	Overall Run
Whiteoak #1	86	Central	Whiteoak Run
South River Falls	83	Central	South River
Lewis Falls	81	Central	Hawksbill Cr.
Dark Hollow Falls	70	Central	Hogcamp Br.
Rose River Falls, Upper	67	Central	Rose River
Big Falls, Doyles River	63	South	Doyles River
Whiteoak #2	62	Central	Whiteoak Run
Whiteoak #6	60	Central	Whiteoak Run
Whiteoak #5	49	Central	Whiteoak Run
Jones Run Falls	42	South	Jones Run
Whiteoak #4	41	Central	Whiteoak Run
Whiteoak #3	35	Central	Whiteoak Run
Twin Falls	29	North	Overall Run
Little Falls, Doyles R.	28	South	Doyles River
Rose River Falls, Lower	22	Central	Rose River

(NOTE: The waterfalls on Whiteoak Run are numbered from top to bottom.)

Measurements were made by Robert Momich and Gary Miller (Volunteers in the Parks) using a Wallace and Tiernan Altimeter accurate within 2 ft. One might consider an unrestricted drop of water a waterfall and a steeply slanting, downhill rush of water a cascade. Shenandoah Park falls of water are usually a combination; in particular, the tops and bottoms of the Park waterfalls are often indefinite and so the establishment of recording stations for the above measurements was necessarily arbitrary.

SHENANDOAH NATIONAL PARK
NORTHERN DISTRICT

The Appalachian Trail in the Northern District of Shenandoah National Park has its northern terminus on US 522 near Front Royal, its southern terminus in Thornton Gap where US 211 crosses Skyline Drive. It includes a total of 27.8 miles of trail, and Section 1 and Section 2 in this guidebook.

In the Northern District of the Park, open areas that were once fields, orchards and farmlands are long gone, so that good viewpoints are limited to occasional rock outcroppings. Through most of this area the Trail and Skyline Drive parallel each other closely, with many intersections, making the Trail readily accessible. However, the deep woods through which it passes makes the hiker feel remote from civilization.

For the first 3.5 miles the Trail is along easements, passing property of the National Zoological Park Conservation Center, the Northern Virginia 4-H Educational Center and private property in Harmony Hollow. From here the Trail enters Shenandoah National Park and soon reaches the crest of the Blue Ridge.

Numerous side trails and fire roads can be used in conjunction with the *AT* for a variety of walking trips, including some circuit hikes. For more information, see section titled "Side Trails", also PATC publication: *Circuit Hikes in Shenandoah National Park.*

Maps: PATC Map #9; USGS map of Shenandoah National Park, Northern Section, 1969, scale 1:62,000 and 7 1/2' quads for Front Royal, Bentonville, Chester Gap, Luray, Thornton Gap, and Washington, Va.

Section 1
US 522 to Gravel Springs Gap
13.3 miles   PATC Map #9

General Description
  From US 522, just below Lake Front Royal (940 ft.), the
AT leads south along the edge of National Zoological
Park Conservation Center property. It crosses SR 602
and reaches an elevation of 1,475 ft. at SR 601. From
here it climbs steadily via graded trail, crossing into
Shenandoah National Park a short distance before
reaching the crest of the Blue Ridge where it comes into
the old road from Chester Gap to Compton Gap (former
route of the *AT*). The Trail follows the Compton Gap Rd.
south to Skyline Drive at Compton Gap (2,415 ft.), then
climbs over Compton Mtn. and North and South Marshall Mtns. before reaching Gravel Springs Gap. The *AT*
either crosses Skyline Drive or comes quite close to it in
several places so that all parts of it are easily accessible.
Spring water is available in several locations near the
Trail.

Trail Approaches
  The northern end of this section begins at US 522, just
west of Lake Front Royal and 3.2 miles east of its
junction with Va 55 in Front Royal.
  The southern end is on Skyline Drive, SDMP 17.7, at
its intersection with old Brownstown-Harris Hollow Road
in Gravel Springs Gap. Paved parking for 12 cars here.

Side Trails
  The Dickey Ridge Trail, Bluff Trail, Lands Run Gap
Road, Hickerson Hollow Trail, Mt. Marshall Trail, Big
Devils Stairs Trail, Jordan River Trail, and Browntown
Trail offer good hiking. For details see "Side Trails".
Also refer to PATC publication: *Circuit Hikes in Shenan-
doah National Park.*

Accommodations

There are many motels and restaurants in Front Royal and a number of private campgrounds in the Front Royal area.

The Tom Floyd Wayside is located along the *AT*, 3.1mi. south of US 522. This is a primitive camping area with a few tent sites and a rain shelter, to be used by long distance *AT* hikers only.

Trail Description, North to South

0.0 *AT* crosses US 522 just below Lake Front Royal (940 ft.) then leads south and crosses stile into field, property of National Zoological Park Conservation and Research Center. Trail follows bridges over a stream and swampy area, Sloan Creek Swamp, then climbs along edge of fields. (With help of field glasses, one may see various zoo animals high on hill.)

0.4 Enter woods. (In early May there are showy orchises along Trail here).

0.9 Climb stile and immediately beyond reach summit of hill.

1.4 Cross SR 602, a dirt road. (Trail leaves National Zoological Park property here and enters property of Northern Virginia 4-H Educational Center. Trail is protected by easements across this property.) Just beyond road cross Moore Run.

1.6 Beyond a wet weather stream come to field. Midway across field are good views of fruit orchards in Harmony Hollow.

2.1 Cross wet weather creek.

2.2 Cross through narrow fence opening. (Trail leaves 4-H Educational Center land here and follows narrow easements on private property. STAY ON TRAIL.)

2.4 Side trail leads right 0.2mi. through PATC property to parking area on SR 601. In 0.1mi. come to farm road and follow it right. Pass white house on left of *AT*.

2.6 Come to SR 601 at sharp turn on road. (PATC parking lot is 0.4mi. down SR 601. Main road through Harmony Hollow, SR 604, is 0.7mi.) *AT* follows SR 601 few feet, turns left onto footpath, passing through gap in rock wall, then crosses small creek, *Barking Dog Spring*. Trail now climbs by switchbacks toward crest of Blue Ridge.

3.1 Enter Tom Floyd Wayside, primitive camping area with tent sites and rain shelter for use of long distance *AT* hikers only. No open fires permitted here. *Ginger Spring* is 800 ft. to right of *AT* here.

3.6 Cross private road.

3.7 Trail begins ascent via rock steps, winding back and forth up to viewpoint.

3.8 Rock outcropping known as Possum Rest offers western views towards Dickey Ridge and Massanutten Mountain. (Blueberries found here.) Trail turns left at viewpoint and enters Shenandoah National Park. In 0.1mi. turn right at PATC sign.

4.1 Horse trail, former Compton Gap Road. Follow it right (blazed both white and yellow). (To left horse trail leads 0.5mi. down to SR 610 at the Park boundary. Via 610 it is 1.8mi. farther to US 522 at Chester Gap. Until 1974 this was route of *AT*.)

5.3 Springhouse Rd., yellow-blazed. (A self-registration backcountry permit booth at this junction. Backpackers intending to camp in Park should stop here and follow instructions for writing their own backcountry camping permits.)

5.6 Reach trail junction marked by concrete post. (To right, Dickey Ridge Trail leads 9.2mi. north to Front Royal town limits and entrance to Skyline Drive, SDMP 0.0. Interesting Fort Windham Rocks are 0.2mi. from *AT* on this trail. To left of *AT*, a Park service road leads 0.4mi. to Indian Run Maintenance Bldg, not available for camping. *Spring* is 250 ft. from service road, on left, about 0.1mi. before reaching building.

5.9 Cross to right(south) of Skyline Drive, SDMP 10.4,

in Compton Gap (2,415 ft.). (Paved parking area for 14 cars here.) Ascend Compton Mtn. by switchbacks. (A patch of white clintonia, speckled wood lily, along Trail here and a small clump of yellow lady's slippers. The latter bloom in mid-May, the former in early June.)

6.7 Signpost marks short blue-blazed trails leading right and left to viewpoints. Both are ungraded and offer only rough footing but are worthwhile. (Trail on left leads 0.2mi. to an interesting outcrop of columnar basalt. To see columnar structure it is necessary to climb down below the rocks. Top of outcrop affords good view east. Trail to right of *AT* leads over top of Compton Mtn. (2,909 ft.) and down 0.2mi. to rocky ledge offering excellent views to west and north.)

7.1 Pass *Compton Springs*. (The first is to left of Trail, second is 100 ft. downhill and to right.) About 150 ft. beyond springs, *AT* crosses small stream fed by them. *AT* descends fairly steeply for about 0.5mi. then levels off. (Much mountain laurel, early June, and pink azalea, mid-May, between here and Jenkins Gap.)

7.9 Cross yellow-blazed Jenkins Gap Trail in Jenkins Gap (2,398 ft). (Paved parking area for 14 cars just off Skyline Drive at Jenkins Gap. Mt. Marshall Trail can be reached by walking south along Skyline Drive about 0.3mi.)

8.0 Cross abandoned road diagonally. Trail climbs unnamed mountain then passes through area of old apple trees.

9.4 Trail passes along foundations of an old building.

9.6 Cross to left of Skyline Drive at Hogwallow Gap, SDMP 14.2 (2,739 ft.). (Some parking available.) Trail ascends gently through Hogwallow Flats area.

10.2 Pass short trail 30 ft. left to *Hogwallow Spring*, unmarked and easy to miss. (Most springs in Park along *AT* are marked with concrete post.)

11.1 Reach summit of North Marshall (3368 ft.). (The name of this mountain grows out of fact that these lands were formerly part of Blue Ridge holdings of John

Marshall, noted Chief Justice of the United States from 1801 to 1835. Along crest of mountain, cliffs to right of Trail offer many good views to west.) As Trail descends, just where it jogs sharply to left, there is one outstanding viewpoint. At next switchback some high cliffs on left of *AT* are worth scrambling onto. (These cliffs are quite visible from Skyline Drive south of Mt. Marshall.)

11.7 Cross to right(west) of Skyline Drive, SDMP 15.9 (3,087 ft.). (Paved parking area for 12 cars just before Drive.)

12.3 Summit of South Marshall, 3,212 ft. Trail descends gradually with ledges on right affording splendid views.

13.3 Gravel Springs Gap at intersection of old Browntown-Harris Hollow Rd. with Skyline Drive, SDMP 17.7 (2,666 ft.). (To right, Browntown Trail, yellowblazed, leads northwest down mountain. To left, Harris Hollow Trail, also yellow-blazed, descends the hollow. See "Side Trails".)

Trail Description, South to North

0.0 West of Skyline Drive at its intersection with Browntown Trail (yellow-blazed), SDMP 17.7 (2,666 ft.). (Browntown Trail follows route of old Browntown-Harris Hollow Rd. northward down the mountain. East of the Drive the first 0.3mi. of old road serves as Harris Hollow Trail as well as an access road to Gravel Springs Hut. (See "Side Trails".) *AT* follows Browntown Trail for few feet, then turns right and ascends gradually. Ledges on left, near top of mountain, afford splendid views.

1.0 Summit of South Marshall, 3,212 ft.

1.6 Cross to right(east) of Skyline Drive, SDMP 15.9 (3,087 ft.). (Paved parking area for 12 cars here.) Ascend North Marshall by switchbacks. Near top, where Trail jogs sharply left, high cliffs on right are worth a scramble. At next bend of Trail is an excellent view of Blue Ridge to south. (Cliffs of North Marshall are quite visible from Skyline Drive south of mountain.)

2.1 Crest of ridge. Cliffs to left of Trail offer many good views to west.

2.2 Summit of North Marshall, 3,368 ft. (The name of this mountain grows out of fact that these lands were formerly a part of Blue Ridge holdings of John Marshall, noted Chief Justice of the United States from 1801-1835.) Trail now descends gradually.

3.1 Pass short trail leading right 30 ft. to *Hogwallow Spring.* (Piped spring and 0asy to miss.) Continue to descend, very gently, through Hogwallow Flat.

3.7 Cross to left of Skyline Drive at Hogwallow Gap, SDMP 14.2 (2,739 ft.). (Some parking available here.) For 0.5mi. *AT* proceeds across relatively level terrain.

3.9 Foundations of old building on right. Trail climbs unnamed mountain, passing through old orchard, with many of old fruit trees persisting, although now topped by black locust trees.

5.3 Cross abandoned road diagonally. (Old road leads left 0.1mi. to an old quarry.)

5.4 Cross yellow-blazed Jenkins Gap Trail in Jenkins Gap, 2,398 ft. (Parking space for 14 cars in Jenkins Gap just off Drive. To left Jenkins Gap Trail descends mountain; to right it leads 150 ft. to Skyline Drive and Mt. Marshall Trail. See "Side Trails".) Trail now passes through a level area containing extensive growth of mountain laurel (blooms early June) and pink azalea (blooms late May). Beyond, Trail ascends fairly steeply.

6.2 *Compton Springs.* First is to left of trail. Second is 100 ft. uphill to right.

6.6 Signpost at top of climb marks short blue-blazed trails leading left and right to viewpoints. Though ungraded and offering only rough footing, both trails are worthwhile. (Trail on right leads down 0.2mi. to interesting outcrop of columnar basalt. To see columnar structure it is necessary to climb down below rocks. Top of outcrop affords good view east. Trail on left leads over crest of Compton Mtn. (2,909 ft.) and down 0.2mi. to a rocky ledge offering excellent views to west and north.)

AT continues along ridge of Compton Mtn. for about 0.2mi. then descends, passing several large boulder-like outcrops of basalt. (At least one clump of yellow lady slipper, blooms mid-May, and some white clintonia, blooms early June, along this stretch of Trail.)

7.4 In Compton Gap cross to right side of Skyline Drive, SDMP 10.4 (2,415 ft.). (Parking for 14 cars here.) *AT* follows the old Compton Gap-Chester Gap Road, both white and yellow blazes, continuing along Blue Ridge crest. (Skyline Drive swings northwest here along Dickey Ridge down which it descends into Front Royal.)

7.7 Intersection with blue-blazed Dickey Ridge Trail (left) and service road (right) to Indian Run Maintenance Bldg. (Dickey Ridge Trail begins here and leads northwest 9.2mi. to entrance to Skyline Drive at Front Royal town limits. Fort Windham Rocks are 0.2mi. from *AT* along this trail. Service road leads 0.4mi. to Indian Run Maintenance Bldg, not available for camping. *Spring* 250 ft. to left of service road about 0.1mi. before reaching building.)

8.0 Springhouse Road, yellow-blazed. At this junction is a self-registration backcountry permit booth. Backpackers who intend to camp in Park should stop here and follow instructions for writing their own backcountry camping permits.

9.1 Turn left from Compton Gap Trail onto narrower footpath (white-blazed only). (Compton Gap Trail, yellow-blazed, continues down mountain. See "Side Trails". This was route of *AT* until 1974.)

9.4 Turn left at PATC sign.

9.5 Rock outcropping known as Possum Rest offers western views toward Dickey Ridge and Massanutten Mountain. (Blueberries can be found here.) Trail turns right at viewpoint and leaves Shenandoah National Park.

9.6 Descend via rock steps.

9.7 Cross private road.

10.1 Enter Tom Floyd Wayside, primitive camping for *AT* long distance hikers. No open fires permitted. Spur trail leads left 150 ft. to rain shelter.

10.2 Spur trail leads left 800 ft. to *Ginger Spring*. Leave wayside.

10.6 Bear right, diagonally, across old road. In 200 ft. cross small creek and pass through gap in rock wall.

10.7 Come to SR 601 at sharp corner of road. (It is 0.4mi. down SR601 to PATC parking area and 0.3mi. farther to main road through Harmony Hollow.) Immediately turn right onto farm road passing white house on right side of *AT*. Follow farm road for about 750 ft., then turn left onto footpath. (Property to left of farm road and *AT* here belongs to PATC.)

10.9 Trail leads left from *AT* 0.2mi. to PATC parking area on SR 601.

11.1 Cross through narrow gap in fence onto *AT* easement on property of Northern Virginia 4-H Educational Center.

11.4 Come into field. Good view of Harmony Hollow and its fruit orchards from center of this field.

11.7 Turn sharply right into woods and immediately cross wet weather creek .

11.9 Cross small creek, Moore Run, then dirt road, SR 602. *AT* enters property of National Zoological Park Conservation and Research Center, following an *AT* easement. Trail now ascends.

12.4 Summit of hill. In 100 ft., cross stile.

12.9 Enter field. From this vantage point and with help of field glasses, the hiker may be able to spot various zoo animals in fenced-in areas across highway. *AT* descends along edge of fields, passing below dam of Lake Front Royal.

13.3 Cross bridges over Sloan Creek Swamp and reach US 522. *(AT* crosses highway here and continues on an *AT* easement through property of National Zoological Conservation and Research Center.)*

Section 2
Gravel Springs to Thornton Gap
14.5 miles   PATC Map #9

General Description

From Gravel Springs (2,666 ft.) the *AT* climbs to the
second peak of Hogback (3,475 ft.), its highest elevation
in the Northern District of the Park. It descends over
1000 ft. to Elkwallow Gap then ascends several lesser
high points and the summit of Pass Mtn. before descending to Thornton Gap (2,307 ft.). Near Range View Cabin
and also on Pass Mountain the Trail passes through
areas that were once quite open. Large old oak trees
with widespreading low branches are being crowded by
slender young forest trees. The old oaks remind the hiker
that these areas were open fields in the pre-Park days
during which these oaks grew to maturity.

Side Trails

At 3.8mi. the Big Blue-Tuscarora Trail connects with
the *AT*. This trail offers a 220 mile route west of the
AT, rejoining it northeast of Carlisle, Pa. For more
information see "Side Trails"; also PATC publication:
Guide to the Big Blue Trail. The Gravel Springs-Thorn-
ton Gap area is rich with side trails, too many to enu-
merate here. See "Side Trails"; also see PATC publication: *Circuit Hikes in Shenandoah National Park*.

Trail Approaches

The northern end of this section is on Skyline Drive,
SDMP 17.7, at intersection with old Browntown-Harris
Hollow Rd. Paved parking area for 12 cars.

The southern end is in Thornton Gap, SDMP 31.5,
where US 211 crosses Skyline Drive. Trail is 0.2mi. west
of Skyline Drive.

Accommodations

Two open-faced huts are available for the long distance *AT* hiker. Gravel Springs Hut is 0.2mi. south of Gravel Springs Gap and another 0.2mi. down the Bluff Trail. Pass Mtn. Hut is 1.2mi. north of Thornton Gap and 0.2mi. down a spur trail. Range View Cabin, a locked PATC cabin requiring advance reservations, is located 5.1mi. south of Gravel Springs Gap. See "Accommodations and Facilities".

Mathews Arm Campground, SDMP 22.2, near the Trail 4.4mi. south of Gravel Springs Gap, offers extensive camping facilities, no reservations accepted. (It is closed entire 1991 season for repair of storm damage. Reopening scheduled for 1992.) Meals are available at Panorama Restaurant in Thornton Gap and lunches can be purchased at the Elkwallow Wayside, SDMP 24.0. None of these facilities is open during the cold months.

Trail Description, North to South

0.0 Intersection of old Browntown-Harris Hollow Rd. with Skyline Drive, SDMP 17.7 (2,666 ft.). (Paved parking area for 12 cars here.) *AT* crosses to left(east) side of Drive and parallels old Harris Hollow Rd. for several hundred feet. (This road, on left of *AT*, is utilized as access road to Gravel Springs Hut, 0.3mi. Harris Hollow Trail, yellow-blazed, follows route of old road down mountain on western side. See "Side Trails".)

0.2 *AT* turns right at concrete post where Bluff Trail comes in on left. (Bluff Trail starts here, descends by switchbacks to Gravel Springs and hut in 0.2mi. See "Side Trails".) *AT* passes through extended level area.

1.3 Cross to right side of Skyline Drive, SDMP 18.9.

1.5 Spur trail to left leads 100 ft. to Skyline Drive, SDMP 19.4, at junction of Keyser Run Fire Rd. on east side of Drive. Paved parking area to be completed by late 1991. Keyser Run Fire Rd. leads south along east slopes of Blue Ridge. See "Side Trails".

1.8 *AT* reaches top of Little Hogback. Fine outlook from ledge 30 ft. to right of Trail.

1.9 Spur trail, at signpost, leads straight ahead 50 ft. to Little Hogback Parking Overlook on Skyline Drive, SDMP 19.7. *AT* veers right and descends, passing below overlook. Trail then ascends steeply, by switchbacks, up east face of first peak of Hogback.

2.5 Ridge crest; continue along ridge.

2.6 Pass few feet to left of first peak of Hogback (3,420 ft.).

2.7 Hogback Spur Trail leads left, downhill, 0.2mi. to walled-in *spring* which is within sight of Skyline Drive. *AT* ascends.

2.8 Pass hang glider launching area with good view into Browntown Valley.

2.9 Pass radio towers on summit of second peak of Hogback, 3,474 ft. Trail follows tower road across its turnaround area, then goes to right of road and descends. Trail crosses to left of road in 0.1mi.

3.1 *AT* comes into tower road just before it reaches the Drive. (Here old road trace leads left 300 ft. to Drive.) Cross to left of Skyline Drive, SDMP 20.8. (Junction with Sugarloaf Trail, leading left, is 50 ft. beyond the Drive.) Ascend toward third peak of Hogback, 3,440 ft. Near top a side trail leads right 15 ft. to a spot offering splendid view north over Browntown Valley and Dickey Ridge. Skyline Drive is directly below; enormous rocks here.

3.4 Cross to right of Skyline Drive, SDMP 21.1. (Paved parking area to be completed late 1991.) Continue along crest of Hogback Mtn.

3.7 Side trail leads left 30 ft. to summit of fourth peak, 3,440 ft., with view south, now mostly overgrown. From fourth peak, *AT* descends.

3.8 Junction with Big Blue-Overall Run Trail. (The Big Blue-Tuscarora forms a 220 mile loop, rejoining the *AT* near Carlisle, Pa. See "Side Trails".)

4.1 Spur trail on right leads 50 ft. to summit of Sugarloaf. *AT* continues to descend.

4.4 Cross to left of Skyline Drive, SDMP 21.9. (Entrance road to Mathews Arm Campground is 0.2mi.to right along Drive. Rattlesnake Point Overlook, 3,105 ft., is 50 yds. left of *AT* on Drive. Views east over Piney Branch.) Pass Rattlesnake Point, a large rock formation, to right of Trail.

4.7 Junction with Piney Branch Trail which leads left from *AT*. Immediately beyond, *AT* comes to Range View Cabin service road and follows it left a few feet before turning left away from it. (To right passes Piney River Ranger Station and continues to Skyline Drive.)

5.0 Pass under powerline.

5.1 Post marks second side trail leading 0.1mi. to Range View Cabin. *Spring* is below cabin. (Cabin is a locked structure. Advance reservations required. See "Accommodations and Facilities".) In 200 ft. *AT* crosses access road to cabin. (A few feet down road Piney Ridge Trail takes off from right of road, just as road bends left toward cabin.) *AT* descends gently toward Elkwallow Gap.

5.9 Cross to right of Skyline Drive, SDMP 23.9 (2,480 ft.). (Elkwallow Wayside is 200 yds. south on Drive. Lunches available spring, summer, fall. Elkwallow Picnic Area is beyond wayside. No overnight accommodations.) *AT* swings right, then circles wayside and picnic area. Cross Elkwallow Trail 250 ft. beyond Drive. (To left, trail leads 0.1mi. to wayside; to right, it is 1.9mi. to Mathews Arm Campground.)

6.2 Trail leads left 200 ft. to Elkwallow Picnic Area. *AT* turns sharply right here and descends.

6.4 *Spring* marked with concrete post is to left of Trail.

6.5 Junction with Jeremys Run Trail which is straight ahead. *AT* turns sharply left at this junction, crosses creek in 100 ft. and ascends.

7.5 Reach crest of narrow ridge and follow it.

8.6 Junction with blue-blazed Thornton River Trail. (Thornton River Trail crosses Skyline Drive in 0.3mi.

then descends along a branch of Thornton River to eastern Park boundary.)

9.8 Trail leads left 0.1mi. to Neighbor Mtn. (Parking area on Skyline Drive, SDMP 26.8.)

10.1 Intersection with yellow-blazed Neighbor Mountain Trail. (To left horse trail continues to Skyline Drive, SDMP 28.1, in 1mi. passing near Byrds Nest #4. See "Side Trails".) AT now tops the rise, then descends following the main ridge.

10.3 *AT* leaves ridge crest and slabs southwest side of ridge.

11.0 Where *AT* bends sharply right a blue-blazed trail leads left 0.5mi. to Byrds Nest #4, for day use only. (*Piped water* available at picnic shelter, May through October.) *Spring,* marked with concrete post, is to right of Trail, 100 ft. farther along *AT*.

11.2 Spur trail on left leads 0.1mi. to Beahms Gap Parking Overlook on Skyline Drive, SDMP 28.5.

11.4 Cross to left of Skyline Drive, SDMP 28.6. *AT* ascends gently from here.

11.5 Intersection with yellow-blazed Rocky Branch Trail.

12.1 Rocky area affords wintertime views to right of Kemp Hollow, The Neighbor and Knob Mtn.

12.5 Reach summit of Pass Mtn., 3,052 ft.

13.3 Pass Mountain Trail leads left. (Pass Mountain Hut is 0.2mi. down trail. Hut for use of long distance *AT* hikers only. *Spring* is few feet behind hut.) A short distance farther along AT is enclosed *spring* to right that provides water for a drinking fountain at Pass Mountain Overlook along Skyline Drive.

14.1 *AT* comes to service road and follows it to right for 150 ft., then turns off road to right.

14.4 Trail descends bank to service road within sight of Drive. Follow road to Drive and cross it.

14.5 Cross US 211 at a point 0.2mi. west of Skyline Drive in Thornton Gap, SDMP 31.5 (2,307 ft).

Trail Description, South to North

0.0 Intersection with US 211 at a point 0.2 west of Skyline Drive in Thornton Gap, SDMP 31.5 (2,307 ft.). Trail leads uphill through woods.

0.1 Cross to right side of Skyline Drive and follow service road for few feet; then turn left, up bank, into woods.

0.4 *AT* turns left onto service road, follows it about 150 ft., then turns left, away from road. Trail ascends gradually.

1.2 Pass Mountain Trail leads right 3mi. to its lower terminus on US 211. (Pass Mtn. Hut is 0.2mi. from *AT* down this trail. *Spring* is few feet behind the hut. Hut for use of long distance *AT* hikers only. See "Accommodations and Facilities".)

2.0 Wooded summit of Pass Mtn., 3,052 ft.

2.4 *AT*, descending, passes through rocky area with wintertime views west of Kemp Hollow, Neighbor Mtn. and Knob Mtn.

3.0 Intersection with yellow-blazed Rocky Branch Tr.

3.1 Trail crosses to left(west) of Skyline Drive, SDMP 28.6, in Beahms Gap.

3.3 Spur trail leads right 0.1mi. to Beahms Gap Parking Overlook on Skyline Drive, SDMP 28.5.

3.5 Cross well-defined old road trace. Just beyond, trail on left leads 100 ft to *spring* (concrete signpost). A few feet farther along *AT* a blue-blazed trail leads right 0.5mi. to Byrds Nest #4. (For day use only. Piped-in *water* available here May through October.) Trail now slabs southwest side of ridge.

4.2 Reach ridge crest and follow it.

4.3 Top of rise. In 200 ft. reach junction with yellow-blazed Neighbor Mountain Trail. (To left leads to peak of "The Neighbor", then continues down to Jeremys Run. See "Side Trails".)

4.7 Spur trail leads right 0.1mi. to parking area on Skyline Drive, SDMP 26.8. Beyond this junction the *AT* continues along crest of long narrow ridge for over 2mi., then descends.

5.9 Junction with blue-blazed Thornton River Trail. (Right leads 0.3mi. to Skyline Drive, then follows branch of Thornton River to Park boundary.)

8.0 Cross creek. In 100 ft., where *AT* turns sharply right, is intersection with Jeremys Run Trail. (See "Side Trails".)

8.1 On right of *AT* a short trail, marked with concrete signpost, leads to *spring*.

8.3 Trail straight ahead leads 200 ft. to Elkwallow Picnic Area. *AT* turns sharply to left here to swing around developed area of Elkwallow Picnic Area and Wayside.

8.5 Intersect the Elkwallow Trail. (To left this trail leads 1.9mi. to Mathews Arm Campground; to the right it leads 0.1mi. to Elkwallow Wayside. Lunches available spring, summer, fall. Closed 1991 season.) In 250 ft. *AT* crosses to right of Skyline Drive, SDMP 23.9 and ascends gently.

9.4 Cross service road to Range View Cabin, a locked structure requiring advance reservations from PATC Headquarters. (See "Accommodations and Facilities". To right, road leads down 0.1mi. to cabin. *Spring* is below cabin. To left, road leads 0.6mi. to Piney River Ranger Station and Skyline Drive, SDMP 22.1.) In 200 ft. spur trail leads right 0.1mi. to Range View Cabin.

9.5 Pass under powerline.

9.8 Turn right onto access road and follow it a few feet before leaving it again as road bends to left. Immediately ahead is junction with Piney Branch Trail which leads right from *AT*. (See "Side Trails".)

10.1 Cross to left side of Skyline Drive, SDMP 21.9. Rattlesnake Point is to left of Trail as you reach the Drive. (Rattlesnake Point Overlook (3,105 ft.) is on Drive, 50 yds. right of *AT*, with views east over Piney Branch. To left of *AT*, 0.2mi. along Drive, is entrance road to Mathews Arm Campground.) *AT* now ascends.

10.4 Spur trail on left leads 50 ft. to summit of Sugarloaf.

10.7 Junction with Big Blue-Overall Run Trail. (Big Blue-Tuscarora Trail provides a 220mi. loop, rejoining *AT* near Carlisle, Pa. See "Side Trails".)

10.8 Side trail leads right 30 ft. to summit of fourth peak of Hogback, 3,440 ft., with overgrown view south. Continue along ridge, descending slightly.

11.1 Cross to right of Skyline Drive, SDMP 21.1. (Paved parking area to be completed here late 1991.) Ascend third peak of Hogback, 3,440 ft. Just beyond top, side trail leads 15 ft. to spot offering splendid view north over Browntown Valley and Dickey Ridge. (Skyline Drive is directly below; enormous rocks here.)

11.4 Junction with new Sugarloaf Trail which leads right. In 50 ft. cross Skyline Drive, SDMP 20.8. Follow tower access road few feet, then bear right off road. (An old road trace leads right here, 300 ft. to Skyline Drive.) In 400 ft. *AT* crosses to left of access road.

11.6 Trail follows road across its turnaround area, reaching summit of second peak of Hogback, 3,475 ft., highest point in Northern District. Antenna towers are to left of Trail. Descend.

11.7 Graded trail to right leads 0.2mi. downhill to walled-in *spring* which is within sight of Skyline Drive. *AT* now ascends.

11.9 Pass few feet to right of first peak of Hogback, 3,420 ft. Continue along ridge crest, then descend steeply by switchbacks down east face of mountain.

12.6 Spur trail, at signpost, leads right 50 ft. to Little Hogback Overlook on Skyline Drive, SDMP 19.7. *AT* veers left here, and climbs.

12.7 Top of Little Hogback; fine outlook from ledge 30 ft. to left of Trail. *AT* now descends gradually.

13.0 Spur trail to right leads 100 ft. to Skyline Drive, SDMP 19.4, at junction of Keyser Run Fire Road on east side of Drive. Paved parking area to be completed here late 1991. (See "Side Trails".)

13.2 Cross to right side of Skyline Drive, SDMP 18.9. Trail passes along an almost level area.

14.3 Junction with Bluff Trail. *AT* bears left, paralleling old Browntown-Harris Hollow Rd. from here to Drive. (Bluff Trail starts here and descends by switchbacks to *Gravel Springs* in 0.2mi. and Gravel Springs Hut 50 ft. beyond. See "Side Trails".)

14.5 Cross to the left side of Skyline Drive, SDMP 17.7 (2,665 ft.), at its intersection with old Browntown-Harris Hollow Rd. (Paved parking area for 12 cars here. Harris Hollow Rd., right of Drive and *AT*, is utilized as service road to Gravel Springs Hut for 0.3mi. Harris Hollow Trail, yellow-blazed, follows route of old road down mountain. See "Side Trails".)

SUMMARY OF DISTANCES ALONG THE *AT*
Northern District

	Miles	
	N-S	S-N
US 522	0.0	27.8
Indian Run Maintenance Bldg.	5.6	22.2
	+ 0.4	+ 0.4
Compton Gap	5.9	21.9
Jenkins Gap	7.9	19.9
North Marshall summit	11.1	16.7
Gravel Springs Gap	13.3	14.5
Gravel Springs Hut	13.4	14.4
	+ 0.2	+ 0.2
Hogback, 2nd peak (tower)	16.2	11.6
Big Blue Trail	17.3	10.7
Piney Branch Trail	18.0	9.8
Range View Cabin	18.4	9.4
	+ 0.1	+ 0.1
Piney Ridge Trail	18.4	9.4
Elkwallow Gap, Skyline Drive crossing	19.2	8.6
Jeremys Run Trail	19.7	8.1
Thornton Hollow Trail	22.6	5.2
Neighbor Mtn. Trail	23.4	4.4
Byrds Nest #4	24.3	3.5
	+ 0.5	+ 0.5
Beahms Gap, Skyline Drive crossing	24.7	3.1
Pass Mtn.	25.8	2.0
Pass Mtn. Hut	26.6	1.2
	+ 0.2	+ 0.2
US 211, Thornton Gap	27.8	0.0

SUMMARY OF DISTANCES BY SKYLINE DRIVE
TO POINTS ON *AT*
Northern District

SDMP N to S		S to N
0.0	Park Entrance; US 340 east of Front Royal	31.5
10.4	Compton Gap; *AT* crossing	21.1
12.3	Jenkins Gap; *AT* is 0.1mi. to west	19.2
14.2	Hogwallow Gap; *AT* crossing	17.3
15.9	*AT* crossing just south of North Marshall Mtn.	15.6
17.7	Gravel Springs Gap; *AT* crossing	13.8
18.9	*AT* crossing	12.6
19.4	Keyser Run Fire Road; *AT* is 100 ft. via spur trail	12.1
19.7	Little Hogback Parking Overlook; *AT* is 50 ft. north via spur trail	11.8
20.8	*AT* crossing, sag between second and third peaks of Hogback	10.7
21.1	*AT* crossing, between third and fourth peaks of Hogback	10.4
21.9	Rattlesnake Point; *AT* crossing 0.3mi. north of Mathews Arm Campground	9.6
23.9	Elkwallow Gap; *AT* crossing 200 yds. north of wayside	7.6
24.2	Elkwallow Picnic Area; *AT* is 200 ft. from second parking area via spur trail	7.3
26.8	Neighbor Mtn. Trail parking area; *AT* is 0.1mi. west via spur trail	4.7
28.5	Beahms Gap Overlook; *AT* is 0.1mi. west of Drive via spur trail	3.0
28.6	Beahms Gap; *AT* crossing	2.9
31.5	Thornton Gap; *AT* crosses US 211 0.2mi. west of Drive	0.0

SHENANDOAH NATIONAL PARK
CENTRAL DISTRICT

This district begins where US 211 crosses the Blue Ridge and intersects Skyline Drive in Thornton Gap, SDMP 31.5, at a point 9 miles east of Luray, 7 miles west of Sperryville, and 83 miles from Washington, D.C. The southern end is at Swift Run Gap, SDMP 65.7, where US 33 crosses the Blue Ridge. From Swift Run Gap it is 7 miles west to Elkton, 8 miles east to Stanardsville, and 110 miles to Washington, D.C. The Central District includes Section 3, Section 4, and Section 5 for a total of 34.4 miles of the *AT*.

The Blue Ridge crest is higher in this part of the Park than in the northern and southern parts. The highest peak in the Park, Hawksbill, just south of Skyland, has an elevation of 4,050 feet. The *AT* reaches its highest point in the Park, 3,812 ft., on Hazeltop Mtn. which is 4 miles south of Big Meadows Campground. Skyline Drive reaches its highest altitude, 3,680 ft., at the northern entrance to Skyland.

The Central District of Shenandoah National Park is the part most widely used by the motoring public, by campers, and by hikers. The *AT* is heavily used, as are the chief side trails. Favorite short hikes include the Stony Man and Forest Nature Trails, the Bearfence and *AT* loop, the Passamaquoddy and *AT* loop, the Dark Hollow Falls Trail, the trails up Hawksbill, and the Limberlost Trail. Longer favorites are the Whiteoak Canyon Trail, the trails up Old Rag Mountain, and the stretch of *AT* from Thornton Gap (Panorama) to Marys Rock. There are also special trails for horseback riding, with a stable at Skyland.

There are two campgrounds in this district, the largest at Big Meadows and another at Lewis Mountain. Skyland, Big Meadows, and Lewis Mountain have lodging facilities available, in season, for tourists.

The Skyland resort antedates the Park, having been developed by George F. Pollock in the early 1900s. Camp Hoover, on the eastern slope of the Blue Ridge near Big

Meadows, was a summer retreat for President Herbert Hoover (1923-33). It is now managed by the Park Service but is still reserved for use by presidential guests. For more information about the history of this area, read "Skyland Before 1900" by Jean Stephenson in the July 1935 PATC Bulletin and the books, *Skyland*, by George Freeman Pollock (Washington, Judd and Detwiler, 1960), *Herbert Hoovers's Hideaway* by Darwin Lambert (Shenandoah Natural History Assoc. Inc., Luray, Va. 1971), and *The Undying Past of Shenandoah* by Darwin Lambert (Roberts Rinehart, Inc. 1989).

Maps

PATC Map #10; also USGS map of Shenandoah National Park, Central Section, 1969, scale 1:62,500, and USGS 7 1/2' quads, scale 1:24,000 for: Thornton Gap, Old Rag, Big Meadows, Fletcher, Elkton East, and Swift Run Gap. (USGS quads covering parts of the Central District not traversed by the *AT* include Luray, Washington, Va., Stanley, Madison, and Stanardsville.)

Section 3
Thornton Gap to Skyland

9.3 miles   PATC #10

General Description

From US 211 in Thornton Gap, 2,307 ft., the Trail climbs to the ridge crest just beyond Marys Rock, 3,514 ft. Here a side trail leads to one of the most outstanding panoramic views in the entire Park. The Trail then follows the ridge crest, climbs over The Pinnacle, 3,730 ft., passes below the Jewell Hollow Overlook and continues on to the Pinnacles Picnic Area. Until Hughes River Gap the Trail stays a little below the ridge crest on the western side. As the western slopes are generally quite steep in this area there are many good views westward.

From Hughes River Gap, the *AT* climbs to the cliff tops of Little Stony Man then continues ascending to within 0.4mi. of the summit of Stony Man, formed by the erosion of layer upon layer of ancient lava flows. From here the Trail descends gently to the Nature Trail Parking Area at the end of the section.

There are no dependable sources of water on the *AT* along this stretch of trail except the piped water, available "in season" at Panorama, Byrds Nest #3, Pinnacles Picnic Area, and Stony Man Mountain Parking Overlook. The springs at Meadow Spring and Shaver Hollow (difficult to find) are each 0.3mi. downhill from the *AT*.

Trail Approaches

The northern end is on US 211 in Thornton Gap, 0.1mi. west of Skyline Drive, SDMP 31.5.

The southern end is at Stony Man Nature Trail Parking Area, SDMP 41.7.

Side Trails

The Park is wide on the eastern side of the Drive in this area and there are many trails. One group of trails is centered around "Hazel Country", that area near the Hazel River and Hazel Mountain. These interconnect with trails in the Nicholson (Free State) Hollow and Corbin Cabin area. (Since the mountaineers who once lived in Nicholson Hollow were reputed to be so mean they were "a law unto themselves", the local sheriffs were afraid to enter the hollow; hence the name "Free State". See George F. Pollock's book, *Skyland*.) Skyland area also includes a wide variety of trails. See "Side Trails". Also refer to PATC publication: *Circuit Hikes in Shenandoah National Park*.

Accommodations

In season, Panorama, at the northern end of the section, offers meals but no lodging facilities. Skyland has an excellent restaurant, a lodge, and cottages. A stable is maintained here and there is a network of horse trails as well as hiking trails in this area. Reservations may be made by calling 1-800-999-4714. The nearest public campground is at Big Meadows, SDMP 51.2, about 9 miles south of Skyland.

There are no huts available for camping in this section. An open-faced shelter, Byrds Nest #3, is available for day use only. Corbin Cabin, a locked structure reached via the Corbin Cabin Cut-Off Trail, is 1.4mi. east of Skyline Drive, SDMP 37.9. For its use reservations must be obtained in advance from PATC Headquarters. See "Accommodations and Facilities".

Trail Description, North to South

0.0 This section of *AT* begins at Trail's intersection with US 211, about 0.1mi. west of Skyline Drive, SDMP 31.5 (2,307 ft.). Proceed through woods, passing west of Panorama Restaurant. (Spur trail here leads left to parking area at Panorama.) *AT* ascends steadily along northern and then eastern slopes of mountain.

1.7 Spur trail leads right 0.1mi. to northern tip of Marys Rock. Views from this point are unsurpassed anywhere in Park. (Highest point, 3,514 ft., is reached by climbing to top of huge rock outcrop; dangerous in wet or windy weather. The rock is granodiorite and geologists have determined its age to be over one billion years!) Beyond junction, *AT* follows ridge crest south, with occasional views westward, then descends gradually.

2.4 In a sag Meadow Spring Trail intersects *AT*. (Meadow Spring Trail leads left, downhill, passing *Meadow Spring* on left in 0.3mi.) *AT* continues along ridge crest which is narrow here. There is an excellent view to west from a rock outcrop 0.1mi. farther along Trail.

2.7 Reach another good viewpoint. Trail switches back to left, then descends toward sag at base of The Pinnacle.

3.0 *AT* comes into service road and follows it right 180 feet to Byrds Nest #3. (To left, service road leads 0.3mi. to Skyline Drive,SDMP 33.9. Piped *water* available at shelter during warmer months. See "Accommodations and Facilities".) Beyond shelter *AT* ascends gradually.

3.8 Obscure spur trail, right, leads 100 feet to fine view north.

3.9 Fifty feet to right of *AT* are jagged rocks forming north peak of The Pinnacle. Beyond, *AT* leads along level ridge crest for a short distance, affording splendid views of sheer western slopes of this ridge.

4.0 Pass to left of highest point of The Pinnacle, 3,730 ft. Descend through heavy growth of mountain laurel (blossoming in early June).

4.7 Cross blue-blazed Leading Ridge Trail. (To left, trail leads 0.1mi. to the Drive. See "Side Trails".) *AT* now passes through some tall white pine, descending gently.

4.8 *AT* passes below the Jewel Hollow Overlook.

5.0 Side trail, left, leads back 75 ft. to Jewell Hollow Overlook, SDMP 36.4 (3,335 ft.). *AT* ascends gradually along crest of a narrow ridge. There are fine views westward across Jewell Hollow.

5.1 *AT* comes up to, then parallels to right, entrance road to Pinnacles Picnic Area, SDMP 36.7. At fork in path *AT* follows unpaved right fork which leads around picnic area. Follow white blazes! Trail route is through tall laurel.

5.3 Trail passes toilets and drinking fountain. (*Water* available here "in season".) Enter woods, ascend slightly, then descend.

5.7 An impressive old white pine grows to left of *AT* here. In 0.1mi. *AT* passes under powerlines. Trail then ascends knob at head of Nicholson Hollow.

6.1 Where *AT* switchbacks sharply to right, descending, there is an excellent viewpoint. *AT* here is close to, but above, Skyline Drive and presents an unobstructed view of Nicholson Hollow and Old Rag Mountain beyond.

6.2 Abandoned trail leads 0.3mi. downhill to right to *spring* near location of razed Shaver Hollow Shelter. From this intersection, *AT* continues with several gentle dips and climbs.

6.8 Cross Crusher Ridge Trail, blue-blazed, which here follows an old woods road known as Sours Lane. (See "Side Trails".)

7.0 Junction with blue-blazed Nicholson Hollow Trail. (It is 0.1mi. to the Drive. See "Side Trails".)

7.3 A side trail, left, leads 200 feet to south end of Stony Man Mountain Overlook in Hughes River Gap, SDMP 38.6 (3,097 ft.). Drinking *water* and toilets here, "in season". Continuing around head of Nicholson Hollow, *AT* parallels the Drive and ascends.

7.7 Spur trail, left, leads 150 ft. to Little Stony Man Parking Area on Skyline Drive, SDMP 39.1. Ascend Stony Man Mountain gradually, by long switchbacks, first left, then right.

8.0 At trail junction, take left fork. (Right fork is Passamaquoddy Trail leading 1.4mi. to Skyland Lodge; Passamaquoddy is a Maine Indian word translating as "abounding in pollock" - as in George Freeman Pollock, founder of Skyland. This is former *AT* route. See "Side Trails".)

8.3 Reach cliff tops of Little Stony Man. (Climbers frequently "top rope" here.) Continue ascent, climbing more gradually.

8.9 Trail junction. (Here the hiker may ascend summit of Stony Man via a 0.4mi. loop, descend to the Stony Man Nature Trail via horse trail, or continue south on *AT*.) *AT* turns left here and descends gradually.

9.3 Reach Nature Trail Parking Area and end of this section. (To right it is 0.3mi. on paved road to Skyland Lodge and Dining Hall; to left 0.1mi. to Skyline Drive, SDMP 41.7.)

Trail Description, South to North

0.0 This section of the *AT* starts at the Stony Man Nature Trail Parking Area, near northern entrance to Skyland, SDMP 41.7. Ascend gently.

0.4 Trail junction. Turn right here and continue on *AT* toward Little Stony Man. (Straight ahead is the 0.4mi. loop around summit of Stony Man Mountain. To left, a spur trail connects with Skyland-Stony Man Mountain Horse Trail.)

1.0 Reach cliffs of Little Stony Man. From here trail descends steeply by switchbacks.

1.3 Base of Little Stony Man cliffs.(Skyland Lodge is 1.4mi. left(south), on Passamaquoddy Trail, former *AT*, which passes under sheer cliffs of Stony Man.)

1.6 Spur trail, right, leads 150 ft. to Little Stony Man Parking Area on Skyline Drive, SDMP 39.1. *AT* drops well below the Drive, then parallels it, clinging to steep western slopes of main ridge.

2.0 Spur trail, right, leads 200 ft. to south end of Stony Man Mountain Parking Overlook in Hughes River Gap, SDMP 38.6 (3,097 ft.). Drinking *water* (in season) and toilets here. *AT* now descends.

2.3 Trail junction. (To right, blue-blazed Nicholson Hollow Trail leads 0.1mi. to Skyline Drive, SDMP 38.4, then continues into Nicholson Hollow. See "Side Trails".)

2.5 Intersection with blue-blazed Crusher Ridge Trail. (This trail utilizes an old road known as Sours Lane. See "Side Trails".) *AT* descends, passes over a slight rise, then descends again.

3.1 To left a trail leads downhill 0.3mi. to *spring* near location of former Shaver Hollow Shelter. From nebulous intersection *AT* ascends.

3.2 Where *AT* switchbacks sharply to left there is an excellent viewpoint. *AT* is immediately above Skyline Drive here and offers an unobstructed view of Nicholson Hollow and Old Rag Mountain beyond.

3.5 Pass under powerlines. About 0.1mi. farther, notice impressive old white pine growing to right of *AT*. From here Trail ascends over knob, then descends to reach Pinnacles Picnic Area.

3.9 Come onto paved path in picnic area and bear left, following *AT* blazes. In 200 ft. turn left at drinking fountain (*water* in season). Pass toilets and follow path through tunnels of mountain laurel. Trail now follows picnic area path, paralleling entrance road to the Pinnacles Area for about 0.1mi.

4.2 Bear left, away from road. Descend gradually along narrow ridge crest. Fine views westward over Jewell Hollow.

4.3 Spur trail, right, leads 75 ft. to Jewell Hollow Parking Overlook, SDMP 36.4. *AT* passes below overlook.

4.5 Pass second spur trail leading back to overlook. Trail now ascends gently through some tall white pines.

4.6 Cross Leading Ridge Trail, blue-blazed, which leads right 0.1mi. to Skyline Drive and left over Leading Ridge. See "Side Trails". *AT* now ascends, passing through thick growth of mountain laurel.

5.3 Pass to right of highest point of The Pinnacle, 3,730 ft. For a short distance Trail follows level ridge crest with excellent views. Pass, on left, jagged rocks forming north peak of The Pinnacle. From here Trail descends to a sag at base of The Pinnacle.

5.5 Pass obscure trail, left, leading 100 ft. to fine view north. *AT* descends by switchbacks along a rocky, picturesque ridge.

6.3 Reach Byrds Nest #3 which has piped *water*, in season. (See "Accommodations and Facilities".) Beyond shelter, *AT* follows access road for 180 ft. then turns left, away from road. (Road leads 0.3mi. to Skyline Drive, SDMP 33.9.) From road, *AT* ascends slightly by switchbacks on east slope of ridge, passing viewpoint at 6.7mi., then bearing right along ridge. Descend into slight sag.

6.9 Junction with Meadow Spring Trail which leads right, downhill, passing *Meadow Spring* on left in 0.3mi. and ending at US 211. (See "Side Trails".) From trail junction *AT* follows ridge crest. At large rock outcrop, the southern tip of Marys Rock, *AT* swings to right of ridge and starts to descend.

7.6 Spur trail leads left 0.1mi. to exposed northern tip of Marys Rock. (Views from this point are unsurpassed anywhere in Park. Here there are splendid views of Central and Northern Districts of the Park, the Massanuttens, Great North Mountain and Alleghenies to west, and the rolling hills of Virginia Piedmont to the east. Highest point, 3,514 ft., is reached by climbing to top of rock outcrop of granodiorite. It can be dangerous in icy, wet, or windy weather. Geologists believe the rock of Marys Rock is over one billion years old!) From trail junction *AT* descends steadily to Thornton Gap, at first through laurel and scrub oak. Here there are splendid views of Hazel Mtn. to southeast, of the Massanuttens, Great North Mountain and Alleghenies to west, Oventop Mtn. with its many peaks to northeast, and the Blue Ridge as far north as Mt. Marshall.

9.2 Spur trail, right, leads into Panorama Upper Parking Area. *AT* passes to left and below Panorama Restaurant.

9.3 Junction with US 211, about 0.1mi. west of Skyline Drive in Thornton Gap, SDMP 31.5 (2,307 ft.).

Section 4
Skyland to Fishers Gap
6.5 miles   PATC Map #10

General Description

Most of the Blue Ridge in this area was at one time covered by a series of lava flows. Today this lava, in its present form of greenstone, is the rock seen in the various rock outcrops along Skyline Drive and along the Appalachian Trail in this section. On the western side of the ridge, where the slope is very steep, the old layers of lava show as a series of vertical cliffs, one above another. The route of the *AT* below Crescent Rocks, along Hawksbill and Franklin Cliffs, follows these cliff shelves from one level to another thus affording a very rugged and photogenic section of trail.

Hawksbill Mountain is the highest in the Park. The *AT* slabs its northwestern slope; side trails lead to the summit, 4,040 ft. Native red spruce and balsam fir can be found in disjunct colonies at high elevations from Hawksbill to Stony Man Mountain, and from The Pinnacles to Marys Rock. They do not grow along the *AT* north of this area until one reaches Vermont or south of this area until one reaches Mt. Rogers, 5,729 ft. and nearby Whitetop in southwest Virginia.

Trail Approaches

The northern end is at Stony Man Nature Trail Parking Area on Skyline Drive, SDMP 41.7.

The southern end is in Fishers Gap, SDMP 49.3, at intersection with Red Gate Fire Road just north of Fishers Gap Overlook.

Side Trails

As in Section 3, the Park is wide here, especially to the east of Skyline Drive. The lovely Whiteoak Canyon-Cedar Run circuit hike is in this area. The scenic rock-sculptured top of Old Rag Mountain beckons the hiker there. Several routes lead to the top of Hawksbill Mountain. For details see "Side Trails". Also refer to PATC publication: *Circuit Hikes in Shenandoah National Park.*

Accommodations

Public accommodations are open at Skyland from mid-April through November. The lodge and cottages can accommodate 350 persons. There is a stable here with a network of horse trails in the area. For information and lodging reservations call 1-800-999-4714 or write to: ARA Virginia Sky-Line Co. Inc., Box 727, Luray, VA 22835.

Rock Spring Hut, 1.9mi. north of Fishers Gap, is available for long distance *AT* hikers. One locked cabin, Rock Spring, also 1.9mi. north of Fishers Gap, may be reserved in advance from PATC Headquarters. See "Accommodations and Facilities". Byrds Nest #2, an open-faced shelter for day use only (no fires), is atop Hawksbill Mtn. It can be reached from the *AT* in 0.9mi. via the Hawksbill Trail from Hawksbill Gap.

Trail Description, North to South

0.0 This section of *AT* begins at Stony Man Nature Trail Parking Area near Skyline Drive, SDMP 41.7. From parking lot, cross paved road (watch for posts and blazes) and enter woods. Ascend gradually.

0.2 Intersection with dirt service road leading right 0.2mi. to Skyland Dining Hall and Lodge and left to water tank. At top of climb, reach open field with large green water tank. (Do NOT camp here!) *AT* now begins a gradual descent.

0.8 Cross paved Skyland Road which leads left to Skyline Drive and right to Skyland development.

1.1 Trail leads along cliffs on western edge of ridge under Pollock Knob, 3,560 ft. (named for George Pollock, founder of Skyland). There are occasional views to right from Trail.

1.6 Where *AT* begins descent by switchbacks, there is a spectacular view of Hawksbill Mtn. and Ida Valley. Beyond, *AT* parallels Drive, passing through a thicket of laurel.

2.1 Reach open area. Spur trail, left, leads uphill 300 ft. to Timber Hollow Parking Overlook on Skyline Drive, SDMP 43.3.

2.2 Trail climbs over small ridge, then descends gently, slabbing steep western slopes of Blue Ridge. Here Trail passes some picturesque contorted trees. A big oak on right extends a "sitting limb".

2.8 Concrete post marks spur trail on right leading uphill 0.1mi. to junction a few feet north from Crescent Rock Parking Overlook, SDMP 44.4, to Bettys Rock (lovely views). *AT* next passes under cliffs of Crescent Rock. Excellent views of Nakedtop and Hawksbill Mtn. from Trail along here.

3.3 Reach Hawksbill Gap. (Trail to right leads downhill 450 ft. to *spring*. To left, uphill, it is 300 ft. to Hawksbill Gap Parking Area on the Drive, SDMP 45.6 (3,361 ft.). On east side of Drive here is start of Cedar Run Trail. From Hawksbill Gap Parking Area, Hawksbill Trail leads steeply up for 0.8mi. to Byrds Nest #2 and summit of Hawksbill just beyond. During summers of 1989 and 1990 the summit of Hawksbill, 4,050 ft., was site of a peregrine falcon release program reintroducing falcon to Park. On rare, magnificent days, skyline of Washington, D.C., including Washington Monument, can be seen along with grandstand view of mountains. From summit, Hawksbill Trail descends southward to Upper Hawksbill Parking Area on Drive, SDMP 46.7.) From Hawksbill Gap, *AT* ascends then slabs steep northern face of Hawksbill Mtn., passing under cliffs in a wild, rugged setting. (This is home of rare Shenandoah salamander. Splendid views, looking backward, of Crescent Rocks, Stony Man, and Old Rag Mtn; also northward views of Ida Valley and Luray.)

4.3 Reach sag between Hawksbill and Nakedtop. Trail to left leads 0.9mi. to summit of Hawksbill. See "Side Trails".

4.6 *AT* comes out of deep woods into old orchard now rapidly being overgrown with black locust, sumac, and pines. Road entering from left is used as service road to Rock Spring Cabin. It appears as a grassy meadow. Do NOT camp here! To left it is 0.2mi. to Skyline Drive, SDMP 47.8. Twenty feet farther along *AT* signpost marks graded spur trail leading right 0.2mi. downhill to Rock Spring Cabin, a locked structure, and to Rock Spring Hut, available for long distance *AT* hikers only. (See "Accommodations and Facilities".) A *spring* is 50 yds. north of cabin.

5.2 Spur trail, left, marked by post, leads 150 ft. uphill to Skyline Drive at Spitler Knoll Parking Overlook, SDMP 48.1. Beyond overlook *AT* continues, again slabbing western slopes of main Blue Ridge.

6.0 Pass concrete post marking obscure trail leading left, uphill 0.3mi., to north end of Franklin Cliffs Overlook.

6.3 Pass second trail, marked by post but equally obscure, which leads left 0.3mi. to south end of Franklin Cliffs Overlook, SDMP 49.0 (3,135 ft.).

6.5 Intersect Red Gate Fire Road in Fishers Gap. (This road was known as Gordonsville Turnpike in days before Shenandoah National Park. To right it leads down mountain to SR 611. To left it is 350 ft. to northern end of Fishers Gap Parking Overlook, SDMP 49.3 (3,061 ft.). East of Drive is Rose River Fire Road leading to Dark Hollow Falls Trail. See "Side Trails".)

Trail Description, South to North

0.0 Intersection of *AT* and Red Gate Fire Road in Fishers Gap. (To right(east) it is 350 ft. to Skyline Drive just north of Fishers Gap Parking Overlook, SDMP 49.3 (3,061 ft.). To east of Drive is Rose River Fire Road leading to Dark Hollow Falls Trail. See "Side Trails".)

0.2 Pass post marking spur trail (may be difficult to follow) leading right 0.1mi. to south end of Franklin Cliffs Overlook, SDMP 49.0 (3,135 ft.). From here *AT* passes below Franklin Cliffs then along ledge above more cliffs. Birdfoot violets bloom here in May. (Cliffs, composed of altered basaltic rock, are result of erosion of ancient lava beds laid down in layers 100 to 250 ft. thick for total thickness of 2-3,000 ft. and later tilted about 90 degrees.)

0.5 Post marks obscure trail, right, which leads 0.3mi. to northern end of Franklin Cliffs Overlook. *AT* continues to slab west side of ridge.

1.3 Spur trail, right, marked by post, leads 150 ft. uphill to Skyline Drive at Spitler Knoll Parking Overlook, SDMP 48.1. *AT* now ascends gradually, passing old road at 1.5mi. Trail soon levels off, then descends gently.

1.9 *AT* comes into slightly open area. Post marks spur trail which leads left 0.2mi. downhill to Rock Spring Hut, for use by long distance *AT* hikers, and Rock Spring Cabin, a locked building requiring advance reservations. (See "Accommodations and Facilities".) *Spring* is 150 ft. north of cabin. Twenty feet farther along *AT* an old road, which serves as Park access road to cabin, leads 0.2mi. to Drive, SDMP 47.8. This road appears to be a grassy meadow. Do NOT camp here! *AT* passes old orchard rapidly being overgrown with pine, sumac, and locust.

2.2 Reach sag between Hawksbill and Nakedtop. Trail to right leads 0.9mi. to summit of Hawksbill. (See "Side Trails.") From sag *AT* slabs northern face of Hawksbill, passing below steep cliffs, home of rare Shenandoah salamander. Good views to north of Ida Valley and Luray, views ahead of Crescent Rock, Stony Man and Old Rag Mountain.

3.2 Reach Hawksbill Gap and trail intersection. (To left trail leads downhill 0.1mi. to *spring*. To right it is 300 ft. uphill to Hawksbill Gap Parking Area on the Drive, SDMP 45.6 (3,361 ft.). From parking area, Hawksbill Trail leads steeply to summit of Hawksbill, 4,050 ft., highest point in SNP. In summers of 1989 and 1990 summit of Hawksbill was site of peregrine release program, reintroducing falcon to Park. On rare, magnificent days skyline of Washington, D.C., including Washington Monument, along with grandstand view of mountains everywhere, can be seen from here. Byrds Nest #2, an open-faced shelter for day use only (no fires), is just below summit. See "Side Trails".)

3.6 *AT* passes under cliffs of Crescent Rock. These, like those of Franklin Cliffs, are eroded remnants of ancient lava beds.

3.7 Side trail, marked by concrete post, leads right, uphill 0.1mi., to northern end of Crescent Rock Parking Overlook, SDMP 44.4. (Trail from there leads 0.3mi. to Bettys Rock. In crannies along exposed rocks of Bettys Rock one may find three-toothed cinquefoil, a northern plant, blooming in late spring and early summer.)

4.6 In open area, spur trail, right, leads uphill 300 ft. to Timber Hollow Parking Overlook on Drive, SDMP 43.3. From junction *AT* parallels Drive, passing through thicket of mountain laurel, blooming in early June. Trail then ascends by switchbacks to Pollock Knob, 3,560 ft. Good views of Hawksbill Mtn. and Ida Valley.

5.0 Reach top of ridge with splendid views of Hawksbill Mtn. and Ida Valley. Trail now follows cliffs along west side of Pollock Knob, with fine views west. Trail ascends slightly, then follows corral fence to Skyland stables.

5.7 Horse trail leads right to Skyline Drive and beyond to Whiteoak Canyon and Big Meadows. *AT* continues ahead, crossing blacktop trail at stables, then crossing paved Skyland Road before entering woods. *AT* now ascends gently. At top of hill, reach open area and large green water tank. (Do NOT camp here!) Begin gradual descent.

6.2 Intersection with dirt service road leading left 0.2mi. to Skyland Dining Hall and Lodge. *AT* continues gradual descent.

6.5 Reach paved Skyland Road near northern entrance to Skyland, SDMP 41.7. (To left it is 0.3mi. on paved road to Skyland Lodge and Dining Hall.) Follow concrete posts, crossing road to Nature Trail Parking Area.

Section 5
Fishers Gap to Swift Run Gap
18.6 miles   PATC Map #10

General Description

From Fishers Gap, 3,061 ft., the *AT* skirts the Big
Meadows developed area, then continues on to Milam
Gap where it crosses Skyline Drive. It climbs to the
summit of Hazeltop where the *AT* reaches its highest
elevation in Shenandoah National Park, 3,816 ft. It
descends to Bootens Gap before climbing two low mountains, Bush and Bearfence; the latter is very scenic. The
AT skirts the Lewis Mountain developed area, climbs
over Baldface Mtn., drops down to skirt the South River
Picnic Area, then follows an old road over a spur of
Saddleback Mtn., finally descending to Swift Run Gap,
2,367 ft.

Trail Approaches

The northern end of this section is on Skyline Drive
just north of Fishers Gap Overlook, SDMP 49.3, at
intersection with Red Gate Fire Road, 350 ft. west of the
Drive.

The southern end is at Swift Run Gap, SDMP 65.5,
where entrance road from US 33 joins Drive. It is 7 miles
east of Elkton and 8 miles west of Stanardsville via US
33.

Side Trails

In the Big Meadows area there are many trails and a
number of circuit hikes that are popular. The Dark
Hollow-Rose River Loop circuit is a favorite one. The
Rapidan Fire Road and several trails lead eastward from
Skyline Drive and the *AT* to Camp Hoover, located
within the Park on the Rapidan River. On Laurel Prong
near Camp Hoover one can find rosebay rhododendron,
(R.maximum). The Lewis Spring Falls Trail combined

with the Lewis Spring service road and the *AT* make a spectacular circuit.

Farther south is the short, but very scenic, South River Falls Trail. An excellent circuit hike can be made from Pocosin Cabin by using the Pocosin Fire Road, the Pocosin Trail, the South River Fire Road, the South River Falls Trail, and the *AT*. See "Side Trails"; also see PATC publication: *Circuit Hikes in Shenandoah National Park.*

Many blue-blazed trails, fire roads and old roads beckon the hiker. Some are well marked and easy to follow, but others may be poorly marked or badly overgrown and should be attempted only by the experienced woodsman.

Accommodations

The Big Meadows developed area, SDMP 51.2, just south of Fishers Gap, includes a lodge and cottages offering meals and lodging for 350 persons. It also contains a wayside (meals and supplies available most of the year), stables (wagon rides only), gas station, the Byrd Visitor Center, and a large camping area for both tents and trailers. Big Meadows campground has standard facilities for campers--store, ice, laundry, showers, etc.--and is open all year except January and February. During the summer and fall, campground reservations may be made through Ticketron by calling 1-800-452-1111 and using either Visa or MasterCard. The lodge is open mid-May through October and the Byrd Visitor Center is open all year. Lewis Mountain has a campground, open summer only, cabins mid-May through October, and a camp store. For information and lodging reservations at Big Meadows and Lewis Mtn., call 1-800-999-4714 or write to: ARA Virginia Sky-Line Co. Inc., Box 727, Luray, VA 22835.

The open-faced Bearfence Mountain Hut, 9.1mi. north of Swift Run Gap, is available for long distance *AT* hikers with backcountry permits. One locked structure, Pocosin Cabin, is near the trail here but must be reserved in advance. A second cabin, Jones Mountain Cabin, is located too far to the east for easy accessibility from the *AT*. See "Accommodations and Facilities".

Trail Description, North to South

0.0 Intersection with Red Gate Fire Road 350 ft. west of Skyline Drive, SDMP 49.3, 3,061 ft. (To right fire road leads down mountain to SR 611. East of Drive is Rose River Fire Road and Dark Hollow Falls. See "Side Trails".)

0.1 Pass below Fishers Gap Overlook. (Look for blooms of hepatica in spring and clematis in summer.) Pass post marking spur trail, left, which leads 100 ft. to Fishers Gap Parking Overlook.

0.2 Pass to right of split rock. Ascend gradually. Pass through beautiful hemlock grove. Continue to ascend, crossing small stream twice.

1.0 *David Spring* is 50 ft. to right of *AT*. A trail comes in from left. (See Big Meadows inset on back of PATC Map #10.) *AT* skirts north edge of Big Meadows Campground. (Several short unmarked trails lead left to campground.) Openings along *AT* give fine views north and west - Hawksbill Mtn. is in foreground, Stony Man Mtn. is farther away, and, in the distance, Knob Mtn. and Neighbor Mtn. Across Page Valley, Signal Knob can be seen at northern end of Massanutten range.

1.3 Cross a small rocky knob, the Monkey Head. Views here also. Beyond, *AT* skirts western edge of ridge.

1.5 Pass below open-air amphitheater of Big Meadows.

1.6 Concrete post marks trail intersection. *AT* is straight ahead. (Trail to right, downhill, leads 1.2mi. to Lewis Falls. Trail to left, the Lodge Trail, leads to Amphitheater Parking Area.

1.9 Pass under sheer cliffs of Blackrock. Rocks to right of *AT* provide a grandstand view west of Shenandoah Valley, the Massanuttens, Great North Mountain, and the distant Alleghenies.

2.1 Trail to left of *AT* leads 0.1mi. to Blackrock viewpoint and another 0.2mi. to Big Meadows Lodge. *AT* continues along western slope of ridge, descending, with occasional views to west from rocks to right of Trail.

2.5 Cross service road. (To left it is 0.3mi. to Skyline Drive, SDMP 51.4, at a point 0.1mi. south of Big Meadows Wayside. Meals and supplies are available at wayside most of the year. Harry F. Byrd Sr. Visitor Center located here, also. (To right of *AT* service road leads downhill about 150 ft. to small pumphouse to right of road. Turn left off road onto footpath that leads 0.5mi. downhill to Lewis Falls.) Beyond service road intersection *AT* passes outlet of housed-in *Lewis Spring*. Trail continues through woods, descending gradually.

3.1 Reach Tanners Ridge Cemetery on right. Cross Tanners Ridge Road. (Road, gated at Drive and Park boundary, leads right 1.4mi. to Park boundary where it becomes SR 682. To left it leads 0.1mi. to Drive, SDMP 51.6.) From here to Milam Gap *AT* is a level path.

3.3 Pass *spring* 50 ft. to left of *AT*. Beyond, pass through stands of pioneering locust.

4.2 Cross Skyline Drive, SDMP 52.8, just south of Milam Gap, 3,257 ft. (Parking space for 20 vehicles on west side of Milam Gap.) *AT* bears east through a field. Concrete post marks Mill Prong Trail which leads left from *AT*. Beyond junction, *AT* ascends north ridge of Hazeltop.

4.6 Bear right along ridge crest. From rock to left of Trail is wintertime view of Doubletop and Fork Mtns. (Former President Herbert Hoover's Camp is in Rapidan Valley between these peaks.) *AT* ascends very gradually along ridge crest. Here may be found a fine stand of stiff gentians among white and purple asters in autumn.

5.7 Reach north end of Hazeltop.

6.1 Cross wooded summit of Hazeltop, 3,812 ft., highest point of *AT* in SNP. A wooden sign marks summit. A few red spruce and balsam can be found here.

6.6 Junction with blue-blazed Laurel Prong Trail, leading left 2.8mi. to Camp Hoover. (See "Side Trails". This is one of few trails in Park that passes through areas with rosebay rhododendron, or great laurel, which blooms in late June or early July. Other wild flowers found here include false lily-of-the-valley, trillium, and wild iris.)

7.0 In Bootens Gap, 3,243 ft., cross gated Conway River Fire Road. (Skyline Drive, SDMP 55.1, is 50 ft. to right with parking space for five cars. To left road leads down mountain to Va 230. See "Side Trails".) *AT* descends gradually for 0.2mi. then continues with little change in elevation, paralleling Skyline Drive.

7.7 Ascend gradually, following western slope of Bush Mtn.

7.9 *AT* approaches within 150 ft. of Drive. Ascent continues for about 0.2mi., then Trail is level for about 0.2mi. before again ascending along ridge of Bearfence Mtn.

8.4 Trail intersection. (To right, blue-blazed trail leads 0.1mi. to Bearfence Mountain Parking Area on Skyline Drive, SDMP 56.4. Naturalist-led hikes start here in summer. To left, a blazed trail leads to spectacular jagged rocks of Bearfence Mtn. Views from rocks are excellent. This is a rough trail requiring use of hands in some places. In 0.3mi. it connects with graded loop trail over Bearfence Mtn. The two trails, with *AT*, make a rough figure eight.

8.6 Bearfence Mtn. Loop Trail (graded) leaves *AT* on left. (Views along this trail are rewarding. Loop trail is only 150 ft. longer than the stretch of *AT* between junctions.)

8.8 Bearfence Loop Trail comes in from left. *AT* now descends by switchbacks. From a rock ledge near top there is a splendid view to east.

9.4 In gap, cross yellow-blazed Slaughter Trail. (Slaughter Trail leads 0.1mi. to access road to Bearfence Hut, then down to Park boundary. To right it is a few feet to

Skyline Drive, SDMP 56.8. Across the Drive it continues as Meadow School Trail. See "Side Trails".)

9.5 Spur trail, left, leads downhill 0.1mi. to Bearfence Mountain Hut, to be used by long distance *AT* hikers only. (*Spring* is 50 ft. south of hut, frequently dry in summer. See "Accommodations and Facilities".) *AT* now ascends gradually the north slope of Lewis Mtn. As Trail levels off at about 3,400 ft., several paths lead right, first to Lewis Mtn. Picnic Area (*water* available "in season") and then to Lewis Mtn. Campground. Camp store on campground road is open May through October.

10.4 Post marks trail, right, leading 300 ft. to campground. (*Water* fountain "in season" directly across camp road.)

10.5 Pass trail intersection. (To right, trail leads to campground; to left the obscure Lewis Mtn. East Trail, blue-blazed, ends in less than one mile.)

11.1 Old road descends left toward Pocosin Hollow; to right, Skyline Drive is only a few feet away. *AT* soon bears away from Drive.

12.0 Pass *spring* to right of Trail. (In early May vast fields of trillium, chickweed, cutleaf toothwort, plus yellow and purple violets can be found here.)

12.2 Cross Pocosin Fire Road. (To right, fire road leads 0.1mi. to Skyline Drive, SDMP 59.5; to left it is 0.1mi. downhill to Pocosin Cabin. See "Side Trails"). Beyond fire road intersection, *AT* ascends gradually.

12.3 Graded spur trail leads left, 250 ft. downhill, to Pocosin Cabin and *spring* just south of cabin. (This is a locked cabin and reservations must be made in advance from PATC Headquarters. See "Accommodations and Facilities". From cabin there is a fine view east over Conway River Valley. Three mountains can be seen across valley. Local mountaineers called them, from right to left: Panther, Bear Stand, and Sawney Macks. These names are not recognized on current maps. "Pocosin" is said to be of Indian derivation meaning "dismal" or swamp.)

12.4 Pass *spring* to right of trail.

12.5 *AT* ascends steeply by switchbacks for 0.1mi. (At top is view north of Lewis Mtn., Hazeltop, Jones Mtn., and Fork Mtn. crowned with a radio transmitter tower.) *AT* next passes through a relatively flat area known as Kites Deadening, now completely wooded. (A deadening was an area where the early settlers, instead of felling trees to clear the land for a field, saved time and effort by ringing them - removing the lower bark - thus killing the trees without the task of cutting them down. They would then plant their crops amid the "deadened" trees.)

13.5 Reach crest of Baldface Mtn., 3,600 ft.

13.8 Rocks to right of Trail offer views to west. *AT* begins gentle descent of Baldface Mtn.

14.2 Cross old road which leads left past an old quarry. (To right, road leads 0.1mi. past site of former CCC camp, then to Skyline Drive, SDMP 61.8.)

15.1 Cross South River Fire Road, yellow-blazed. (To left road leads 0.8mi. to blue-blazed trail which goes right to South River. Follow a footpath for 0.1mi. up river to base of South River Falls. To right fire road leads 0.3mi. to Skyline Drive, SDMP 62.7 (2,960 ft.). See "Side Trails".)

15.6 Cross graded South River Falls Trail. (To left trail leads 1.5mi. downhill to South River Falls. To right it is 0.1mi. to eastern edge of South River Picnic Area. *Water* is available here "in season".)

15.9 In pine thicket old road comes in on right from the Drive, SDMP 63.1. *AT* turns left onto this road and follows it.

16.1 *AT* takes right fork of road. (Left fork is blue-blazed Saddleback Trail which leads 0.3mi. to South River Maintenance Bldg. where there is a *spring* 200 feet west of building. Trail continues to south and west to rejoin *AT* in 1.4mi.)

16.5 At bend in Trail an old road comes in from left. *AT* ascends.

16.7 Still following old road, reach top of rise, just west of westernmost peak of Saddleback Mtn., 3,296 ft. There is much trillium along Trail here in early May.

17.2 Junction with Saddleback Mtn. Trail which comes in from left.

17.9 *AT* turns left off old road.

18.3 Trail passes under powerline.

18.5 Pass side trail on left which leads 100 yds. to a cemetery.

18.6 Reach Skyline Drive, where US 33 crosses the Drive in Swift Run Gap, SDMP 65.5 (2,367 ft.).

Trail Description, South to North

0.0 This section begins on eastern side of Skyline Drive in Swift Run Gap, SDMP 65.5, 2,367 ft., where entrance road from US 33 joins the Drive. Trail ascends through woods.

0.1 Pass a side trail, right, which leads 100 yds. east to a cemetery.

0.3 *AT* passes under powerline.

0.7 Trail turns right onto old road which it follows over Saddleback Mtn., passing west of summit. Follow old road for about 2mi.

1.4 Saddleback Mtn. Trail, blue-blazed, leads right from *AT* for 1.1mi. to South River Maintenance Bldg. where there is a *spring* 200 ft. west of building.

1.9 Still following old road, *AT* reaches top of rise just west of westernmost peak of Saddleback Mtn., 3,296 ft. (One may find a profusion of trillium blooming here in early May.) Trail now descends.

2.1 At sharp left bend in *AT* an old road comes in from right.

2.5 At junction of old roads, *AT* follows left fork. (Right fork is Saddleback Trail which leads 0.3mi. to South River Maintenance Bldg.)

2.7 *AT* turns right off old road and passes through a pine woods. (Road bears left and leads 0.1mi. to Skyline Drive, SDMP 63.1.) *AT* skirts eastern side of South River Picnic Area.

3.0 Cross graded South River Falls Trail. (To left trail leads 0.1mi. to picnic area. *Water* available here "in season". To right trail leads steeply downhill for 1.5mi. to lovely South River Falls.)

3.5 Cross South River Fire Road, yellow-blazed. (To left it is 0.2mi. to Skyline Drive, SDMP 62.7 (2,960 ft.). See "Side Trails".) *AT* begins long gentle ascent of Baldface Mtn.

4.4 Cross old road which leads, right, past an old quarry. (To left road leads past site of former CCC camp 0.1mi. to Skyline Drive, SDMP 61.8.)

4.8 Rocks to left of Trail offer views to west.

5.1 Reach summit of Baldface Mtn., 3,600 ft., then descend gently.

5.9 *AT* passes through a relatively flat area known as Kites Deadening, now completely wooded. (Instead of felling trees for a field, the early settlers saved time and effort by ringing the trees and removing the lower bark, thus killing them without the task of removing them. They would plant their crops amid the "deadened" trees.)

6.0 View north of Lewis Mtn., Hazeltop, Jones Mtn. and Fork Mtn. with radio transmitter tower. Trail descends steeply by switchbacks for 0.1mi.

6.2 Pass *spring* to left of trail.

6.3 Spur trail leads 250 ft. right, downhill, to Pocosin Cabin, 3,120 ft., and *spring* south of cabin. (Pocosin is a locked cabin which may be reserved in advance at PATC Headquarters. See "Accommodations and Facilities." From cabin there is a fine view east over Conway River Valley. Three mountains can be seen across valley. Local mountaineers called these, from right to left: Panther, Bear Stand and Sawney Macks; these names are not shown on today's maps. The word "Pocosin" is said to be of Indian derivation meaning a "dismal" or swamp.) Beyond spur trail *AT* descends gently.

6.4 Cross Pocosin Fire Road. (To left fire road leads 0.1mi. to Skyline Drive, SDMP 59.5. To right it leads back to Pocosin Cabin. See "Side Trails".)

7.5 Where *AT* is close (30 ft.) to the Drive, an old road leads right and descends toward Pocosin Hollow. *AT* soon ascends.

8.1 Pass trail intersection. (To left trail leads to Lewis Mountain Campground. To right blue-blazed Lewis Mountain East Trail leads along ridge crest of Lewis Mtn., then disappears.)

8.2 A post marks trail, left, which leads 300 ft. to Lewis Mtn. Campground. (*Water* fountain "in season" directly across camp road. Camp store is located on road.) *AT* now descends gently. Several paths, unmarked, lead left to camping area and then picnic area of Lewis Mtn. *Water* available "in season".

9.1 Spur trail, right, leads downhill 0.1mi. to Bearfence Mtn. Hut. (*Spring* 50 ft. to right of hut, is frequently dry by late summer. Hut is for use of long distance *AT* hikers. See "Accommodations and Facilities".)

9.2 Cross yellow-blazed Slaughter Trail. (To right it joins access road to Bearfence Mtn. Hut. To left it leads to Skyline Drive, SDMP 56.8. See "Side Trails".)

9.8 Junction with Bearfence Loop Trail which leads right. (Views on this short trail are very rewarding. Loop Trail is only 150 ft. longer than *AT* between junctions.)

10.0 Loop Trail reenters *AT* from right.

10.2 Cross blue-blazed trail. (To left trail leads 0.1mi. to Bearfence Mtn. Parking Area on Skyline Drive, SDMP 56.4. Hikes led by a SNP naturalist start here during summer. To right trail leads to spectacular jagged rocks of Bearfence Mtn.; they offer excellent views. This rough trail requires use of hands in some places. It connects with loop trail over Bearfence Mtn. making a rough figure eight with *AT*.) Beyond intersection *AT* remains rather level for 0.3mi. then descends gradually along western slope of Bush Mtn.

11.6 In Bootens Gap, 3,243 ft., cross Conway River Fire Road. (Skyline Drive, SDMP 55.1, is 150 ft. to left, with parking space for 5 cars; to right leads down mountain to Va 230. See "Side Trails".) *AT* now starts ascent of Hazeltop Mtn.

12.0 Pass blue-blazed Laurel Prong Trail on right. (It leads 2.8mi. down to Camp Hoover, passing through one of few areas in Park where rosebay rhododendron (R.Maximum) grows.) *AT* continues to ascend.

12.5 Cross wooded summit of Hazeltop, 3,812 ft., highest point on *AT* in SNP. Wooden sign marks summit. (A few red spruce and balsam here.) *AT* now descends gently.

13.0 Along a level area there is a fine stand of stiff gentians mixed with purple and white asters, blooming in autumn. Beyond this area Trail again descends.

14.0 Trail bears left, due west. From a rock to right of *AT* at this turn is a good wintertime view of Doubletop and Fork Mtns. (Former President Hoover's Camp is in Rapidan Valley between these peaks.)

14.4 Come into overgrown field. Concrete post marks Mill Prong Trail leading right from *AT*. (This trail, of which first 0.1mi. is blue-blazed, leads 1.8mi. to Camp Hoover. See "Side Trails".) A few feet farther, just south of Milam Gap, *AT* crosses Skyline Drive, SDMP 52.8. (This is only crossing of Drive in Central District of Park. On west side of Milam Gap is parking for 20 cars.) Cross a field and enter woods.

15.3 Pass *spring* 50 ft. to right of *AT*.

15.5 Cross Tanners Ridge Road with cemetery on left. (To right it is 0.1mi. to Drive, SDMP 51.6; to left leads out of Park. See "Side Trails".)

16.1 Pass outlet of housed-in *Lewis Spring*. Immediately beyond, cross Park service road. (To right, road leads 0.3mi. to Skyline Drive, SDMP 51.4. To left, road leads to Lewis Falls in 0.6mi. Follow road down about 150 ft. to small pumphouse on right of road. Turn left off road onto footpath that continues downhill 0.5mi. to falls.) *AT* ascends steadily along western slope of ridge with occasional views from rocks to left of Trail.

16.5 Trail to right of *AT* leads 0.1mi. to Blackrock Viewpoint and 0.2mi. farther to Big Meadows Lodge. (About 50 yds. north of Blackrock Trail is incredible view west encompassing length of Massanuttens and beyond to Great North Mountain and the Alleghenies.) Continuing on *AT*, pass under sheer cliffs of Blackrock in 0.2mi.

17.0 Trail intersection marked by concrete post. (Trail to left leads back 1.2mi. to Lewis Falls; to right leads up to amphitheater and picnic area.) *AT* now passes below Big Meadows Amphitheater.

17.3 Cross small rocky knob, the Monkey Head, where there are views. Beyond *AT* skirts north edge of Big Meadows Campground. Several small unmarked trails lead right to camping area. Openings along *AT* give fine views north and west. (Hawksbill Mtn. is in foreground, Stony Man Mtn. farther away and, in the distance, Knob Mtn., The Neighbor, and, across Page Valley, Signal Knob is at northern end of Massanutten range.

17.6 Reach northern end of campground. *David Spring* is 50 ft. to left of *AT*. *AT* now descends. (A large, disjunct colony of gray birch, southernmost stand of this northern tree, is found here.) Begin gradual descent to Fishers Gap. Cross small stream twice. Pass hemlock grove.

18.4 Pass to left of split rock.

18.5 Spur trail leads right 100 ft. to Fishers Gap Parking Overlook on Skyline Drive. Pass below overlook. (Look for blooms of hepatica in spring and clematis in summer.)

18.6 Intersection with Red Gate Fire Road, 350 ft. west of Skyline Drive, just north of Fishers Gap Parking Overlook, SDMP 49.3 (3,061 ft.). (Across Drive, Rose River Fire Rd. leads down mountain, crossing Hogcamp Branch in 1mi. Dark Hollow Falls is a few hundred feet above crossing. See "Side Trails".)

SUMMARY OF DISTANCES ALONG THE *AT*
Central District

	Miles N-S	S-N
Thornton Gap and US 211	0.0	34.0
Marys Rock summit	1.7 + 0.1	32.3 + 0.1
Meadow Spring Trail	2.4	31.6
Byrds Nest #3	3.0	31.0
Pinnacles Picnic Area	5.4	28.6
Nicholson Hollow Trail	7.0	27.0
Stony Man Parking Overlook	7.3	26.7
Little Stony Man Parking Area	7.6	26.4
Stony Man Nature Trail Parking	9.0	25.0
Whiteoak Canyon Trail	9.7 + 0.1	24.3 +0.1
Hawksbill Gap	12.2	21.8
Byrds Nest #2 and summit of Hawksbill	12.2 +0.8	20.8 + 0.9
Rock Spring Cabin	13.5 + 0.2	20.5 + 0.2
Rock Spring Hut	13.5 + 0.2	20.5 + 0.2
Fishers Gap	15.4	18.6
Big Meadows - Amphitheater area	17.0	17.0
Lewis Spring Service Road	17.9	16.1
Skyline Drive crossing, Milam Gap	19.6	14.4
Hazeltop Mtn. summit	21.5	12.5
Bearfence Mtn. Loop Trail	24.0	10.0
Bearfence Mtn. Hut	24.9 + 0.2	9.1 + 0.2
Lewis Mtn. Campground	25.9	8.1
Pocosin Cabin	27.6 + 0.1	6.4 + 0.1
South River Falls Trail	31.0	3.0
Swift Run Gap and US 33	34.0	0.0

SUMMARY OF DISTANCES BY SKYLINE DRIVE TO POINTS ON THE *AT*
Central District

SDMP N-S		Miles S-N
31.5	US 211 at Thornton Gap	34.0
33.5	Buck Hollow Trail, 0.7mi. from *AT*	32.0
33.9	Service Road to Byrds Nest #3; 0.3mi. to *AT*	31.6
36.4	Jewell Hollow Overlook	29.1
36.7	Pinnacles Picnic Area	28.8
37.9	Shaver Hollow Parking Area	27.6
38.4	Nicholson Hollow Trail; 0.1mi. to *AT*	27.1
38.6	Stony Man Mtn. Overlook	26.9
39.1	Little Stony Man Parking Area	26.4
41.7	Skyland, North Entrance; 0.3mi. to *AT*	23.8
42.5	Skyland, South Entrance, 0.1mi. to *AT*	23.0
43.3	Timber Hollow Overlook	21.2
44.4	Crescent Rock Overlook	21.1
45.6	Hawksbill Gap	19.9
48.1	Spitler Knoll Parking Overlook	17.4
49.0	Franklin Cliffs Overlook	16.5
49.3	Fishers Gap	16.2
51.2	Big Meadows developed area; 0.1mi. to *AT*	14.3
51.6	Tanners Ridge Fire Road; 0.1mi.l to *AT*	13.9
52.8	Milam Gap; *AT* crossing	12.7
55.1	Bootens Gap	10.4
56.4	Bearfence Mtn. Parking Area; 0.1mi. to *AT*	9.1
56.8	Slaughter Trail	8.7

57.5	Lewis Mtn. Campground; 0.1mi. to *AT*	8.0
59.5	Pocosin Fire Road; 0.1mi. to *AT*	6.0
62.7	South River Fire Road; 0.2mi. to *AT*	2.8
62.8	South River Picnic Area; 0.3mi. to *AT*	2.7
63.1	Service Road to South River Maintenance Bldg; 0.1mi. to *AT*	2.4
65.5	Swift Run Gap	0.0

(Summary of Distances by Skyline Drive
to Points on the *AT* - continued from page 93)

SHENANDOAH NATIONAL PARK
SOUTHERN DISTRICT

In the northern end of this district, the Appalachian Trail commences where US 33 (Spotswood Trail) crosses the Blue Ridge at Swift Run Gap, SDMP 65.5 (2,367 ft.). The southern end is in Rockfish Gap where US 250 and I-64 cross Skyline Drive. The Southern District of the Park includes Section 6, Section 7, Section 8, and Section 9 in this guidebook for a total of 44.9 miles.

The Southern District is the wildest and least developed area of the Park. Much of it has wilderness status. The *AT* follows the main crest of the Blue Ridge, is rarely far from Skyline Drive and crosses it often.

There are many interesting side trails and fire roads which can be used in conjunction with the *AT* for interesting hiking trips. Some points of particular interest are the Doyles River-Jones Run Loop Trail, Big Run Loop Trail, Riprap Ravine and Blackrock. Traveling south, the *AT* leaves the Park at Jarman Gap and, except for a short stretch on Calf Mountain, passes through a corridor of land acquired by the National Park Service for the Trail. See "Side Trails"; also PATC publication: *Circuit Hikes in Shenandoah National Park.*

There is one large campground in this district, Loft Mountain Campground, and one campground for groups only, Dundo Group Campground.

Maps

PATC Map #11; also USGS map of Shenandoah National Park, Southern Section, scale 1;62,500, and U.S. 7 1/2' quads: Swift Run Gap, McGaheysville, Browns Cove, Crimora and Waynesboro East. (Other quads covering areas of the Southern District not traversed by the *AT* include Grottoes, Elkton East and Crozet.

Section 6
Swift Run Gap to Simmons Gap
9.6 miles   PATC Map #11

General Description

The highest elevation of the *AT* in the Southern District of the Park is reached near the summit of Hightop Mtn., 3,587 ft. This means a climb of over 1,200 ft. traveling in either direction. Open ledges to the west of the summit afford excellent views south and west.

Trail Approaches

Access to the northern end of this section is at the junction of US 33 and Skyline Drive, SDMP 65.5, on east side of Drive, about 300 ft. north of bridge and directly opposite place where entrance road from US 33 reaches the Drive in Swift Run Gap; marked by concrete post.

The southern end is in Simmons Gap, SDMP 73.2, at intersection of Simmons Gap Fire Road and Skyline Drive, 7.7 miles south of the Swift Run Gap-US 33 entrance to Skyline Drive. .

Side Trails

Because SNP is very narrow through most of this section there are few side trails and those that do exist lead out of the Park.

Accommodations

There are no public accommodations along this section. Closest public lodgings, open only during warmer months, are at Lewis Mtn., SDMP 57.5, in the Central District of the Park. There is neither gasoline nor food available at Swift Run Gap.

Hightop Hut, 3.4 miles south of Swift Run Gap, is available for use by long distance *AT* hikers only. See "Accommodations and Facilities".

Trail Description, North to South

0.0 From concrete post on east side of Skyline Drive, SDMP 65.5, *AT* follows pedestrian footway along edge of bridge. Beyond bridge, cross to right side of Skyline Drive and climb bank. Trail shortly comes into old road which it follows for few feet.

0.1 Trail turns sharply left from old road and climbs. It soon levels off and follows an old farm road through what remains of an apple orchard, then descends gently.

1.3 In grassy sag, Trail crosses to left(east) of Skyline Drive, SDMP 66.7 (2,637 ft.). From sag trail ascends steeply, by switchbacks, northern slope of Hightop Mtn.

2.7 As *AT* nears summit there are two excellent viewpoints from ledges to right of Trail, one about 100 ft. farther along Trail than the other. In another 100 ft. spur trail, left, leads 350 ft. to site of former Park Service lookout tower at summit of Hightop Mtn., 3,587 ft. No view from summit. *AT* now descends.

2.9 Protected *spring* at foot of large boulder just to left of *AT*. Trail continues to descend.

3.4 Spur trail leads right 0.1mi. to Hightop Hut, for use by long distance *AT* hikers only. (See "Accommodations and Facilities". *Spring* is 400 ft. downhill from hut on graded trail.)

3.5 Cross dirt road. (Service road leads right to Hightop Hut and left to Smith Roach Gap Fire Road.) *AT* descends steadily.

4.6 Trail crosses Smith Roach Gap Fire Road, then turns right and parallels it to Skyline Drive.

4.7 Cross to right(west) of Skyline Drive in open Smith Roach Gap, SDMP 68.6 (2,622 ft.). Trail continues with little change in elevation around east and south sides of Roundtop Mtn., affording wintertime views of Powell Gap and Flattop Mtn. Continue along ridge crest.

5.8 Summit of Little Roundtop Mtn. is 50 yds. to right. View of Powell Gap just as Trail starts to descend steeply western slope of mountain.

6.3 Powell Gap, SDMP 69.9 (2,294 ft.). Cross to left of Drive. *AT* now ascends shoulder of Flattop Mtn.

6.6 Turn sharply left where old road, which *AT* has been following, continues straight ahead. Continue to ascend.

6.8 Excellent views of Roach River Valley (Powell Gap and Bacon Hollow) from rock ledges to left of Trail. Continue to ascend very gently.

8.0 Summit of shoulder of Flattop Mtn. Start gradual descent.

8.1 *AT* comes close to Skyline Drive. Views, especially of Flattop Mtn., 3,325 ft. from open field 50 ft. to left of Trail (beyond wire fence). Trail continues to descend.

8.7 Trail bends right to parallel old road on left, and descends steeply.

9.1 Trail comes into old road and follows it right for about 0.1mi..

9.2 Trail bends right, uphill, and ascends 3 rock steps.

9.4 Descend under powerlines.

9.6 Simmons Gap, SDMP 73.2 (2,253 ft.) at intersection of Simmons Gap Fire Road and Skyline Drive. (A short distance south on road is ranger's office and beyond it are Park Service maintenance facilities. *Water* available here.) *AT* crosses to right(west) of Skyline Drive.

Trail Description, South to North

0.0 Begin at intersection of Simmons Gap Fire Road and Skyline Drive, SDMP 73.2 (2,253 ft.). *AT* follows Simmons Gap Road east of Drive for about 40 ft., then turns left onto path. (A short distance south on road is ranger's office and Park Service maintenance facilities. *Water* available here.)

0.2 Ascend under powerlines.

0.4 Descend 3 rock steps and bend left.

0.9 *AT* turns sharply left while old road continues ahead. Trail continues to ascend.

1.5 Near top of rise, open field about 50 ft. to right of Trail (beyond wire fence) affords views of Flattop Mtn., 3,325 ft.

1.6 Summit of shoulder of Flattop Mtn. *AT* continues along northern ridge crest.

2.8 Excellent views of Roach River Valley (Bacon and Powell Gap Hollows) from rock ledges to right of Trail. *AT* descends gradually.

3.0 Turn sharply right onto well-worn trail, former road, leaving old roadbed (now overgrown) in 0.1mi. Continue descent.

3.3 Powell Gap, SDMP 69.9 (2,294 ft.). Cross to left(west) of Drive. Trail crosses grass, angles along edge of woods, then ascends western slope of Little Roundtop Mtn.

3.8 Summit of Little Roundtop Mtn. is 50 yds. to left of *AT*. Trail continues along ridge crest, then swings around south and east sides of Roundtop Mtn., affording wintertime views of Powell Gap and Flattop Mtn. *AT* continues with little change in elevation.

4.9 Cross to right(east) of Skyline Drive in open Smith Roach Gap, SDMP 68.6 (2,622 ft.). From the Drive, *AT* parallels Smith Roach Gap Fire Road a few feet to right of road for about 300 ft., then crosses road and ascends steadily through woods.

6.1 Cross Hightop Hut service road. (Hut is to left.)

6.2 Spur trail leads left 0.1mi. to Hightop Hut, to be used by long distance *AT* hikers only. (See "Accommodations and Facilities". *Spring* is 400 ft. downhill from hut on graded trail.)

6.7 Piped, covered *spring* at foot of large boulder to right of *AT*. Trail continues to ascend.

6.8 Side trail leads right 350 ft. to site of former Park Service lookout tower at summit of Hightop Mtn., 3,587 ft. No view from summit. About 100 ft. farther along Trail is excellent view from ledges to left of Trail. A little farther yet is second good viewpoint. Beyond, Trail descends sharply, veering east then switchbacking down northern slope of mountain.

8.3 Trail crosses to left(west) of Skyline Drive in grassy sag, SDMP 66.7 (2,637 ft.). *AT* continues along former farm road, ascending slightly, passing through remains of old apple orchard, then descending.

9.5 Trail turns sharply right on old road which comes in from left. It follows road a few feet only, then climbs to its right. Just beyond, Trail drops steeply down to highway bridge which carries Skyline Drive over US 33. *AT* follows pedestrian footway along edge of bridge.

9.6 Concrete post marking *AT* on east side of Drive in Swift Run Gap, SDMP 65.5 (2,376 ft.).

Section 7
Simmons Gap to Browns Gap

12.2 miles   PATC Map #11

General Description

The Shenandoah Park is much wider in this section than in Section 6. Most of the Park west of the *AT* is designated as a wilderness area. A roughly triangular area between the ridges of Rockytop, Brown Mtn. and Loft Mtn., and drained by the tributaries of Big Run, comprises the largest watershed in the Park, 11 square miles.

Elevations in this section range from 2,253 ft. at Simmons Gap to over 3,300 ft. in the area of Big Flat Mtn. (where Loft Mountain Campground is located) and back to 2,599 ft. at Browns Gap. Traveling from the north there are two 600 ft. climbs and one 800 ft. one from Ivy Creek to the summit of Loft Mtn., but little other climbing. Between Loft Mtn. and Big Flat Mtn. the *AT* passes through considerable open area, a pleasant change from wooded territory.

Trail Approaches

The northern end of this section begins on the west side of Skyline Drive, at its junction with Simmons Gap Fire Rd, SDMP 73.2. This is 7.7 miles south of Swift Run Gap and US 33.

The southern end starts at its junction with Madison Run Road about 100 ft. west of Skyline Drive, SDMP 82.9, in Browns Gap.

Side Trails

The greater width of the Park here gives space for a wide variety of trails. The Big Run Loop Trail and the Doyles River-Jones Run Trails are both loop trails, connected at each of their ends with either the *AT* or Skyline Drive. There are, in addition, other blue-blazed trails, a number of horse trails, and three gated Park fire roads - Simmons Gap Rd., Browns Gap Rd., and Madison Run Fire Rd. For details see "Side Trails". Also refer to PATC publication: *Circuit Hikes in Shenandoah National Park.*

Accommodations

The Loft Mtn. developed area includes a wayside, camp store, campground with shower and laundry facilities, picnic grounds and two nature trail. Open dates vary between April and November, no reservations accepted.

One open-faced hut, Pinefield Hut, 2.1mi. south of Simmons Gap, is available for long distance *AT* hikers only.

One locked cabin, the Doyles River Cabin, 2.2mi. north of Browns Gap, may be reserved in advance from PATC Headquarters. See "Accommodations and Facilities".

Trail Description, North to South

0.0 West side of Skyline Drive, at junction with Simmons Gap Fire Rd., SDMP 73.2 (2,253 ft.). (A short distance to south on fire road is ranger's office and beyond it Park Service maintenance facilities. *Water* available here.) Trail ascends northwestern face of Weaver Mtn.

1.1 Top of Weaver Mtn. Descend gently through sparse, scraggly woods, primarily black locust.

1.9 Cross to left(east) of Skyline Drive at Pinefield Gap, SDMP 75.2. Continue through level area.

2.1 Cross access road to Pinefield Hut, for use by long distance *AT* hikers only.(See "Accommodations and Facilities". *Spring* is located along this road, 20 yds. left of *AT* but is dry much of year. Hut is 150 yds. farther. A second *spring* is 250 ft. behind hut.) Trail now ascends.

2.3 *AT* comes within 100 ft. of Skyline Drive.

2.7 At spot where *AT* turns sharply left, Skyline Drive is approximately 200 ft. to right. (Twomile Run Parking Overlook is 0.1mi. north, SDMP 76.2.) *AT* continues to ascend.

3.1 Reach unnamed summit, 3,050 ft., then descend gently.

3.7 North end of Ivy Creek Overlook, SDMP 77.5. *AT* passes along overlook, then parallels Drive a few feet farther.

3.9 Ascend unnamed peak, 3,080 ft., then descend.

4.4 Trail reaches excellent viewpoint with Skyline Drive immediately below Trail. (View covers area from Trayfoot Mtn. on left to Rockytop on right.) *AT* continues to descend.

5.1 Cross Ivy Creek in lovely miniature canyon at elevation of 2,550 ft. Trail starts ascent of Loft Mtn., longest climb in this portion of *AT*, climbing along east bank of Ivy Creek for 0.2mi., then bearing left away from it.

5.8 Spur trail leads right 0.1mi. to Ivy Creek Maintenance Bldg.(no camping permitted) and a *spring*.

6.1 *AT* passes to right of peak of Loft Mtn., about 3,320 ft., and follows ridge crest. For next mile or so, as far as Big Flat Mtn., *AT* passes through Patterson Field, an area that was once a 240 acre pasture. (Grass has been replaced by blackberry vines and other shrubby growth. Black locust now covers much of the land, but in the midst of the young woods stand several old oak trees with very large low-spreading branches, showing that these oaks gained their maturity while the land was still open pasture.)

6.7 Panoramic (270 degree) view from Trail. A short distance farther Deadening Nature Trail (see Loft Mtn. inset, back of PATC Map #11), a Park Service trail, enters from right and follows *AT*. (This interpretive trail starts from Skyline Drive at entrance to Loft Mtn. Campground, SDMP 79.5, climbs to *AT*, follows it south about 0.1mi., then descends to starting point.)

6.8 Deadening Nature Trail leaves *AT*. *AT* begins descent toward sag between Loft Mtn. and Big Flat Mtn.

7.4 *AT* crosses old road in sag. (Right leads to paved Loft Mtn. Campground road. Left is a dead-end.)

7.9 Spur trail leads right, uphill, to Loft Mtn. camp store which is open "in season", generally mid-May through October. (Store carries complete line of groceries. Adjoining laundromat is equipped with coin-operated washers, dryers, and showers.) Trail climbs gently toward Big Flat Mtn., 3,387 ft.

8.1 *AT* circles clockwise around Loft Mtn. Campground. Excellent views, east, then south, and finally to west, as *AT* swings around camping area on summit of Big Flat Mtn. *AT* is almost level here. Concrete posts at 8.5mi. and 9.0mi. mark side trails leading to campground.

9.2 Concrete post marks trail leading right 0.3mi. to Loft Mtn. Amphitheater.

9.7 Excellent panoramic view, from left to right: Rockytop, Brown Mtn., Rocky Mtn., Rocky Mount, and to right (east) of Drive, Loft Mtn. *AT* continues to descend.

10.0 *AT* intersects Doyles River Trail. (Skyline Drive, SDMP 81.1, is 200 ft. to right. Big Run Parking Overlook is 250 ft. south on Drive. To left *AT* passes below Doyles River Cabin and *spring* in 0.3mi. (Cabin must be reserved in advance at PATC Headquarters. See "Accommodations and Facilities".) From Doyles River Trail intersection *AT* closely parallels Skyline Drive and is relatively level.

10.9 Trail passes through Doyles River Parking Overlook, SDMP 81.9.

11.1 Trail follows ledges with wintertime views south.

11.3 *AT* crosses to right(west) of Skyline Drive, SDMP 82.2, with fine view from Drive of Cedar Mtn. and Trayfoot Mtn.

11.6 Junction with Big Run Loop Trail. (Big Run Loop Trail, 4.2mi. long, runs from here to Big Run Parking Overlook, SDMP 81.1, near Doyles River Trail.) Beyond junction, *AT* gradually descends.

12.2 Concrete post marks junction with Madison Run Fire Road 100 ft. right of Skyline Drive, SDMP 82.9 (2,599 ft.) in Browns Gap. (See "Side Trails". Browns Gap was used several times by Gen. Stonewall Jackson during Civil War's Valley Campaign.)

Trail Description, South to North

0.0 Browns Gap. (Gen. Stonewall Jackson used this gap several times during Valley Campaign of Civil War.) Start of this section is at junction with Madison Run Rd. (western portion of old Browns Gap Rd.) about 100 ft. to left(west) of Skyline Drive, SDMP 82.9, in Browns Gap, 2,599 ft., and is marked by concrete post. Trail ascends, gaining 250 ft. in elevation, then levels off.

0.6 Big Run Loop Trail, blue-blazed, leads left 4.2mi. to its northern trailhead at Big Run Parking Overlook, SDMP 81.1.

0.9 *AT* crosses to right of Skyline Drive, SDMP 82.2, with fine view of Cedar Mtn. and Trayfoot Mtn.

1.1 Trail follows ledges affording wintertime views south.

1.3 Trail passes through Doyles River Parking Overlook, SDMP 81.9.

2.2 *AT* intersects Doyles River Trail. (Skyline Drive is 200 ft. to left, SDMP 81.1, just north of Big Run Parking Overlook. Doyles River Trail leads right, passing below Doyles River Cabin and *spring* in 0.3mi. Cabin must be reserved in advance at PATC Headquarters. See "Accommodations and Facilities".) *AT* now ascends Big Flat Mtn., 3,389 ft.

2.5 Excellent panoramic view, from left to right, of: Rockytop, Brown Mtn., Rocky Mtn., Rocky Mount, and, to the right(east) of the Drive, Loft Mtn.

3.0 Concrete post marks side trail leading left 0.3mi. to Loft Mountain Amphitheater. *AT* now skirts southern and eastern edges of Loft Mtn. Campground for about a mile, with good views west, then south, and finally due east. Concrete posts at 3.2mi. and 3.7mi. mark side trails leading left to campground.

4.3 Trail leads left, uphill, to Loft Mtn. camp store, usually open mid-May through October. (Store carries complete line of groceries. Laundromat with coin-operated washers, dryers, and showers, adjoins store.) For next mile or so, to summit of Loft Mtn., Trail passes through Patterson Field, once a 240 acre pasture. (Now the grass has been replaced by berry vines, other shrubby growth and black locust trees. In the midst of the young woods stand several old oak trees with very large, low-spreading branches indicating that these oaks gained their maturity while the land was still pasture.)

4.8 Trail crosses old road. (To left, road leads to paved road to Loft Mtn. Campground. To right is dead-end.)

5.4 Ridge crest of Loft Mtn. Deadening Nature Trail enters *AT* from left. (Nature Trail starts on Skyline Drive at entrance to Loft Mtn. Campground, SDMP 79.5, joins *AT*, follows it north 0.1mi., then descends to starting point. See inset, back of PATC Map #11.) Excellent 270 degree panoramic view about 150 ft. farther along *AT*.

6.1 Trail passes slightly to left of peak of Loft Mtn., 3,320 ft., then starts descending toward Ivy Creek.

6.4 Trail leads left 200 yds. to Ivy Creek Maintenance Bldg. and *spring* (no camping here). *AT* continues to descend, following right bank of Ivy Creek.

7.1 Trail crosses Ivy Creek, very picturesque, at an elevation of about 2,550 ft., then ascends.

7.8 Excellent viewpoint showing area from Trayfoot Mtn. on left to Rockytop on right. Skyline Drive is immediately below Trail. *AT* continues to ascend for 0.2mi., then descends.

8.5 South end of Ivy Creek Overlook, SDMP 77.5. Trail passes along overlook, then ascends gently for 0.5mi.

9.1 Unnamed summit, 3,080 ft. Trail descends through patches of white pine, interspersed with areas of locust and young oak.

9.5 At spot where *AT* turns sharply right, spur trail leads left approximately 200 ft. to Skyline Drive, 0.1mi. south of Twomile Run Parking Overlook.

9.9 *AT*, still descending, again comes within 100 ft. of Drive.

10.1 *AT* crosses access road to Pinefield Hut. (Hut available for use of long distance *AT* hikers only. *Spring* 20 yds. to right along this road is often dry. Hut is 0.1mi. farther with another *spring* behind it.)

10.3 *AT* crosses to left(west) of Skyline Drive at Pinefield Gap, SDMP 75.2. Trail now ascends, winding through sparse, scraggly woods, primarily black locust.

11.1 Top of Weaver Mtn. Trail descends along north-western side of ridge.

12.2 *AT* reaches Simmons Gap at junction of Simmons Gap Fire Road and Skyline Drive, SDMP 73.2 (2,253 ft.). (A short distance to south on fire road is ranger's office and beyond it Park Service facilities. *Water* available here. See "Side Trails".)

Section 8
Browns Gap to Jarman Gap

15.1 miles

PATC Map #11

General Description

The highlight of this section is Blackrock, a tumbled mass of large, lichen-covered blocks of stone, interesting of itself but also a spot for splendid views. As in Section 7, this part of the Park is quite wild and most of it is designated a wilderness area. Rhododendron, which is quite scarce in the Park, is found along the Riprap Trail and along the *AT* in the same general area. Mountain laurel is very plentiful in this area, especially along the Moormans River Fire Road east of the Drive from Blackrock Gap.

From Browns Gap the Trail climbs to Blackrock, drops 750 ft. to Blackrock Gap, then, after a succession of short climbs and dips, gradually ascends to over 3,000 ft. The final five miles to Jarman Gap, 2,173 ft., is primarily downhill.

Trail Approaches

The northern end of this section begins in Browns Gap, SDMP 82.9. This is 17.4 miles south of the Swift Run Gap entrance to Skyline Drive from US 33 or 22.5 miles north of the Rockfish Gap entrance from US 250. A concrete post marks junction of *AT* and Madison Fire Road 100 ft. west of Skyline Drive. *AT* crosses the Drive here then continues on east side.

The southern end begins in Jarman Gap, SDMP 96.9, 8.5mi north of the Rockfish Gap entrance to Skyline Drive from US 250/I-64. The *AT* is at junction with Bucks Elbow Mtn. Fire Road, 0.1mi. east of Skyline Drive.

Side Trails
There are many worthwhile side trails in this section. Some lead to places of special interest such as Riprap Ravine, Calvary Rocks, Trayfoot Mtn., and the falls on both Jones Run and Doyles River. The old Moormans River Road, former route of the *AT*, leads from Jarman Gap down the south fork of the Moormans River and up the north fork to Blackrock Gap. See "Side Trails". Also refer to PATC publication: *Circuit Hikes in Shenandoah National Park.*

Accommodations
The Dundo Group Campground, SDMP 83.7, is for organized youth groups only, from May through October. The remainder of the year it may be used by the public for picnicking. Reservations may be made with Park Headquarters (703) 999-2229. There is no store here and no shower or laundry facilities.
One open-faced hut, Blackrock Hut, 3.0mi. south of Browns Gap, is available for long distance *AT* hikers only. See "Accommodations and Facilities".

Trail Description, North to South

0.0 Concrete post marks junction of *AT* and Madison Run Fire Road, 100 ft. west of Skyline Drive, SDMP 82.9 (2,599 ft.). *AT* crosses diagonally to left side of Drive, then ascends gently.
0.4 Trail skirts eastern side of Dundo developed area, SDMP 83.7, for next 0.2mi. Several unmarked paths lead up to Dundo. *Water* may be obtained there May through October.
0.6 *AT* turns sharply left. A trail to right leads to Dundo.
1.2 Intersection with Jones Run Trail. (Jones Run Parking Area is 100 ft. to right. Left leads down Jones Run then ascends Doyles River Trail to return to *AT*.

See "Side Trails".) *AT* now passes through remnants of old apple orchard.

1.4 Cross to west side of Skyline Drive, SDMP 84.3, and ascend very gently.

2.1 *AT* and Trayfoot Mtn. Trail come within few feet of each other and run parallel but do not cross. After 0.1mi., *AT* bears right away from road, and circles north, west, and south sides of Blackrock, 3,092 ft. (This area is reminiscent of New Hampshire's White Mountain terrain above tree-line. View from rocks is excellent.)

2.4 Blue-blazed Blackrock Spur Trail leads right from *AT* at its highest elevation at Blackrock and follows ridge leading to Trayfoot Mtn.

2.5 *AT* crosses Trayfoot Mtn. Trail, then descends steadily toward Blackrock Gap, following east side of narrow ridge. (An old road parallels Trail on western side of ridge, just out of sight.)

3.0 Spur trail, left, leads steeply down 0.2mi. to Blackrock Hut. (Hut located in deep ravine. *Spring* 10 yds. in front of it. Hut for use of long distance *AT* hikers only. See "Accommodations and Facilities".) In 100 ft., *AT* crosses to west of old road, parallels it for 0.2mi., then joins it and follows it down to intersection with Skyline Drive.

3.5 Cross to left of Skyline Drive, SDMP 87.2, and continue along east side for quarter mile.

3.7 Cross Moormans River Fire Road, yellow-blazed, in Blackrock Gap, SDMP 87.4 (2,321 ft.). (Moormans River Fire Road follows north fork of river down to Charlottesville Reservoir, then climbs along south fork of river to Skyline Drive at Jarman Gap, hiking distance 9.4mi. This is former route of *AT*.) From road intersection *AT* climbs over small knob, then descends to sag at 4.8mi., with Skyline Drive 50 ft. to right. Trail now climbs over second small knob.

5.5 Trail crosses to right(west) of Skyline Drive, SDMP 88.9, in sag, then climbs.

6.2 Junction with blue-blazed Riprap Trail, at summit of knob, 2,988 ft. (Riprap Trail, Wildcat Ridge Trail and *AT* make excellent circuit of 9.3mi. See "Side Trails".) *AT* descends steeply.

6.6 Graded trail, left, leads to Riprap Parking Area on Skyline Drive, SDMP 90.0. Trail continues to descend steeply another 0.1mi., then more gradually. For next 2mi. Trail alternately climbs and dips gently. Occasional rhododendron (Catawba).

9.3 Intersection with Wildcat Ridge Trail. (Wildcat Ridge Parking Area, SDMP 92.1, is to left.) *AT* ascends gently.

9.6 *AT* crosses to left(east) of Skyline Drive, SDMP 92.4, and continues to ascend, reaching summit, 3,080 ft., in 0.5mi. (Beyond summit are wintertime views of peaks in George Washington National Forest, Pedlar District, south of Rockfish Gap.) Trail descends to slight sag, reclimbs to about same elevation, then descends fairly steeply toward Turk Gap.

11.6 *AT* passes concrete post marking start of Turk Branch Trail, then crosses to right side of Skyline Drive at Turk Gap, SDMP 94.1 (2,610 ft.).

11.8 Turk Mtn. Trail leaves *AT*, right, and follows side ridge which shortly divides into two ridges, one Turk Mtn., the other Sawmill Ridge. (The hiker will find 1.1mi. side trip to top of Turk Mtn. via blue-blazed Turk Mtn Trail well worth his time. See "Side Trails".) In 250 ft., *AT* reaches crest and starts long gentle descent.

13.2 Cross to left of Skyline Drive, SDMP 95.3, in deep sag at north edge of Sawmill Run Parking Overlook. Trail now climbs. Looking backwards while ascending, there are views of Turk Mtn., Sawmill Ridge and city of Waynesboro.

13.8 Summit of unnamed hill, 2,453 ft. As Trail starts to descend, views to east of Bucks Elbow Mtn.

14.2 Cross grass-covered pipeline diagonally to right. Continue to descend.

14.6 South Fork of Moormans River, a small creek here; follow creek along west bank to source.

14.9 Cross Moormans River Fire Road. (Road leads right 0.1mi. to Skyline Drive at Jarman Gap, SDMP 96.8, 2,173 ft.) In 200 ft., pass *spring* on left, then climb.

15.1 Bucks Elbow Mtn. Fire Road, 100 yds. east of Skyline Drive, SDMP 96.9, and end of section. (To right, road leads to Skyline Drive at intersection with Moormans River Fire Road in Jarman Gap; left leads out of Park and along ridge of Bucks Elbow Mtn. to radio tower.)

Trail Description, South to North

0.0 Junction of *AT* and Bucks Elbow Mtn. Fire Road. Trail descends.

0.2 Pass *spring* on right of *AT*. In 100 yds. cross Moormans River Fire Road. Continue descent along west bank of South Fork of Moormans River at its upper end.

0.5 *AT* leaves creek and ascends unnamed hill. Partway up it crosses a grass-covered pipeline area diagonally to right.

1.3 Summit of hill, 2,453 ft. Looking backwards, toward east, is view of Bucks Elbow Mtn. As Trail begins to descend, there are forward views of Turk Mtn., Sawmill Ridge, and city of Waynesboro.

1.9 *AT* crosses to left(west) of Skyline Drive, SDMP 95.3, in sag at north edge of Sawmill Run Parking Overlook.

3.3 Summit of knob, 2,650 ft.; in 250 ft., Turk Mtn. Trail, blue-blazed, leads left 0.9mi. to summit of Turk Mtn. (Worthwhile side trip.)

3.5 Turk Gap, SDMP 94.1 (2,625 ft). *AT* crosses to east side of Skyline Drive. Concrete post marks junction of *AT* with Turk Branch Trail. Trail ascends 400 ft., dips gently, then ascends second summit with about same elevation as first. (Backward views in winter of peaks in George Washington National Forest, Pedlar District, south of Rockfish Gap.) Trail now descends.

5.5 *AT* crosses to west of Skyline Drive, SDMP 92.4.

5.8 Junction with Wildcat Ridge Trail. (Wildcat Ridge-Riprap Trail make 6.2mi. loop with *AT*. See "Side Trails".) *AT* continues along western side of ridge crest, passing through one of few areas in SNP having (Catawba) rhododendron.

8.3 Trail ascends steeply 0.5mi. around slope of Riprap Hollow.

8.5 Graded trail to right leads to Riprap Parking Area on Skyline Drive, SDMP 90.0.

8.9 Summit of knob, 2,988 ft. Riprap Trail comes in from left. *AT* descends.

9.6 In sag, cross to right of Skyline Drive, SDMP 88.9. *AT* climbs over small knob.

10.3 Trail comes into sag with Skyline Drive 150 ft. to left. *AT* climbs second knob then descends steadily.

11.4 Cross Moormans River Fire Road in Blackrock Gap, SDMP 87.4 (2,329 ft.). Trail continues along east side of Drive for quarter mile.

11.6 *AT* crosses to left(west) of Drive, SDMP 87.2, ascends old road for 0.2mi., then angles off slightly to left of road and parallels it.

12.1 Trail crosses to east of old road. In 100 ft., graded trail leads right, steeply down for 0.2mi., to Blackrock Hut. (Hut for use of long distance *AT* hikers only, located in very deep ravine. *Spring* 10 yds. in front of hut.) *AT* continues to ascend along eastern side of ridge. (Old road runs parallel on left.)

12.6 Junction with Trayfoot Mtn. Trail. In 300 ft. *AT* begins circling Blackrock, 3,092 ft. (Blackrock is reminiscent of terrain above tree-line on Mt. Washington. Views excellent.)

12.7 Graded trail leads left along ridge leading to Trayfoot Mtn.

12.9 *AT* and Trayfoot Mtn. Trail come within few feet of each other but do not cross. They are parallel about 0.1mi. *AT* bears off to left. (Blue-blazed trail leads 750 ft. to Skyline Drive, SDMP 84.7. Parking for several cars.)

13.7 Cross to right side of Skyline Drive, SDMP 84.3. Trail passes through remnants of old apple orchard.

13.9 Junction with Jones Run Trail. (To left leads to Jones Run Parking Area, SDMP 84.1; to right descends Jones Run then ascends Doyles Run to rejoin *AT* in 4.7mi.) *AT* continues with little change in elevation.

14.4 *AT* turns sharply to right; trail straight ahead leads to Dundo developed area. (*Water* available May through October.) Beyond Dundo, Trail descends gently.

15.1 *AT* reaches Browns Gap where Skyline Drive intersects old Browns Gap Road, then crosses Drive, SDMP 82.9 (2,599 ft.).

Section 9
Jarman Gap to Rockfish Gap

8.0 miles   PATC Map #11

General Description

Except for a short distance over the northern summit of Calf Mtn. utilized by the *AT* with the owner's permission, the Appalachian Trail from Rockfish Gap to Jarman Gap is located entirely within a corridor of land purchased by the National Park Service. Views are excellent from summit of Calf Mtn. and Bear Den Mtn. Rock outcrops on the summits in this section consist of a green shale, rather than greenstone, the basaltic rock so predominant along the ridge crest in the Shenandoah Park itself.

From Jarman Gap the *AT* climbs Calf Mtn., descends to Beagle Gap where it crosses Skyline Drive, climbs over Bear Den Mtn., drops to McCormick Gap where it recrosses the Drive, climbs up Scott Mtn., then slabs along the western side of the ridge as it drops gradually toward Rockfish Gap. Descending steeply to Skyline Drive just before reaching the Gap, it follows the Skyline Drive bridges over I-64/US 250, where the section ends, as does the Drive, at SDMP 105.4.

Trail Approaches

The northern end of this section begins at the Bucks Elbow Mtn. Fire Road, about 0.1mi. east of Skyline Drive in Jarman Gap, SDMP 96.8. (Bucks Elbow Mtn. Fire Road is the more southerly of the two roads that intersect at Skyline Drive. The other is Moormans River Fire Road.) Jarman Gap is 8.5 miles north of the I-64/US 250 entrance to Skyline Drive at Rockfish Gap.

The southern end is at the south end of the Skyline Drive overpass of I-64/US 250 in Rockfish Gap, SDMP 105.4, on east side of Drive.

Side Trails
  None other than old roads.

Accommodations
  Gasoline, restaurant, and lodging facilities are available at Rockfish Gap and in Waynesboro, 4 miles northwest via US 250. The Calf Mtn. Shelter, completed by PATC in 1984, is available for overnight use.

Trail Description, North to South

0.0 From Bucks Elbow Mtn. Fire Road in Jarman Gap, ascend southward.

0.4 *Spring* to left of Trail.

0.5 Pass under powerlines.

1.0 Side trail leads right to *spring* in 0.2mi. and Calf Mtn. Shelter in 0.3mi. (This is a PATC shelter, available for overnight use, not to be confused with picnic shelters and huts within the Park.)

1.3 Trail enters open area and follows pasture road through grass and staghorn sumac.

1.6 Cairn marks summit of Calf Mtn., 2,974 ft. (Excellent spot for watching mid-September hawk migrations.) Continue along ridge.

1.7 Descend through pines and cross stone fence.

2.2 *AT* passes to left of Little Calf Mtn., 2,910 ft. Trail descends.

2.5 Cross Skyline Drive in Beagle Gap, SDMP 99.5 (2,523 ft.). Trail ascends open slopes of Bear Den Mtn.

3.1 Bare summit of Bear Den Mtn., 2,885 ft. (Police radio installation here.) Continue past second summit, 2,810 ft.

4.3 Cross Skyline Drive in McCormick Gap, SDMP 102.1 (2,434 ft.). From Gap, climb stile and follow dirt road a few feet, then turn right from road and ascend steeply through brush and locust trees.

4.5 Trail ceases to climb and begins to slab western side of ridge, just below ridge crest.

5.6 Meet old trail and follow it south.

6.1 Come to another old trail and continue south.

6.3 Pass through gate, and shortly pass trail leading west, then another gate.

6.8 Pass through a third gate.

7.2 Trail to right leads 0.2mi. to southern entrance station of Skyline Drive.

7.8 Reach Skyline Drive and follow it south.

8.0 End of section at south end of Skyline Drive, on bridge over I-64/US 250 in Rockfish Gap, SDMP 105.4 (1,902 ft.) (For continuation see: *Guide to the Appalachian Trail in Central and Southwest Virginia* and PATC Map #12.)

Trail Description, South to North

0.0 Skyline Drive at south end of overpass over I-64/US 250 in Rockfish Gap. Trail follows footway along right(east) side of Drive.

0.1 Cross I-64/US 250, utilizing Skyline Drive overpass. Continue along right side of Drive.

0.2 At concrete post and *AT* trail marker, turn right away from Drive. Ascend steeply.

0.8 Trail leads left 0.2mi. to southern entrance station of SNP. Backpackers can obtain camping permits here.

1.2 Pass through gate.

1.7 Pass through second gate and in few feet pass trail leading west; pass through third gate.

1.9 At trail junction avoid right fork.

2.4 At another trail junction avoid right fork.

3.5 Trail starts to descend.

3.7 Cross Skyline Drive in McCormick Gap, SDMP 102.1 (2,434 ft.). Ascend through pine thicket, then across open land along ridge of Bear Den Mtn.

4.9 Bare summit of Bear Den Mtn., 2,885 ft. (Police radio installation here.) Trail descends northeastward.

5.5 Cross Skyline Drive in Beagle Gap, SDMP 99.5 (2,532 ft.). Trail ascends Calf Mtn.

5.8 Pass slightly to right of Little Calf Mtn., 2,910 ft.

6.4 Open summit of Calf Mtn., 2,974 ft. (Excellent spot for watching mid-September hawk migrations.)

7.0 Blue-blazed trail leads to *spring* in 0.2mi. and Calf Mtn. Shelter in 0.3mi. (This is a PATC shelter available for overnight use. Not to be confused with picnic shelters and huts within the Park.)

7.5 Pass under two powerlines.

7.6 *Spring* to right of Trail.

8.0 Bucks Elbow Mtn. Fire Road, 0.1mi. east of Skyline Drive at Jarman Gap, SDMP 96.8 (2,175 ft.).

SUMMARY OF DISTANCES ALONG *AT*
Southern District

	Miles	
	N-S	S-N
Swift Run Gap	0.0	44.9
Hightop Hut	3.4 + 0.1	41.5 + 0.1
Smith Roach Gap, Skyline Drive crossing	4.7	40.2
Powell Gap, Skyline Drive crossing	6.3	38.6
Simmons Gap, Skyline Drive crossing	9.6	35.3
Pinefield Hut	11.7 + 0.1	33.2 + 0.1
Ivy Creek Overlook, Skyline Drive	13.3	31.6
Loft Mtn. Camp Store	17.5	27.4
Doyles River Trail	19.6	25.3
Doyles River Cabin	19.6 + 0.3	25.3 + 0.3
Big Run Loop Trail, north end	19.6	25.3
Big Run Loop Trail, south end	21.2	23.7
Browns Gap, Skyline Drive crossing	21.8	23.1
Jones Run Trail	23.0	21.9
Blackrock	24.2	20.7
Blackrock Hut	24.8 + 0.2	20.1 + 0.2
Blackrock Gap, Moormans River Fire Road	25.5	19.4
Riprap Trail	28.0	16.9
Wildcat Ridge Trail	31.1	13.8
Turk Gap, Skyline Drive crossing	33.4	11.5
Skyline Drive crossing, just north of Sawmill Ridge Overlook	35.0	9.9

Jarman Gap, 0.1mi. east of Skyline Drive	36.9	8.0
Calf Mtn. Shelter	38.0 + 0.3	6.9 + 0.3
Beagle Gap, Skyline Drive crossing	39.4	5.5
McCormick Gap, Skyline Drive crossing	41.2	3.7
Rockfish Gap, US 250/I-64	44.9	0.0

(Summary of Distances Along *AT* - continued from Page 119)

SUMMARY OF DISTANCES BY SKYLINE DRIVE
TO POINTS ON *AT*
Southern District

SDMP N-S		S-N
65.5	Swift Run Gap	39.9
68.6	Smith Roach Gap	36.8
69.9	Powell Gap	35.5
73.2	Simmons Gap	32.2
75.2	Pinefield Gap	30.2
77.5	Ivy Creek Overlook	27.9
79.5	Loft Mtn. developed area (1.3mi. to *AT*)	25.9
81.1	Doyles River Trail	24.3
81.9	Doyles River Parking Overlook	23.5
82.9	Browns Gap	22.5
84.1	Jones Run Trail (100 ft. to *AT*)	21.3
84.7	Trayfoot Mtn. Trail (0.1mi. to *AT*)	20.7
87.4	Blackrock Gap	18.0
90.0	Riprap Trail Parking Area (300 ft. to *AT*)	15.4
92.1	Wildcat Ridge Trail Parking Area (0.1mi. to *AT*)	13.3
94.1	Turk Gap	11.3
95.3	Sawmill Run Parking Overlook	10.1
96.8	Jarman Gap (0.1mi. to *AT*)	8.6
99.5	Beagle Gap	5.9
102.1	McCormick Gap	3.3
105.4	Rockfish Gap	0.0

SIDE TRAILS
SHENANDOAH NATIONAL PARK

In addition to the Appalachian Trail that traverses the Park from one end to the other, there are three classes of trails in SNP. Blue-blazed trails are for foot-travelers only. Most of these, like the *AT* itself, are maintained by volunteers, members of the Potomac Appalachian Trail Club. Yellow-blazed trails, including fire roads, are classified as horse/foot trails; they are primarily maintained by Park personnel, although several horse riding groups have been assigned maintenance for specific trails. Park-maintained nature trails and stroller trails, usually quite short, are not blazed but are marked by signposts.

For all trails the trailheads and trail junctions are marked by concrete posts with aluminum bands which indicate direction and usually distance to the next trail junction or other landmark. It is wise, when hiking in a new area of the Park, to carry a guide book or map with you as the aluminum bands are sometimes removed by vandals.

Trail descriptions have been grouped according to area to facilitate planning of hikes. The PATC publication, *Circuit Hikes in Shenandoah National Park*, will also be useful in hike planning. The three PATC maps of the Shenandoah Park (#9 - Northern District, #10 - Central District, #11 - Southern District) are valuable for use in conjunction with the guide. USGS 7 1/2' quadrangle maps are available but are chiefly of value for bushwhacking and exploring.

In giving detailed trail data in this section, description is given in one direction only. The distances indicated on the left are those in the direction indicated. Those to the right are the distances in the reverse direction.

INDEX OF SIDE TRAILS

Trails in Southern District

NORTHERN DISTRICT
SHENANDOAH NATIONAL PARK

DICKEY RIDGE TRAIL

9.2 miles   blue-blazed

This is a very popular trail because of its accessibility and gentle grade. The northern end is at the northern entrance to Skyline Drive. The trail parallels the Drive much of the way, crossing it at SDMP 2.1, again at Low Gap, and yet again at Lands Run Gap. The southern terminus is on the Appalachian Trail near Compton Gap, SDMP 10.4. Most of the climb along Dickey Ridge is between the northern end and the summit of Dickey Hill and involves a change in elevation of about 1,700 ft. The remainder of the route consists of gentle ups and downs.

There are few views from this trail. Where it climbs nearly to the top of Dickey Hill there are glimpses west of the Shenandoah Valley. (Summit has been cleared because of a federal navigational installation, Vortac.) Near the southern end of the trail, the Fort Windham Rocks are of considerable interest.

Access

Northern terminus is on south side of US 340 at southern limits of Front Royal.

Southern terminus is on *AT*, 0.3mi. north of Compton Gap, SDMP 10.4.

Trail Description

Front Royal to *AT* near Compton Gap

0-0-9.2 Southern side of US 340. Trail cuts across open area of Shenandoah Park's northern entrance and crosses to right side of Skyline Drive at Entrance Parking Area, SDMP 0.0. From here trail ascends very gently along small creek. Although close to Drive here, it is effectively isolated from it by trees and a jungle of

Japanese honeysuckle. At about 1.4mi. it turns sharply right away from creek and climbs more steeply.

1.9-7.3 Cross to left of Skyline Drive, SDMP 2.1. Continue to ascend. In about 0.5mi. trail comes quite close to Drive at Shenandoah Valley Overlook where there is good view of Front Royal and Signal Knob in the Massanuttens. Large patch of Virginia bluebells right on trail in this area, probably planted by a long ago resident. Expect to find bluebells in bloom latter part of April.

4.0-5.2 Skyline Drive is slightly above and to right of trail here. Several side trails lead to Dickey Ridge Visitor Center, SDMP 4.6. Fox Hollow Trail, a Park interpretive trail, cuts across Dickey Ridge Trail directly below visitor center.

4.5-4.7 Cross Snead Farm Road (dirt). (To right road leads few feet to Drive, just opposite exit road of Dickey Ridge Picnic Area, SDMP 5.1. To left, road leads into old apple orchard and site of Snead Farm.)

5.3-3.9 Trail skirts ridge, just below summit of Dickey Hill. Summit can be reached by a short scramble and offers sweeping views. From here trail descends gently.

5.7-3.5 Snead Farm Loop Trail enters on left. (Blue-blazed loop trail, 0.7mi. long, has its lower end on Snead Farm Road, offering a nice circuit route.)

7.0-2.2 Low Gap, SDMP 7.9. Cross to right of Skyline Drive.

8.0-1.2 Lands Run Gap, SDMP 9.2. Cross to left of Drive.

8.6-0.6 Yellow-blazed Springhouse Road. (Trail leads left for 0.7mi. to join Compton Gap Road and *AT* 0.3mi. north of point where Dickey Ridge Trail itself joins *AT*.)

9.0-0.2 Pass Fort Windham Rocks on left. They are interesting to climb upon.

9.2-0.0 Junction with *AT*, which is here coincident with Compton Gap Road, at a point on *AT* 0.3mi. from Compton Gap, SDMP 10.4. (To left in 0.3mi. a self-registration backcountry permit booth is at junction of

AT and Springhouse Rd. *AT* follows road for another 1.2mi. then turns left and descends into Harmony Hollow, reaching US 522 in 3.8 additional miles. Compton Gap Horse Trail leads down to Park boundary. As SR 610 it continues to US 522 at Chester Gap. Distance from Dickey Ridge Trail to Chester Gap via this route, 3.7mi.)

FOX HOLLOW TRAIL

1 mile   not blazed
The interpretive trail starts from Skyline Drive directly across from the Dickey Ridge Visitor Center. It descends about 0.5mi. then ascends through the former Fox Farm to complete the circuit. See PATC Map #9, inset on back, or check map displayed outside visitor center. A self-guiding leaflet, with map, can be purchased at visitor center.

SNEAD FARM ROAD

0.6 miles   not blazed
A leisurely circuit hike of 2.5mi. can be made with this road, along with the Snead Farm Loop Trail and a segment of Dickey Ridge Trail, starting at Dickey Ridge Picnic Area.

Trail Description
0.0 Snead Farm Road leaves Skyline Drive, SDMP 5.0, just across from exit road of Dickey Ridge Picnic Area.
0.3 Road leads left, downhill, from Snead Farm Road, soon coming to dead end.
0.7 Snead homesite at end of road. House is gone but barn is still standing. Concrete post at road's end marks lower end of Snead Farm Loop Trail.

SNEAD FARM LOOP TRAIL

0.7 miles   blue-blazed

Lower end of this trail is at end of Snead Farm Road. Upper end is on Dickey Ridge Trail, joining latter about 0.3mi. south of summit of Dickey Hill. From here via Dickey Ridge Trail it is 1.2mi. north(right) to return to Snead Farm Road and Skyline Drive.

LANDS RUN GAP ROAD

2.0 miles   yellow-blazed

Lands Run Gap Road leaves Skyline Drive, SDMP 9.2, in Lands Run Gap and descends west side of Blue Ridge to Park boundary where it connects with SR 622. About 0.5mi. from Skyline Drive road crosses Lands Run. Creek immediately below road here is very pretty, falling rapidly in a series of cascades.

Access

Upper end is on Skyline Drive, SDMP 9.2, in Lands Run Gap.

To reach lower end, drive to Browntown (which is about 6mi. east of Bentonville via SR 613 and 7 miles southwest of Front Royal on SR 649). Turn east in Browntown onto SR 634. In 1mi. turn left onto SR 622. Reach fire road in 1mi. from this junction.

HICKERSON HOLLOW TRAIL

1.2 miles   yellow-blazed

This trail leads from Lands Run Gap, SDMP 9.2, northward down one of branches of Happy Creek into Harmony Hollow. It ends outside Park where it meets SR 600 about 0.5mi. from SR 604, main road through Harmony Hollow. (The land is posted along stretch of trail between Park boundary and SR 600.)

A circuit hike could include the *AT* from SR 601 in Harmony Hollow, uphill to its junction with Dickey Ridge Trail, that trail to Lands Run Gap, and Hickerson Hollow Trail back down mountain, then road walk down SR 600 and SR 604, up SR 601 to start, for total distance of about 7mi.

JENKINS GAP TRAIL

1.5 miles   yellow-blazed
From end of SR 634, about 2 miles east of Browntown, trail climbs west side of Blue Ridge, crosses Skyline Drive at Jenkins Gap just north of Jenkins Gap Overlook, SDMP 12.3, then continues to Mt. Marshall Trail.

About 1 mile of trail is west of Drive. This section has nice gradient and is particularly attractive when mountain laurel, which is quite plentiful along trail, blooms around first week in June. Lowest 0.2mi. is outside Park. Remember that access to Park boundary across private land depends upon goodwill of landowner. Posted trail closures must be respected. Trail intersects *AT* about 0.1mi. west of Drive.

East of Drive trail descends, passes below Jenkins Gap Overlook, then climbs back to reach Mt. Marshall Trail, joining it at a point on latter 0.1mi. from Skyline Drive.

BROWNTOWN TRAIL

3.4 miles   yellow-blazed
This trail utilizes western portion of route of pre-Park Browntown-Harris Hollow Road. From Gravel Springs Gap, it runs down west side of Blue Ridge, descending in switchbacks. Grade is gentle and there are occasional glimpses of Hogback Mtn. and Gimlet Ridge through the trees.

Access

Upper trailhead is on Skyline Drive at Gravel Springs Gap, SDMP 17.7. In 50 ft. it intersects *AT*.

Lower end of trail can be reached by driving to Browntown (6mi. east of Bentonville via SR 613 and 7mi. southwest of Front Royal via SR 649). From Browntown follow SR 631 for about 1mi. Where SR 631 turns sharply right, old Browntown Road is straight ahead. Room for two cars to park. *Do not* drive up old Browntown Road but start hiking here.

Trail Description

SR 631 to Skyline Drive

0.0-3.4 Junction with SR 631. Follow old road along creek, Phils Arm Run. Land is posted on both sides of road so stay on road.

0.2-3.2 Take right fork and immediately cross creek. (Left fork leads through gate into field.)

0.8-2.6 Where road forks, take right fork straight ahead. In few yards road forks again, and again take right fork straight ahead. (Avoid other roads to right which are gated.) Road soon begins to climb.

1.1-2.3 Cross into SNP. Road, now trail, is gated here. Continue to climb and soon begin series of switchbacks. Occasional views of Hogback Mtn. and Gimlet Ridge.

3.4-0.0 Pass gate. In few feet intersect *AT* and a few feet farther reach Skyline Drive, SDMP 17.7.

COMPTON GAP FIRE ROAD-COMPTON GAP HORSE TRAIL-SR 610

4.0 miles   white (*AT* portion) and yellow-blazed

This fire road/horse trail leads northeast along the Blue Ridge crest from Compton Gap for 2.2mi. Here it leaves the Park and becomes SR 610 which continues another 1.8mi. to Chester Gap where US 522 crosses the mountain (the last 340 ft. of road is SR 665). The *AT*, until

1974, followed this route from Compton Gap to Chester Gap and continued across US 522 following at first near the mountain crest, then on through woods to reach Mosby Shelter in another 2.5mi. The present route of the *AT* follows the fire road from Compton Gap for 1.7mi. then turns north away from it.

Access

The upper end of the fire road is on Skyline Drive, SDMP 10.4 in Compton Gap.

The lower end is on US 522 in Chester Gap, 3.2mi. east of junction of US 522 and Va 55 in Front Royal.

Trail Description
Compton Gap to US 522

0.0-4.0 Junction with Skyline Drive, SDMP 10.4 (2,415 ft.). *AT* hikers traveling north will cross Drive at this junction after descending Compton Mtn. From here *AT* and fire road/horse trail are coincident for next 1.7mi.

0.3-3.7 Dickey Ridge Trail leads left to Windham Rocks in 0.2mi. then continues to Skyline Drive. To right is service road leading 0.4mi. to Indian Run Maintenance Building. Spring is 250 ft. from road, on left, about 0.1mi. before reaching building.

0.6-3.4 Yellow-blazed Springhouse Road leads left 0.7mi. coming into Dickey Ridge Trail 6mi. north of its junction with fire road. Beyond this point horse trail is blocked to motorized vehicles.

1.7-2.3 *AT* turns left, away from horse trail. Beyond this junction horse trail is yellow-blazed only.

2.2-1.8 Pass gate and leave Park. Beyond this point road is SR 610, paved and blue-blazed.

3.9-0.1 Take left fork of road, SR 665, and descend short distance.

4.0-0.0 US 522 in Chester Gap. To left along US 522 it is 1.5mi. to *AT* crossing.

SIDE TRAILS IN NORTH AND SOUTH MARSHALL MOUNTAINS AREA

This group of trails includes the Mt. Marshall Trail, Bluff Trail, Jordan River Trail, Big Devils Stairs Trail and Harris Hollow Trail.

Access:

From *Skyline Drive* there are two points of access. Yellow-blazed Mt. Marshall Trail enters Drive at SDMP 12.6, just south of Jenkins Gap Overlook. (Horses may prefer using Jenkins Gap Trail which leaves Drive just north of overlook, SDMP 12.3.)

At Gravel Springs Gap, SDMP 17.7, yellow-blazed Harris Hollow Trail descends eastward paralleling *AT* for a short distance and in 0.4mi. intersects Bluff Trail near Gravel Springs. One can also follow *AT* from gap and reach start of Bluff Trail in 0.2mi.

From the *east*, main access to area is through town of Washington, Va. From main corner of town go north one block on SR 628, then turn left on SR 622. *To reach Mt. Marshall Trail* follow SR 622 for 2.4mi. then turn right onto SR 625 and follow it about 1mi. to end of state maintenance. Small parking area for 3 to 4 cars here. Sign and blue arrow mark trail which leads right from road. In about 250 yds. turn left onto old roadbed. Trail is not blazed until it enters Park. *To reach bottom of Big Devils Stairs Trail* follow SR 622 for 4mi. from Washington, Va. and 0.1mi. west of stream crossing. *To reach bottom of Harris Hollow Trail* follow SR 622 for about 5mi. from Washington to the head of Harris Hollow. Trail starts just before reaching highest elevation of SR 622. There is a small sign saying "Trail" but no blazes outside Park.

Lower end of Jordan River Trail is reached by turning west in Flint Hill, Va. onto SR 641. Continue ahead and, at a "T" turn left on graveled road, SR 629. Follow SR 629 up the Jordan River to gate. Park here and continue up road on foot. In about 0.1mi. enter SNP.

Trail access across private property depends upon goodwill of landowners. Posted trail closures must be observed.

MT. MARSHALL TRAIL

5.7 miles   yellow-blazed
This trail is valuable in providing access to the Bluff Trail and the Jordan River Trail, also for use in several circuit hikes. The upper 4mi. are almost level. The trail is not blazed outside the Park but is marked at its lower end on SR 625.

Trail Description
Skyline Drive to Harris Hollow (SR 625)
0.0-5.7 Intersection with Skyline Drive, SDMP 12.6, just south of Jenkins Gap Overlook.
0.1-5.6 Yellow-blazed Jenkins Gap Trail leads left 0.5mi. and crosses Skyline Drive.
0.9-4.8 Trail enters wilderness area.
3.5-2.2 Junction with yellow-blazed Bluff Trail. (Bluff Trail leads right 3.8mi. to end on *AT* near Gravel Springs Gap.)
3.9-1.8 Jordan River Trail, yellow-blazed, leads down mountain 1.3mi. following branch of Jordan River to SR 629.
5.1-0.6 Pass chain across road near Park boundary. Yellow blazes end here. Travel across private land beyond this point depends upon goodwill of landowner. Posted closures must be respected.
5.3-0.4 Pass through wooden gate.
5.7-0.0 Trail junction with SR 625 at end of state maintenance. From here it is 1mi. via SR 625 to main road through Harris Hollow, SR 622.

BLUFF TRAIL

3.8 miles   first 0.3mi. blue-blazed
                                        remainder yellow-blazed

"Bluff" was a local name for Mt. Marshall. The trail slabs the southern and eastern slopes of the mountain with a very gentle grade. It provides access to the Big Devils Stairs Trail and is also useful in circuit hikes.

Trail Description
AT to Mt. Marshall Trail, (S to N)

0.0-3.8 Junction with *AT*, 0.2mi. south of Gravel Springs Gap, SDMP 17.7.

0.2-3.6 Intersection with access road for Gravel Springs Hut. Hut, for use of long distance *AT* hikers only, is 100 ft. to right.

0.3-3.5 Harris Hollow Trail enters from left. At this junction blue blazes end, yellow blazes start. Bluff Trail and Harris Hollow Trail are concurrent here.

0.4-3.4 Bluff Trail bends sharply left as Harris Hollow Trail continues straight ahead.

1.6-2.2 Junction with Big Devils Stairs Trail which leads right, downhill, to SR 622 in Harris Hollow.

3.4-0.4 Trail turns sharply right, soon followed by sharp turn to left.

3.8-0.0 Mt. Marshall Trail. (To left it is 3.5mi. to Skyline Drive, SDMP 12.5, at Jenkins Gap; to right it is 0.4mi. to Jordan River Trail and 2.2mi. to lower end of Mt. Marshall Trail on SR 625.)

JORDAN RIVER TRAIL

1.3 miles   yellow-blazed

Although this trail is primarily used by horsemen, it is a pleasant walk for hikers along an abandoned road. About 0.1mi. inside Park boundary are two very tall chimneys just across river, all that is left of what was once a large home. Much higher on the trail there are ruins of a simpler home.

Access

To reach lower end of trail first take US 522 to Flint Hill and turn west onto SR 641. Continue ahead on SR 606 for about 1mi. then turn right onto SR 628 and, at a "T", turn left on graveled road, SR 629. Follow SR 629 up Jordan River to gate and park. Continue beyond gate on foot. Access to Park boundary across private land depends upon goodwill of landowner. Posted trail closures must be respected. In about 0.1mi. enter SNP.

Upper end of trail is on Mt. Marshall Trail in Thorofare Gap. To north it is 0.4mi. to Bluff Trail and 3.5mi. to Skyline Drive.

BIG DEVILS STAIRS TRAIL

2.3 miles   blue-blazed

The Big Devils Stairs canyon is one of the most impressive features of Shenandoah National Park. There is no trail through the canyon, but, with caution, one can climb along the stream all the way through. The trail follows the rim on the eastern side of the canyon. It is not suitable for young children. If parking in Harris Hollow *please do not park in private driveway.* Access to the Park boundary depends upon the goodwill of the landowner. Trail closures must be observed.

Trail Description

Bluff Trail to Harris Hollow (SR 622)

0.0-2.3 Junction with Bluff Trail, 1.6mi. from *AT* and Gravel Springs Gap.

0.2-2.1 Trail follows eastern rim of canyon above creek (a branch of Rush River).

0.6-1.7 Trail continues along rim, following close to cliff edge. Excellent views across canyon and toward south. Once past cliffs trail descends by switchbacks.

1.6-0.7 Cross creek and in a few feet pass Park boundary.

2.3-0.0 Junction with SR 622 in Harris Hollow about 0.1mi. west of creek and 4mi. from Washington, Va.

HARRIS HOLLOW TRAIL

2.8 miles   yellow-blazed

If starting at the lower end of the Harris Hollow Trail, park along SR 622 wherever there is room to pull off. *Please do not block a private driveway.* Trail is not blazed outside the Park but a small sign on SR 622 says "Trail". Where it leaves the gravel road it is again marked by a similar sign. Remember, access to the Park boundary across private land depends on the goodwill of the landowner. Trail closures must be respected.

A *circuit hike* of about 7.5mi. can be made using this trail, the Bluff Trail and Big Devils Stairs Trail, with 1mi. of road walking along SR 622. A *longer circuit*, 11.5mi., would use the Bluff Trail, the Mt. Marshall Trail and a road walk along SR 625 and SR 622.

Trail Description
Skyline Drive to SR 622

0.0-2.8 Junction with Skyline Drive at Gravel Springs Gap, SDMP 17.7. Trail follows access road toward Gravel Springs Hut.

0.3-2.5 Turn left off access road.

0.4-2.4 Bluff Trail. Follow it left for 0.1mi.

0.5-2.3 Continue straight ahead where Bluff Trail bends sharply to left.

0.7-2.1 Reach roadbed of former Harris Hollow Road and turn left along it. (To right Gravel Springs Hut trail leads 0.1mi. up to Gravel Springs Hut. Hut for use of long distance *AT* hikers only.)

1.4-1.4 Cross Park boundary. No blazes beyond this point. Continue down old road. Land is posted on both sides so stay on road.

2.6-0.2 Reach gravel road and follow it right. Where gravel road bends left continue straight ahead on old rutted road.

2.8-0.0 Junction with SR 622, 5mi. from Washington, Va.

TRAILS IN THE RANGE VIEW CABIN AREA EAST OF SKYLINE DRIVE

The Keyser Run Fire Road, Piney Branch Trail and Hull School Trail are the major routes in the area. Trails that intersect one or more of these include Piney Ridge Trail, Little Devils Stairs Trail, Pole Bridge Link, Fork Mtn. Trail, Thornton Hollow Trail, and the *AT*. Many different circuit routes are possible.

Range View Cabin is ideally situated for campers who wish to hike in this area or in the adjacent Mathews Arm-Elkwallow area. Cabin reservations must be made in advance at PATC Headquarters; see "Accommodations and Facilities".

Access
From Skyline Drive:

1. *SDMP 19.4*: Here is upper end of Keyser Run Fire Road. Also at this milepost, but across Drive from fire road, a spur trail goes west to connect with *AT* in 100 ft. One mile down fire road is Fourway, the point where Little Devils Stairs Trail goes to left(east) and Pole Bridge Link Trail goes to right.

2. *SDMP 21.9*: *AT* crosses the Drive here, just south of Rattlesnake Point Overlook. Follow *AT* south for 0.4mi. to reach upper end of Piney Branch Trail and another 0.4mi. to reach intersection with service road to Range View Cabin.

3. *SDMP 22.1*: Here a service road (gated) leads by Piney River Ranger Station and on east to Range View Cabin, intersecting *AT*. Both Piney Branch Trail and Piney Ridge Trail have their upper ends on this road (and on or near *AT*). Upper end of Piney Ridge Trail is a few feet down road from this intersection.

4. *SDMP 25.4*: Thornton River Trail crosses the Drive.

5. *SDMP 28.1*: Hull School Trail descends eastward from Beahms Gap.

From the Piedmont north of Sperryville:

1. *Lower end of Piney Branch Trail:* To reach this point turn northwest from US 511/211 onto SR 612 just north of Thornton River bridge north of town. In 1.3mi. continue ahead on SR 600, following Piney River. Reach junction with SR 653, which enters from left, when 3.3mi. from US 522/211. Park car near this junction. Continue along SR 600 on foot to its end, about 0.1mi. Here Piney Branch Trail leads left, crossing Piney River, then continuing up river for 0.6mi. before entering Park.

Fords of Piney River along lower stretch of Piney Branch Trail may be difficult in wet weather. Hull School Trail and lower end of Piney Ridge Trail are easily reached by this access route.

2. *Lower end of Thornton River Trail:* Turn off US 511/211 as described above but continue on SR 612 where it forks left at its junction with SR 600. About 3.2mi. from junction reach end of state maintenance and park. Continue up road on foot and, in 0.1mi., enter Park. This road, now Thornton River Trail, here yellow-blazed, continues up North Fork of river for 1.4mi. to its junction with Hull School Trail. One can then follow Hull School Trail, right, to reach Fork Mtn. Trail, Piney Branch Trail and Keyser Run Fire Road. Using this route there are no fords of creeks except where Hull School Trail crosses Piney River. Above Hull School Trail Thornton River Trail is blue-blazed.

3. *Lower ends of Little Devils Stairs Trail and Keyser Run Road:* From US 522/211 at southwest side of bridge over Covington River, about 2.5mi. north of Sperryville, turn west onto SR 622. Follow SR 622 for 2mi. to just past bridge over Covington River. Take left fork which is SR 614 and follow it about 3mi. to start of Little Devils Stairs Trail and a parking area. A self-registration backcountry permit booth is located here for those who intend to backpack in this area. Keyser Run Fire Road is a continuation of SR 614 and is gated about 0.2mi. beyond parking area.

KEYSER RUN FIRE ROAD

4.5 miles   yellow-blazed
   This is a pleasant road to hike with an easy gradient most of the way. It is also an important route as it offers access to the Little Devils Stairs Trail, Pole Bridge Link, Piney Branch Trail and other trails in the area. Across the Drive from its upper end a short spur trail leads west to the *AT*, thus extending the number of circuit hikes for which the fire road can be used.

Access:
   Upper end starts at Skyline Drive, SDMP 19.4, at east base of Little Hogback Mtn. A short spur trail (100 ft.) between *AT* and Drive directly opposite fire road gives access from *AT*.
   Access from US 522-211 is via SR 622 and SR 614. (See "Access to Trails in the Range View Cabin Area".)

Trail Description
Skyline Drive to SR 614
   0.0-4.5 From south or "east" side of Skyline Drive, SDMP 19.4, fire road drops very gradually, passing around head of hollow containing Little Devils Stairs.

1.0-3.5 Reach Fourway. To left Little Devils Stairs Trail
leads 2mi. down to SR 614. To right Pole Bridge Link
leads 0.8mi. to Piney Branch Trail.

3.3-1.2 Hull School Trail leads right, reaching Piney
Branch Trail in 0.4mi. and crossing Piney River 0.1mi.
farther. On left of Keyser Run Fire Road is walled-in
Bolen Cemetery.

4.3-0.2 Road is gated.

4.5-5.0 Reach SR 614 at end of state maintenance.
Little Devils Stairs trailhead is here at parking area.

LITTLE DEVILS STAIRS TRAIL

2.0 miles   blue-blazed

This trail follows Keyser Run into the canyon known as
Little Devils Stairs. The canyon area is steep, wild and
picturesque. Its sheer cliffs are outstanding; they offer a
challenge to rock climbers. The trail route is dangerous
in wet or icy weather and even in good weather must be
negotiated with care.

For a circuit hike it is preferable to ascend the Little
Devils Stairs Trail and to descend via the Keyser Run
Fire Road or via the Pole Bridge Link to Piney Branch
Trail, then the Hull School Trail.

Access

The trail's upper end is at Fourway on the Keyser Run
Fire Road, 1mi. from Skyline Drive and the *AT*.

Lower end is reached via SR 622 and 614 from US
522/211. (See "Access to Trails in the Range View Cabin
Area.")

Trail Description

SR 614 to Keyser Run Fire Road at Fourway

0.0-2.0 From parking area at end of state maintenance
of SR 614 trail heads north, immediately crossing two
small creeks. (SR 614 continues into Park as Keyser Run
Fire Road and is gated 0.2mi. beyond parking area.)

0.6-1.4 Trail approaches Keyser Run, stream that cut Little Devils Stairs canyon. Here is old rock wall, part of former dam or bridge. Trail crosses run frequently as it climbs steeply.

1.7-0.3 Trail makes sharp left turn and climbs steeply away from run.

1.8-0.2 Trail crosses rock-edged terrace, former home-site.

2.0-0.0 Reach Keyser Run Fire Road at Fourway. (Directly across road is Pole Bridge Link which joins Piney Branch Trail in 0.8mi. To right Keyser Run Fire Road leads 1mi. to Skyline Drive and *AT*. To left it leads 3.5mi. to SR 614 at Little Devils Stairs trailhead.)

POLE BRIDGE LINK

0.7 miles   blue-blazed
   This trail links the Keyser Run Fire Road and Little Devils Stairs Trail with the Piney Branch Trail.

Trail Description
Keyser Run Fire Road to Piney Branch Trail

0.0-0.7 Fourway intersection on Keyser Run Fire Road, 1mi. from Skyline Drive (and *AT*). Little Devils Stairs Trail starts here, from opposite side of fire road.

0.4-0.3 Intersection with Sugarloaf Trail. To right it is 1.4mi. to *AT* near SDMP 20.8.

0.7-0.0 Intersection with Piney Branch Trail. (To right, via Piney Branch Trail, *AT* is 1.4mi. and Range View Cabin 0.4mi. farther. To left, Hull School Trail is 2.8mi. and lower end of Piney Ridge Trail is 2.4mi.)

PINEY BRANCH TRAIL

6.5 miles   blue-blazed between *AT* and
                                            Hull School Trail
                      yellow-blazed from Hull School Trail
                                            to Park boundary

This trail begins outside the Park at SR 600 and follows Piney River to its source, then continues on to *AT* and crest of Blue Ridge.

A *circuit hike* of 8mi. can be made from Range View Cabin with this trail and the Piney Ridge Trail. *Another circuit* could be : *AT* between Piney Ridge Trail junction and Keyser Run Road, fire road down to Fourway, then Pole Bridge Link and back up Piney Branch Trail to Range View Cabin.

Another favorite circuit of 7.8mi. starts from SR 614. Climb up Little Devils Stairs, then follow Pole Bridge Link, descend Piney Branch Trail to Hull School Trail. Follow Hull School Trail left and descend Keyser Run Fire Road to start. See PATC Map #9 for other possible circuits.

Access

Upper end of trail starts at *AT* and service road leading to Range View Cabin. (See PATC Map #9 inset of Range View Cabin Area.) Start of trail is 0.4mi. north of Range View Cabin and 0.4mi. from Skyline Drive at Rattlesnake Point, SDMP 21.9, via *AT*, and about 0.3mi. from Drive via service road at Piney River Ranger Station, SDMP 22.1.

Lower end of trail is on SR 600. See "Access to Trails in Range View Cabin Area" for details.

Trail Description
AT to SR 600 and 653

0.0-6.5 Intersection with *AT*. Trail leads east at signpost and follows old road down mountain. Follow blue blazes.

1.3-5.2 Cross headwaters of Piney Branch.

1.4-5.1 Junction with Pole Bridge Link Trail which comes in from left. (Via Pole Bridge Link it is 0.8mi. to Fourway on Keyser Run Fire Road.) Turn right at this junction.

4.0-2.5 Junction with Piney Ridge Trail which enters from right. (Range View Cabin is 3.4mi. from this junction via Piney Ridge Trail.)

4.3-2.2 Cross Piney Branch.

4.4-2.1 Junction with Hull School Trail. Blue blazes end here. Turn right. Piney Branch Trail and Hull School Trail are coincident for next 0.2mi.

4.6-1.9 Cross Piney River, then turn left from Hull School Trail and descend old road along Piney River, following yellow blazes.

5.8-0.7 Leave Park and continue down road to SR 600.

6.5-0.0 Junction of SR 600 and SR 653.

PINEY RIDGE TRAIL

3.3 miles   blue-blazed

This trail used along with the Piney Branch Trail provides a *circuit hike* from Range View Cabin.

Access

Upper end of Piney Ridge Trail may be reached by following service road from Skyline Drive, SDMP 22.1, past Piney River Ranger Station south about 0.7mi., crossing *AT* 30 ft. before reaching start of Piney Ridge Trail which leads right from road. (Trailhead is nearly within sight of Range View Cabin at road's end.) One can also start at Rattlesnake Point Overlook and follow *AT* south for 0.8mi. to its intersection with service road, then turn left onto road toward cabin and in 30 ft., reach start of Piney Ridge Trail. Lower end of Piney Ridge Trail is on Piney Branch Trail 0.4mi. above its junction with Hull School Trail.

Trail Description
Range View Cabin Service Road (near *AT*) to Piney Branch Trail

0.0-3.3 Junction with service road, just west of Range View Cabin. Trail bears south, descending along crest of ridge.

2.0-1.3 Pass old cemetery to right of trail; a few feet beyond take left(east) fork at trail intersection. (Straight ahead blue-blazed Fork Mtn. Trail continues along ridge to Hull School Trail.) As one descends one may find traces of an old homesite.

3.3-0.0 Reach Piney Branch Trail 0.4mi. from its junction with Hull School Trail.

FORK MOUNTAIN TRAIL

1.2 miles   blue-blazed

This short trail leads along Fort Mtn. ridge from Piney Ridge Trail southeastward to its intersection with Hull School Trail. It makes a useful link in circuit hikes.

THORNTON RIVER TRAIL

5.2 miles   yellow-blazed east of
                                 Hull School Trail
                                 blue-blazed to west

From SR 612 trail follows an old road up North Fork of Thornton River to Hull School Trail. It climbs up Thornton Hollow, crossing Skyline Drive on a diagonal at SDMP 25.4, then continues on to end at *AT*.

Trail Description
Junction of SR 612 and SR 653 to *AT*

0.0-5.2 From junction of SR 612 and SR 653, continue up SR 612 on foot.

0.6-4.6 State road maintenance ends.

0.7-4.5 Road gated at Park boundary. Spring to right of road just beyond gate. Trail is yellow-blazed from Park boundary to Hull School Trail.

2.0-3.2 Junction with Hull School Trail. Follow road a few feet beyond its sharp turn to right. Thornton River Trail (blue-blazed from here on) turns left away from road. Trail crosses river 3 times in next 0.6mi. Difficult in wet weather.

3.4-1.8 Cross branch of river. Valley is wide here and there are numerous indications of old homesites, traces of old roads, even an old car!

3.6-1.6 From here trail climbs gently but steadily upward through open woods.

4.9-0.3 Skyline Drive, SDMP 25.4. Cross Drive diagonally to left.

5.2-0.0 Reach *AT* at point on *AT* 1.2mi. north of Neighbor Mtn. Parking Area.

HULL SCHOOL TRAIL

4.4 miles   yellow-blazed

This trail makes use of a number of roads that existed before the Park was established - Beahms Gap Road, North Fork (of Thornton) Road, a bit of Keyser Run Road, and a short section long known as "PLD". One end is on Skyline Drive at Beahms Gap, SDMP 28.1; the lower end is on Keyser Run Road at Bolen Cemetery. Trails that intersect it include Thornton River Trail, Piney Branch Trail and Fork Mtn. Trail.

Trail Description
Skyline Drive to Keyser Run Fire Road

0.0-4.4 Skyline Drive, SDMP 28.1. Trail follows route of old Beahms Gap Road, occasionally detouring right or left of it where erosion has damaged old roadbed.

1.5-2.9 Enter area of old homesites. Find double daffodils in bloom first week of April.

1.9-2.5 Old homesite on right. More daffodils.

2.2-2.2 Cross Thornton River and reach Thornton River Trail. Hull School Trail now follows route of former North Fork Road over ridge of Fork Mtn.

2.9-1.5 Summit of Fork Mtn. ridge. (Fork Mtn. Trail, blue-blazed, leads left about 1mi. to end on Piney Ridge Trail.)

3.5-0.9 Junction with Piney Branch Trail. (To right Piney Branch Trail, yellow-blazed, leads out of Park to SR 600.) Cross Piney River.

3.7-0.7 Piney Branch Trail, blue-blazed here, leads left 4.2mi. to *AT*.

4.4-0.0 Keyser Run Fire Road. Just up fire road from junction is walled-in Bolen Cemetery. (To right, Keyser Run Road leads 1.2mi. downhill to parking area for Little Devils Stairs Trail on SR 614. To left, fire road leads 3.3mi. to Skyline Drive and *AT*.)

HOGBACK SPUR TRAIL

0.3 miles   blue-blazed

This short trail runs from Skyline Drive, SDMP 20.4, up to the *AT*. There is a spring near lower end. Upper terminus is less than 0.1mi. north of hang glider launching area, so that main use of this trail is for hang glider enthusiasts.

SUGARLOAF TRAIL

1.4 miles   blue-blazed

This new trail in the area connects the *AT* to Pole Bridge Link, making possible several new circuit hikes. For most of its length it follows a pleasantly graded old road trace through mountain laurel.

Trail Description
AT to Pole Bridge Link Trail
  0.0-1.4 Junction with *AT*, 100 ft. south of Skyline Drive, SDMP 20.8.
  0.1-1.3 Bear right(southeast) onto old road trace.
  1.0-0.4 Pass large flat area to right(west) of trail. Small stream 150 ft. to left of trail.
  1.4-0.0 Junction with Pole Bridge Link Trail. From here it is 0.5mi. left to Fourway and Little Devils Stairs Trail and 0.4mi. right to Piney Branch Trail.

MATHEWS ARM-ELKWALLOW AREA
(west of Skyline Drive)

This trail network includes about a dozen trails from the Big Blue Trail and Mathews Arm Trail on the north to Neighbor Mountain Trail on the south. A study of PATC Map #9 will suggest a number of possible circuit hikes of varying lengths.

Historical note: Mathews Arm was part of a grant of land made by Lord Fairfax to Israel Mathews. Many of Israel's descendants still live in Warren County.

BIG BLUE TRAIL

7.8 miles   blue-blazed
The Big Blue-Tuscarora Trail extends about 220 miles, with its southern terminus on the Appalachian Trail on Hogback Mountain in SNP and its northern terminus, also on the *AT*, near Duncannon, Pa. West of US 340 its route crosses the south branch of the Shenandoah River at the Bentonville Low Water Bridge, then climbs west over the ridges of the Massanutten, crosses the main Shenandoah Valley in the area of Toms Brook, climbs Little North Mountain and zigzags its way west to the Va.-W.Va. state line where it runs generally northeast.

For much of its length within Shenandoah National Park the Big Blue follows Overall Run and is coincident with the Overall Run Trail. Just off the trail, 3.1mi. from the *AT* and 4.6mi. from US 340 via the Big Blue Trail is the beautiful cascade, Overall Run Falls. This is one of the prettiest spots in the Northern District of the Park. The falls here is considered the highest in the Park. *Caution:* The Big Blue Trail is extremely steep near here and the side trail to the base of the falls is very rough.

Access:

To reach southern end of Big Blue Trail, follow *AT* south for 0.4mi. from *AT* crossing of Skyline Drive at SDMP 21.1 or follow *AT* north 0.6mi. from crossing of Drive at SDMP 21.9, just south of Rattlesnake Point Overlook (parking here). Concrete post on *AT* identifies trail here as Big Blue Trail.

Trail Description
AT to US 340

0.0-7.8 Junction with *AT*. Big Blue Trail descends to west. (Big Blue and Overall Run Trail are coincident for first 4.8mi.)

0.7-7.1 Turn sharply right. (Straight ahead a short connecting trail leads 250 ft. to Traces Interpretive Trail and beyond to northern part of Mathews Arm Campground. Follow Traces Trail to left 0.5mi. to reach parking area and entrance road to campground.) Big Blue continues to descend gently, skirting swampy area known as Bearwallow.

2.3-5.5 Mathews Arm Trail, yellow-blazed. Continue ahead on road for 240 ft., then turn left following blue blazes and descend.

2.5-5.3 Short side trail to left leads to view of upper falls, also known as Twin Falls, a small but scenic waterfall.

2.7-5.1 Several short paths lead left to views of Big Falls of Overall Run and valley below. Beyond these trail becomes very steep.

3.1-4.7 Unmarked spur trail leads left 0.2mi. to foot of Overall Falls. (Spur trail is very rugged; dangerous to descend in icy weather.) Beyond junction main trail continues to descend via several switchbacks.

3.7-4.1 Trail crosses to south side of creek.

4.1-3.7 Trail recrosses creek (to north bank).

4.8-3.0 Concrete post marks separation point of Big Blue and Overall Run Trails. Big Blue turns sharply right here and ascends toward Thompson Hollow.

5.0-2.8 Turn 90 degrees left. (Blue-blazed Thompson Hollow Trail continues straight ahead.) Big Blue now follows trace of an old road.

5.5-2.3 Take left fork of old road, heading northwest, then bear around or over several hills with relatively little change in elevation.

6.3-1.5 Begin descent.

6.5-1.3 Make sharp right turn. (An old trail continues ahead, reaching Park boundary in about 100 ft.). Trail now descends along Park boundary, crossing in and out several times.

6.7-1.1 Cross creek and turn left. In 200 ft. leave Park. Ascend gradually along old road.

6.8-1.0 Turn back sharply to right while continuing to climb.

6.9-0.9 Again turn right, returning to Park boundary and following it short distance. Descend gradually through pines, passing pasture on left.

7.3-0.5 Cross gate and turn sharply left, following southwest edge of pasture. At lower corner of pasture, nearly under powerline, bear right downhill, heading directly toward railroad underpass in hollow. (Trail through meadow is marked with stakes, blue-blazed.)

7.6-0.2 Reach farm road and turn left onto it. Pass through railroad underpass.

7.8-0.0 US 340, 1.5mi. south of Bentonville and 1.1mi. north of Overall.

THOMPSON HOLLOW TRAIL

0.4 miles   blue-blazed

One end of this short trail is at the Park boundary at end of SR 630 in Thompson Hollow south of Bentonville. Turn east on SR 613. In about 0.8mi. turn south on SR 630 and drive to end of state maintenance. *Do not block road access.* Follow road through privately owned land a short distance to reach Park boundary and look for post marking trail.

The upper, or southern, terminus of trail is on Big Blue Trail at a point on latter 2.8mi. from US 340 and 0.2mi. from Overall Run.

Now that Overall Run Trail has no outside access, this Thompson Hollow-Big Blue route is shortest approach to Overall Run Falls.

OVERALL RUN TRAIL

5.4 miles   blue-blazed

Most of what was earlier called the Overall Run Trail is now coincident with the Big Blue Trail. Only the lowest section along the run, below the point where the Big Blue turns away from it, remains separate. At present there is no access to lower end of Overall Run Trail from US 340, so trail is not maintained west of Beecher-Overall Connecting Trail.

A pleasant circuit hike can be made, starting at Mathews Arm Campground, by descending Mathews Arm Trail, going left on Beecher Ridge Trail and right on Beecher-Overall Connecting Trail, then ascending via Overall Run Trail, Big Blue and Mathews Arm Trail.

Trail Description
East to West

0.0-5.4 See description of Big Blue Trail for first 4.8mi.

4.8-0.6 Overall Run Trail continues straight ahead. Big Blue Trail turns right toward Thompson Hollow. (This point is 2.5mi. from Mathews Arm Trail and 3mi. from US 340 via Big Blue Trail.)

4.9-0.5 Lower falls of Overall Run is few feet to left.

5.4-0.0 End of maintenance. (Trail is closed to public outside Park.) Beecher-Overall Connecting Trail, blue-blazed, leads left, crossing run and ascending ridge.

BEECHER-OVERALL CONNECTING TRAIL

3.1 miles   blue-blazed

The upper terminus of this trail is on the Beecher Ridge Trail, 2.3mi. down from its upper terminus on the Mathews Arm Trail. The lower terminus is on the Overall Run Trail at its lower end. (*Note:* Overall Run Trail is no longer maintained below this point as there is no hiker access from outside Park.

BEECHER RIDGE TRAIL

3.1 miles   yellow-blazed

This trail leaves Mathews Arm Trail 0.9mi. from northern end of Mathews Arm Campground (1.4mi. from campground registration station) and descends crest of Beecher Ridge. It comes into Heiskell Hollow Trail at a point on the latter 2.5mi. below its upper terminus on Knob Mtn. Trail and 1.5mi. from lower end on SR 697. Beecher-Overall Connecting Trail, blue-blazed, connects Overall Run Trail near its lower end (Overall Run Trail not maintained below junction) with Beecher Ridge Trail, joining it 2.3mi. from Mathews Arm Trail.

A circuit hike can be made starting from Mathews Arm Campground registration station, using the Beecher Ridge and Overall Run Trails (9.5mi.) or a shorter circuit using Beecher Ridge and Heiskell Hollow Trails (7.5mi.).

MATHEWS ARM TRAIL

4.4 miles   yellow-blazed

This old road, most of which is now classified by the Park as trail, leads north from Mathews Arm Campground. After crossing Overall Run it continues on the long ridge, Mathews Arm, from which the campground takes its name, then descends to the Park boundary. It continues outside the Park but no parking is available.

Access

From Skyline Drive, SDMP 22.2, drive down paved entrance road to Mathews Arm Campground and park in lot near registration station. Walk through campground to far end chain gate at "tents only" section of B-loop. Distance from Drive to Tent Area B is 1.1mi. (When campground is closed one must walk full distance. One can follow abandoned section of Mathews Arm Road (kept clear for overhead powerline) from Drive to registration station and avoid some of paved road walking.) Trail description below starts at camp road in Tent Area B.

Trail Description

Mathews Arm Campground to Park boundary

0.0 Mathews Arm Trail is gated as it leaves paved camp road in Tent Area B. Descend gently.

0.1 "Traces" Trail intersects road here.

0.4 Weddlewood Trail leads left to end on Heiskell Hollow trail in 1.3mi.

0.9 Beecher Ridge Trail leads left down Beecher Ridge and over to Heiskell Hollow Trail.

1.3 Cross Overall Run and turn right.

1.4 Intersection with Big Blue Trail. (To right it is 2.3mi. to *AT*; to left it is 5.2mi. to US 340.)

2.7 Trail descends steeply. In 0.6mi. turn sharp left off ridge crest.

4.4 Park boundary. Trail closed to hikers outside Park.

THE TRACES INTERPRETIVE TRAIL

1.7 miles   not blazed

This trail, which loops around Mathews Arm Campground, emphasizes the traces that remain of pre-Park days of this land. It starts at upper end of parking area (near registration station) and circles campground in counter-clockwise direction.

Trail Description

0.0 Sign at edge of parking area.

0.5 Concrete post marks spur trail to campground. In 50 ft. second post marks spur trail which leads right 0.1mi. to Big Blue Trail.

1.1 Interpretive Trail intersects Mathews Arm Road at a point on latter about 0.1mi. from northern end of campground.

1.3 Viewpoint on right.

1.6 Camp road at lower end of parking area.

1.7 Completion of loop at trail's start.

KNOB MOUNTAIN TRAIL

7.6 miles   yellow-blazed

From Mathews Arm Campground this trail follows portion of graveled road leading to sewage treatment plant. Near this area trail goes left and follows ridge, passing over peak of Knob Mtn., descending along ridge crest, then dropping down to Jeremys Run.

A *circuit hike* of 6mi. would include 2.2mi. of Knob Mtn. Trail, Knob Mtn. Cut-Off Trail, upper portion of Jeremys Run Trail, the *AT* back to Elkwallow Gap, then Elkwallow Trail to Mathews Arm Campground.

Access

To reach upper end of trail and road, turn west from Skyline Drive, SDMP 22.2, onto entrance road to

Mathews Arm Campground and drive 0.5mi. to parking area at registration station. (When entrance road to campground is closed, winter and all seasons in 1991, it is necessary to walk down from Drive. One can avoid paved road by following abandoned section of Mathews Arm Fire Road which parallels entrance road a few feet to south.) From parking area follow on foot paved road leading left to yellow chain gate at far end of dump station turn-around. Continue past Wastewater Treatment Plant and Heiskell Hollow Trail on right. Knob Mtn. Trail takes off to left at wooden sign just beyond Heiskell Hollow Trail. Start of trail is 0.9mi. from Skyline Drive.

Lower end is reached via Jeremys Run Trail. See description of that trail.

Trail Description
Mathews Arm Campground to Jeremys Run

0.0-7.5 From loop in paved campground road, follow graveled road beyond chain.

0.4-7.1 Heiskell Hollow Trail junction, yellow-blazed, leads right 4mi. to SR 697 near Compton.

2.2-5.3 To left, Knob Mtn. Cut-Off Trail, blue-blazed, leads 0.5mi. steeply down to Jeremys Run Trail at a point on latter 0.8mi. from *AT*.

4.3-3.2 Trail continues as much narrower footway, immediately climbing over highest peak of Knob Mtn., 2,865 ft., then descending along ridge crest, finally dropping steeply toward Jeremys Run.

7.5-0.0 Cross Jeremys Run and reach Jeremys Run Trail in 50 ft. (From this junction it is 0.8mi. right to Park boundary; to left it is 50 ft. to Neighbor Mtn. Trail. *AT* is 5.4mi. via Jeremys Run Trail and 4.6mi. via Neighbor Mtn. Trail.)

HEISKELL HOLLOW TRAIL

4.0 miles   yellow-blazed
This trail can be used in combination with others in the area - Mathews Arm Trail, Weddlewood Trail, Beecher Ridge Trail and the Big Blue (Overall Run) Trail - for some excellent circuit hikes.

Access

To reach the "upper" or easternmost trailhead follow Knob Mtn. Trail from Mathews Arm Campground. In 0.5mi. from registration station reach trailhead on right.

To reach "lower" or western trailhead follow US 340 to Compton, about 4.5mi. south of Bentonville and 1.8mi. north of Rileyville. Turn east on SR 662. In 0.4mi. turn left onto SR 697 and follow it 0.6mi. to its end. Room for parking here but don't block driveway. As first 0.2mi. of trail is on private property and necessitates passing through barnyard, it is courteous to ask permission before starting. Trail access to Park boundary depends upon goodwill of landowner. Trail closures must be observed. Trail roughly follows south side of Compton Run (or Dry Run) to Park boundary.

Trail Description

Knob Mtn. Trail to SR 697

0.0-4.0 Trailhead on Knob Mtn. Trail, 0.5mi. from Mathews Arm registration station. Descend.

0.7-3.3 Junction with yellow-blazed Weddlewood Trail. (To right leads 1.3mi. to end on Mathews Arm Trail.)

2.5-1.5 Just after crossing Compton Run reach junction with Beecher Ridge Trail, yellow-blazed also. Within next mile trail crosses run 4 times.

3.8-0.2 Pass gate into pasture. Continue to parallel creek until reaching barnyard.

4.0-0.0 Reach SR 697.

WEDDLEWOOD TRAIL

1.3 miles   yellow-blazed

The eastern (upper) end of this short trail is on Mathews Arm Trail 0.5mi. north of paved campground road (1mi. north of campground registration station) and 1mi. south of Big Blue-Mathews Arm Trail junction. Its western (lower) terminus is on Heiskell Hollow Trail 0.7mi. west of latter's upper end on Knob Mtn. Trail (and 1.2mi. from Mathews Arm Campground registration station) and 3.3mi. east of its end on SR 697. Weddlewood Trail utilizes an old roadbed and the slope is a gentle one. Thanks to this trail, one can start outside the Park using either the Big Blue or Heiskell Hollow Trail and make a circuit avoiding campground area.

KNOB MOUNTAIN (JEREMYS RUN) CUTOFF TRAIL

0.5 mile   blue-blazed

This is a short, very steep trail that connects Jeremys Run Trail to Knob Mtn. Trail. It is useful in circuit hikes. One end is on Knob Mtn. Trail 2.2mi. from Mathews Arm Campground; the other is on Jeremys Run Trail 0.8mi. from its upper end on *AT* near Elkwallow Picnic Area.

ELKWALLOW TRAIL

2.0 miles   blue-blazed

This short trail leads from Elkwallow Wayside to registration area (and parking area) of Mathews Arm Campground, roughly paralleling Skyline Drive. It crosses *AT* near edge of wayside area. It is useful in circuit hikes.

One circuit hike, about 5mi. would include the *AT* from Elkwallow Gap north 2.1mi. to its junction with Big Blue (Overall Run) Trail. Descend Big Blue for 0.7mi. Turn left on spur trail toward Mathews Arm Campground. Bear left along Traces Trail, entering paved entrance road to campground at upper end of parking area. Beginning of Elkwallow Trail, with signpost so indicating it, is directly across entrance road. Follow this back to Elkwallow Wayside.

Another possible circuit would include upper portions of Jeremys Run and Knob Mtn. Trails, Knob Mtn. Cut-Off Trail and a short stretch of *AT*.

JEREMYS RUN TRAIL

6.2 miles   upper 5.4mi. blue-blazed
                                     lower 0.8mi. yellow-blazed

Jeremys Run Trail is one of the most delightful routes in the Park. From Park boundary at base of western slope of Blue Ridge, it leads up Jeremys Run in a deep gorge between two projecting spurs, Knob Mtn. and Neighbor Mtn., to the Appalachian Trail at a point 0.3mi. from Elkwallow Picnic Area. The whole of this valley is beautifully forested; the run itself is a continual series of cascades and pools. The hiking is generally easy, with a gentle rise in elevation and numerous rockhopping crossings of the stream. The exception is one very steep stretch, the lowest 0.5mi. to the Park boundary. The valley abounds with wildlife. Deer are frequently seen and bear scat can be found on the trail, though bears themselves are seldom sighted. Jeremys Run is considered one of the fine trout streams in the Park.

A circuit hike of about 6mi. would include 0.8mi. of Jeremys Run Trail, Knob Mtn. Cut-Off Trail, upper portion of Knob Mtn. Trail, Elkwallow Trail and 0.6mi. stretch of *AT*.

Access

Upper and northeast end of trail can be reached by following *AT* south 0.6mi. from Skyline Drive crossing in Elkwallow Gap, SDMP 23.9, or by following a short spur trail from Elkwallow Picnic Area to *AT* and then down *AT* 0.3mi.

Trail Description

AT to Park boundary

0.0-6.2 Junction with *AT*.

0.8-5.4 Junction with Knob Mtn. Cut-Off Trail. In 100 yds. cross first of many fords of Jeremys Run.

3.1-3.1 Cross 11th ford of creek at halfway point of trail.

4.8-4.1 Pass largest waterfalls on Jeremys Run.

5.4-0.8 Junction with Neighbor Mtn. Trail which enters from left. Knob Mtn. Trail enters from right in 50 ft.

5.5-0.7 Cross 16th and final ford.

6.2-0.0 Park boundary.

NEIGHBOR MOUNTAIN TRAIL

5.6 miles   yellow-blazed

The Neighbor Mtn. Trail follows service road toward Byrds Nest #4, circles to east and north of picnic shelter, then bears northwestward as far as its intersection with *AT*. From the *AT* west trail follows long, almost level, ridge to beyond peak of "The Neighbor". It then descends steeply to Jeremys Run where it connects with Jeremys Run Trail and Knob Mtn. Trail, offering a choice of circuit hikes.

A circuit hike of 13.6mi. can be made by following Neighbor Mtn. Trail to Jeremys Run Trail, then right (uphill) on Jeremys Run Trail to *AT* and *AT* south back to starting point.

Access

Upper end of this trail is on Skyline Drive, SDMP 28.1, directly across from Hull School Trail, also yellow-blazed. Hikers may prefer to park in grassy Neighbor Mtn. Trail Parking Area, SDMP 26.8, and either follow short spur trail to *AT* and thence south along *AT* for 0.3mi. to Neighbor Mtn. Trail junction; or they can follow the "spur" horse trail, yellow-blazed, for 0.3mi. from parking area to Neighbor Mtn. Trail.

Trail Description
Skyline Drive to Jeremys Run

0.0-5.6 From Skyline Drive, SDMP 28.1, opposite Hull School Trail, Neighbor Mtn. Trail follows service road toward Byrds Nest #4.

0.1-5.5 Blue-blazed trail leads left 0.1mi. to *AT*.

0.4-5.2 Turn right off service road and circle east and north of Byrds Nest #4. Water available at shelter during summer.

0.9-4.7 Yellow-blazed spur trail leads 0.3mi. to Neighbor Mtn. Trail Parking Area.

1.0-4.6 Concrete post marks intersection with *AT*. (Via *AT* it is 3.9mi. north to Elkwallow Picnic Area and 1.2mi. south to Beahms Gap.)

2.0-3.6 Pass curious rocks known as "The Gendarmes".

2.9-2.7 Peak of "The Neighbor". Trail now descends steeply with switchbacks.

4.7-0.9 Spur trail leads right 50 ft. to Dripping Spring.

5.6-0.0 Jeremys Run Trail. (To left it is 0.8mi. to Park boundary; to right it is 5.4mi. to *AT*.)

ROCKY BRANCH TRAIL

3.2 miles   yellow-blazed

From its trailhead 50 ft. west of Skyline Drive, SDMP 28.1, on the Hull School Trail, this trail heads south, crossing the *AT* in 0.4mi. Two miles from its start it crosses the Drive and descends eastward. It ends on SR 666 at point on road where state maintenance begins.

To reach lower terminus, turn off US 211 just west of Shenandoah Park Headquarters onto SR 674. Turn right in 0.2mi. onto SR 658; in 0.4mi. turn left onto SR 612. Follow SR 612 for 1.3mi. then turn right onto SR 666 and continue to end of drivable road and park. (Room for 1 or 2 cars; do not block driveway.) Blazes begin in several hundred yards when trail enters Park.

PASS MOUNTAIN TRAIL

3.0 miles   blue-blazed

This trail starts on the *AT* 1.2mi. north of Thornton Gap and furnishes access to Pass Mtn. Hut. It descends eastward to a deep sag between Pass Mtn. and Oventop Mtn. (There is no longer a maintained trail along ridge of Oventop Mtn.) Here it turns sharply right and descends to US 211, reaching it directly across from a road construction storage site, approximately 4.5mi. west of Sperryville and 2.5mi. east of Thornton Gap.

Trail Description
AT to US 211

0.0-3.0 Junction with *AT* 1.2mi. north of Thornton Gap and 1.9mi. south of Beahms Gap, SDMP 28.6.

0.2-2.8 Bear to right of Pass Mtn. Hut. (Hut for overnight use of long distance *AT* hikers only.)

0.5-2.5 Come to old road and follow it downhill.

2.4-0.6 Trail turns 90 degrees to right. Pass Mtn. Trail now follows route of former Butterwood Branch Trail and descends along an old road.

3.0-0.0 End of trail at US 211.

SHENANDOAH NATIONAL PARK
CENTRAL DISTRICT

BUCK HOLLOW TRAIL

3.7 miles   blue-blazed

This trail starts from US 211 and climbs to Skyline Drive in 3mi., crossing it near the junction of Hazel Mtn. Trail with the Drive. *A circuit hike* of roughly 7.5mi. can be made by using this trail in conjunction with the Buck Ridge Trail and the Hazel Mtn. Trail.

Access

Lower trailhead is on US 211 3.4mi. west of intersection of US 211 and US 522 in Sperryville; it is 4.6mi. east of Thornton Gap.

Upper end is on Skyline Drive, SDMP 33.4. Park in Meadow Spring Parking Area on east side of Drive.

Trail Description
US 211 to *AT* (N to S)

0.0-3.0 From US 211 trail passes through brushy area.

0.1-2.9 Cross Thornton River and 200 ft. farther cross Buck Hollow steam.

0.2-2.8 Buck Ridge Trail leads left 2.4mi., climbing steeply to Hazel Mtn. Trail and joining it 0.4mi. from Skyline Drive.

1.3-1.7 Just beyond a crossing of Buck Hollow stream an old road leads left. *Beware* of this road when coming downhill. Trail can easily be missed. For next 0.3mi. trail is close to stream and very attractive.

1.6-1.4 While climbing, watch for blazes where trail (an old roadbed) goes right and another old road forks to left. No problem for those heading downhill. Trail is quite pretty all the way to Drive, sometimes passing through areas with large hemlocks, sometimes following stream.

3.0-0.0 Intersection with Skyline Drive, SDMP 33.4. (To reach *AT*, cross Drive diagonally to Meadow Spring Trail.)

MEADOW SPRING TRAIL

0.7 mile   blue-blazed
This short trail connects the *AT* and Skyline Drive at SDMP 33.4. From the *AT* it descends to the east, passing Meadow Spring on the left. (This was site of former PATC cabin which burned in 1946.) Trail continues to descend more steeply to the Drive.

BUCK RIDGE TRAIL

2.4 miles   blue-blazed
This steep trail has its lower end on the Buck Hollow Trail about 0.2mi. from the lower end of the latter on US 211. Its upper end is on the Hazel Mtn. Trail about 0.4mi. from Skyline Drive, SDMP 33.4. It can be used along with the Buck Hollow and Hazel Mtn. Trails for *a circuit hike.*

LEADING RIDGE TRAIL

1.3 miles   blue-blazed
This trail leads northwest from Skyline Drive, SDMP 36.2, and crosses the *AT* in a few hundred feet. It then climbs to a small knob about 0.1mi. west of the *AT* intersection before descending steeply along a ridge, finally coming into Jewell Hollow and passing through private property to reach SR 669. To reach the trail from the valley turn south from US 211 about 1mi. east of Park Headquarters and 2.5mi. west of Thornton Gap. In 0.5mi. turn left onto SR 669 and drive about 0.8mi. Access across private land at the Park boundary is by goodwill of landowner. Posted closures must be respected.

CRUSHER RIDGE TRAIL

3.6 miles   blue-blazed

This trail starts on the Nicholson Hollow Trail a few feet "west" of Skyline Drive and heads north along Crusher Ridge, following an old road once known as Sours Lane. It crosses the *AT* about 0.1mi. from the Drive. After 0.4mi. it begins descent into Shaver Hollow, reaching the Park boundary 2.4mi. from the start. There is no access to this trail from outside the Park.

NICHOLSON HOLLOW-HAZEL COUNTRY TRAIL NETWORK

This area was well populated before the creation of Shenandoah National Park. Now most of the old cabins are gone, but a few, in ruins, can be seen along the trails. There is one cluster, still quite interesting, along the Hannah Run Trail; two can still be seen along the Broad Hollow Trail and another on the Hot-Short Mtn. Trail. Corbin Cabin, on the Nicholson Hollow Trail, has been restored and is maintained in good condition by the PATC. It is available for use by hikers but reservations must be made in advance at PATC Headquarters. The cabin has been placed on the National Register of Historic Places. Its location is ideal for anyone wanting to explore the many trails of the area.

Most of the present trails were originally roads that served the mountain community. There are many other signs of the formerly well-populated area - small orchards, rock walls and the remains of chestnut rail fences, walled springs, even bits of rusting metal. Sometimes one discovers an old family cemetery, the only markers thin slabs of local rock set vertically into the ground. Very often periwinkle was planted around the graves and its bright shiny greenery helps one spot the cemetery plots today.

Nicholson Hollow was named after the Nicholson clan that had homes along the Hughes River. It was also called "Free State" Hollow, reputedly because law enforcement officers avoided entering the hollow because of its ill-tempered and lawless inhabitants. George F. Pollock, in his book, *Skyland*, gives a vivid description of some of the Nicholsons who lived here. The old USGS Stony Man quadrangle map, surveyed in 1927, indicated the location of many of the mountain cabins. A series of articles by H.T. Dockerty, published in the Washington Times and preserved in the PATC scrap books, recorded many legends of the "Free State" Hollow.

Three major trails cross through the area - the Nicholson Hollow Trail which leads up the Hughes River, the Hannah Run Trail and the Hazel Mtn. Trail. Other trails in the area include the Catlett Mtn. Trail, Hot-Short Mtn. Trail, Sams Ridge Trail, Broad Hollow Trail, Corbin Cabin Cut-Off Trail, Corbin Mtn. Trail, Catlett Spur Trail and Indian Run Trail, all blue-blazed; also White Rocks Trail, Hazel River Trail and Pine Hill Gap Trail which are yellow-blazed horse/foot trails. See PATC Map #10 and PATC publication: *Circuit Hikes in Shenandoah National Park*.

NICHOLSON HOLLOW TRAIL

5.9 miles   blue-blazed

This trail leads down through the hollow formed by the Hughes River. The mountaineers who lived here, mostly members of the Nicholson clan, were so feared by the valley folks that even the sheriffs and deputies avoided entering the hollow. Corbin Cabin, located on the Nicholson Hollow Trail, was the pre-Shenandoah Park home of George Corbin. See "Accommodations and Facilities".

The trail runs in a generally southeast direction to SR 600 at its junction with the old Weakley Hollow Road. (This is where Brokenback Run joins the Hughes River.) Difficulty may be experienced in crossing Brokenback Run and the numerous fords of the Hughes River when the water is high.

Trails connecting with the Nicholson Hollow Trail include: Hannah Run Trail, Hot-Short Mtn. Trail, Corbin Mtn. Trail, Indian Run Trail and Corbin Cabin Cut-Off Trail, all blue-blazed.

Access

The upper end of Nicholson Hollow Trail is on the east side of Skyline Drive at SDMP 38.4, and is marked by a concrete post. Parking is in the Stony Man Overlook-Hughes River Gap Parking Area 0.2mi. farther south.

The lower end is reached from Va 231. Turn west onto SR 601 or 602 then SR 707 to Nethers. Bear left onto SR 600 to parking area at junction with Weakley Hollow Road. Another lot is 0.5mi. east on SR 600. Areas may be crowded on weekends. *Cars parked on road are subject to towing.*

Trail Description
Skyline Drive to SR 600 (W to E)

0.0-5.8 From trailhead, descend bank and turn left along an old road which leads through area of scrub oak and laurel, then descends.

0.4-5.4 To right of trail is walled-in Dale Spring.

1.6-4.2 Cross creek.

1.7-4.1 Indian Run Trail leads right to Corbin Mtn. Trail. Nicholson Hollow Trail continues downhill, soon following Hughes River.

1.8-4.0 Corbin Cabin Cut-Off Trail leads left 1.4mi. to Skyline Drive, SDMP 37.9. Corbin Cabin is to right. (See "Accommodations and Facilities".)

1.9-3.9 Pass overgrown field on right. This was once site of Madison Corbin's cabin. Marked spring is on left of trail 250 ft. farther.

2.0-3.8 Old road leads left to Hughes River. Just below road, across river, are ruins of Aaron Nicholson's cabin.

3.4-2.4 Cross to left side of Hughes River at base of deep pool.

3.9-1.9 Hannah Run Trail leads left 3.7mi. to Skyline Drive, SDMP 35.1. Giant hemlocks near junction.

4.0-1.8 Cross Hannah Run.

4.1-1.7 Hot-Short Mtn. Trail, left, follows old road up valley between Short Mtn. and Hot Mtn. reaching Hazel Mtn. Trail in 2.1mi.

4.5-1.3 Corbin Mtn. Trail leads right across Hughes River, then climbs 4.4mi. to end at Old Rag Fire Road.

5.0-0.8 Walled-in spring to left of trail.

5.5-0.3 Leave SNP.

5.7-0.1 Cross to right of Hughes River and 150 ft. farther cross Brokenback Run. Beyond, turn left onto dirt road.

5.8-0.0 SR 600, at its intersection with Weakley Hollow Road.

HANNAH RUN TRAIL

3.8 miles   blue-blazed

This trail extends from Skyline Drive down to the Nicholson Hollow Trail on the Hughes River, with a descent of about 2,000 ft. It passes the ruins of several old mountain cabins.

A circuit hike can be made by using the Catlett Mtn. Trail, Hazel Mtn. Trail, Hot-Short Mtn. Trail and Nicholson Hollow Trail. *Another circuit* may be started by leaving car at Pinnacles Overlook and following trail down to Nicholson Hollow Trail. Follow Nicholson Hollow Trail 2.1mi. to Corbin Cabin then take Corbin Cabin Cut-Off Trail 1.5mi. to Drive. Directly across Drive short spur trail connects with *AT*. Follow *AT* north 1.2mi., turning off on spur trail which leads few feet to Jewell Hollow Parking Overlook. From here it is

1.3mi. along the Drive to your car, for total distance of just under 10 mi.

Access

Upper terminus is on east side of Skyline Drive, SDMP 35.1, at Pinnacles Overlook Parking Area.

Lower terminus is on Nicholson Hollow Trail, 1.9mi. from its lower end on SR 600.

Trail Description

Skyline Drive to Nicholson Hollow Trail

0.0-3.8 Pinnacles Overlook Parking Area. Trail descends steeply with switchbacks. Wintertime views to east over Hazel Country, with Hazel Mtn. as dominant feature.

1.3-2.5 Trail intersection in deep sag, with low knob ahead. Catlett Mtn. Trail leads 1.2mi. to Hazel Mtn. Trail. Hannah Run Trail turns sharply right and again descends.

1.7-2.1 Trail is exceedingly steep, dropping 500 ft. in 0.2mi.

1.9-1.9 Cross Hannah Run. After climbing out of ravine, pass ruins of cabin on right.

2.3-1.5 Pass between ruins of cabins. Spring and an old apple orchard on right. Trail descends along Hannah Run but does not cross it.

3.8-0.0 Cross small stream; in 200 ft. reach Nicholson Hollow Trail. (To left via Nicholson Hollow Trail it is 0.2mi. to Hot-Short Mtn. Trail, 0.6mi. to Corbin Mtn. Trail and 1.9mi. to its lower end at SR 600. To right it is 2.1mi. to Corbin Cabin and 1.8mi. farther to Skyline Drive; via Corbin Cabin Cut-Off Trail it is 1.5mi. to Drive.)

HAZEL MOUNTAIN TRAIL

4.5 miles   yellow-blazed

This old road might well be called the hemlock trail for it passes through hemlock for much of the way. Many of the trees are quite young but in the low areas, along the headwaters of the Hazel River, there are much larger trees, so that it is a veritable "limberlost". For the first 2mi. the trail descends gently along one branch of the Hazel River. It then heads southward and climbs along another branch of the river. From here it passes through a broad level area for another 1.5mi.

From the Hazel Mtn. Trail the Buck Ridge Trail leads northeast in 0.4mi. A mile or so farther along, the White Rocks Trail forks to the left leading northward. Still farther along the Hazel Mtn. Trail are junctions with the Catlett Spur Trail, Hazel River Trail, Sams Ridge Trail, Broad Hollow Trail, Catlett Mtn. Trail, Hot-Short Mtn. Trail, and Pine Hill Gap Trail. The old Hazel School which served the area in pre-Shenandoah Park days was situated near the junction of the Hazel Mtn. Trail with the Sams Ridge-Broad Hollow Trails.

Access

Upper end is on Skyline Drive, SDMP 33.4. Trail begins at south end of Meadow Spring Parking Area on east side of Drive, marked with concrete post.

Lower end is on Pine Hill Gap Trail. From Va 231 turn west onto SR 681 or SR 707 from Nethers. Drive as far as drivable then continue on foot to Gap.

Trail description

Skyline Drive to Pine Hill Gap Trail

0.0-4.5 Skyline Drive, SDMP 33.4. Trail gated at Drive.

0.4-4.1 Where trail turns sharply to right, Buck Ridge Trail leads northeast down ridge to Buck Hollow Trail.

1.6-2.9 At fork take right branch. (Left fork is White Rocks Trail leading to Hazel River Trail.)

1.7-2.8 Cross bridge over branch of Hazel River.

2.2-2.3 Junction with Catlett Spur Trail leading right to Catlett Mtn. Trail. Immediately beyond junction, ford creek, then in 250 ft. ford a second creek; both are branches of Hazel River. Old road now climbs, paralleling last creek. Hemlocks are lovely here.

2.9-1.6 Junction with Hazel River Trail leading left to Park boundary. Beyond junction trail passes to right of bulk of Hazel Mtn.

3.1-1.4 Concrete post marks junction with Sams Ridge-Broad Hollow Trails which are coincident here. (Sams Ridge Trail leads east to SR 600; Broad Hollow Trail leads southeast to SR 681.)

3.4-1.1 Unmarked trail on left leads 0.2mi. to Broad Hollow Trail.

3.6-0.9 Junction with Catlett Mtn. Trail, leading right to Hannah Run Trail.

4.1-0.4 Junction with Hot-Short Mtn. Trail which leads to Nicholson Hollow Trail.

4.5-0.0 Pine Hill Gap Trail leads to Park boundary and Pine Hill Gap.

CORBIN CABIN CUT-OFF TRAIL

1.4 miles   blue-blazed

This is the shortest route from Skyline Drive to Corbin Cabin. It is an old, old trail used by the mountain folk in Nicholson Hollow long before there was a Skyline Drive. Trail is quite steep, descending 1,000 ft. in 1.5mi.

Access

Trail begins on Skyline Drive, directly across from Shaver Hollow Parking Area, SDMP 37.9.

Lower end is on Nicholson Hollow Trail.

Trail Description
Skyline Drive to Nicholson Hollow Trail
   0.0-1.4 From Skyline Drive descend along blue-blazed trail.
   0.5-0.9 Trail turns sharply to left.
   0.7-0.7 Trail switchbacks to right. Footway is rough and rocky for next 250 ft.
   1.1-0.3 Path leads right 180 ft. to graveyard. Only unmarked, upended stones mark graves, as is true of most old family cemeteries in Park.
   1.4-0.0 Cross Hughes River and come to Nicholson Hollow Trail just below Corbin Cabin which is to right. (Corbin Cabin was once home of George Corbin and is typical of mountain cabins which were once numerous in hollows. It has been restored and may be rented by hikers. See "Accommodations and Facilities".)

SAMS RIDGE TRAIL

2.2 miles   blue-blazed
   This trail is one of the trails leading into Hazel Country from east of the mountains.
   A short circuit hike can be made by using this trail in combination with either Broad Hollow Trail, Hazel River Trail or Pine Hill Trail, all of which have their upper ends on the Hazel Mtn. Trail and their lower ends on either SR 681 or SR 600 which forks from SR 681.

Access
   From Va 231 turn west onto SR 681 just north of bridge over Hazel River. Follow SR 681 about 1mi. to road fork. Take right fork which is SR 600 and continue to where SR 600 crosses Hazel River. Walking begins here.

Trail Description
SR 600 to Hazel Mtn Trail (E to W)

0.0-2.2 From SR 600 follow old road up south side of Hazel River.

0.4-1.8 Park boundary. Trail turns left away from road. (Road inside Park becomes Hazel River Trail, yellow-blazed.) Trail now tends away from Park, climbing slope of ridge through private property, then following crest of ridge.

0.6-1.6 Enter SNP, continuing up Sams Ridge.

1.5-0.7 Pass site of mountaineer home. Stone foundation, scattered apple trees and rose bushes are only evidence of former habitation. Good view north of Hazel River Valley. Spring 200 ft. to left of trail.

2.0-0.2 Junction with Broad Hollow Trail coming in from left. From here two trails are coincident.

2.2-0.0 Junction of Sams Ridge-Broad Hollow Trail with Hazel Mtn. Trail. (To left it is 0.5mi. to Catlett Mtn. Trail, 1mi. to Hot-Short Mtn. Trail and 1.4mi. to Pine Hill Gap Trail. To right it is 0.2mi. to Hazel River Trail and 1.5mi. to White Rocks Trail.) The old Hazel School was located near this junction. Spring is 200 ft. to right of junction down abandoned Sams Run Trail.

HAZEL RIVER TRAIL

3.4 miles   yellow-blazed

This horse/foot trail offers yet another route into Hazel Country from the east. It follows up the Hazel River for over 1mi. before swinging left up a subsidiary creek and climbing over a shoulder of Hazel Mtn. to reach its upper end on the Hazel Mtn. Trail. Be prepared to wade the river at trail crossings after heavy rains.

Access

From Va 231 turn west onto SR 681 to fork then right onto SR 600. Drive about 1mi. to crossing of Hazel River.

Trail Description

SR 600 to Hazel Mtn. Trail (E to W)

0.0-3.4 From Hazel River follow private road up south side of River. (Blazes do not begin until Park boundary.) Where road turns right and crosses river *stay* on south side of river.

0.4-3.0 Enter Park. Sams Ridge Trail turns left here.

0.9-2.5 Within next 0.6mi. trail crosses river 4 times (difficult when water is high).

1.8-1.6 Trail junction. At concrete marker, Hazel River Trail turns left up a side creek and climbs. (Straight ahead is White Rocks Trail which soon crosses river and climbs 2.4mi. to end on Hazel Mtn. Trail.)

3.4-0.0 Junction with Hazel Mtn. Trail 0.2mi. northwest of Sams Ridge-Broad Hollow Trail junction and 1.3mi. south of junction with White Rocks Trail.

BROAD HOLLOW TRAIL

2.4 miles   blue-blazed

Like Sams Ridge Trail this trail offers access into Hazel Country from the east. It ascends about 1,400 ft. with its lower end on SR 681 and its upper end coincident with Sams Ridge Trail. It passes several abandoned cabins along route.

A *circuit hike* can be made when this trail is used in combination with Sams Ridge Trail, Hazel Mtn. Trail and Pine Hill Gap Trail.

Access

From Va 231 turn west onto SR 681, just north of bridge over Hazel River. Follow SR 681 about 2.5mi. to trailhead on right of road.

Trail Description

SR 681 to Hazel Mtn. Trail (E to W)

0.0-2.4 Junction with SR 681. In about 50 ft. trail

crosses Broad Hollow Run. In another 250 ft. old road takes off to right of trail.

0.3-2.1 Trail crosses run.

0.5-1.9 Trail recrosses run, continuing up hollow .

0.7-1.7 Two old trails, about 250 ft. apart, lead left to remains of two log buildings. Continue to ascend steeply, with several sharp turns in trail.

1.0-1.4 Pass rocked-up spring and, 150 ft. beyond, a ruined cabin with shingled sides.

1.5-0.9 Pass roofless cabin and another in about a quarter mile.

2.1-0.3 Unmarked trail leads left about 0.2mi. to Hazel Mtn. Trail, coming into latter about 0.2mi. north of Catlett Mtn. Trail junction.

2.2-0.2 Junction with Sams Ridge Trail coming in from right. Two trails coincide for next 0.2mi.

2.4-0.0 Junction with Hazel Mtn. Trail near site of old Hazel School. (To left it is 0.5mi. to Catlett Mtn. Trail, 1mi. to Hot-Short Mtn. Trail and 1.4mi. to Pine Hill Gap Trail. To right it is 0.2mi. to Hazel River Trail and 1.5mi. to White Rocks Trail. Spring is 200 ft. to right of junction, down abandoned Sams Run Trail.)

PINE HILL GAP TRAIL

1.4 miles   yellow-blazed

This trail leads from Pine Hill Gap to the Hazel Mtn. Trail, coming into that trail about 0.4mi. south of the Hot-Short Mtn. Trail junction. To reach the lower end at Pine Hill Gap either drive up SR 681 as far as passable by car or follow SR 707 from Nethers as far as drivable; by either route continue on foot to the Gap, where trail starts. This trail is useful for circuit hikes.

HOT-SHORT MOUNTAIN TRAIL

2.1 miles   blue-blazed

This is an interesting stretch of trail along the valley between Hot and Short Mountains. It connects the Nicholson Hollow Trail with the Hazel Mtn. Trail. From its lower end this trail involves a considerable climb with a change in elevation of about 1,300 ft. It follows up a stream much of the way, utilizing old roads and passing several old homesites.

Trail Description
Nicholson Hollow Trail to Hazel Mtn. Trail

0.0-2.1 This trail begins on Nicholson Hollow Trail at a point 1.7mi. from the latter's intersection with SR 600 where it is joined by Weakley Hollow Road.

0.1-2.0 Turn left and follow trail between stone walls. From here trail ascends.

0.4-1.7 Continue to ascend along a road, with ravine to left.

0.7-1.4 Outcropping of rocks with splendid view of Corbin and Robertson Mtns. across Nicholson Hollow.

0.9-1.2 Notice old homesite across stream to left. In 200 ft. cross stream and follow it up. In another 250 ft. turn sharp left and ascend steeply. Turn right and cross overgrown clearing.

1.3-0.8 Cross stream and continue to ascend.

1.4-0.7 Trail leads through overgrown field with apple trees. To right is view of Hot Mtn.

1.6-0.5 Cross stream again.

1.9-0.2 Old chimney worthy of notice about 100 ft. to right of trail.

2.0-0.1 Enter old road and continue through level section.

2.1-0.0 Junction with Hazel Mtn. Trail. (To left it is 0.5mi. to Catlett Mtn. Trail, 1mi. to Broad Hollow-Sams Ridge Trails and 4.1mi. to Skyline Drive; to right it is 0.4mi. to Pine Hill Gap Trail.)

CATLETT MOUNTAIN TRAIL

1.2 miles   blue-blazed

This trail connects the Hannah Run Trail with the Hazel Mtn. Trail. It affords a pleasant, easy walk along the north slope of Catlett Mtn. through woods, abandoned orchards and small clearings.

A *circuit hike* of 10mi. could start at the end of SR 600 west of Nethers. Follow Nicholson Hollow Trail for 1.7mi. then Hot-Short Mtn. Trail for 2.1mi. Turn left on Hazel Mtn. Trail and follow it 0.5mi. to Catlett Mtn. Trail. Follow Catlett Mtn. Trail 1.2mi. to Hannah Run Trail, Hannah Run Trail 2.5mi. to Nicholson Hollow Trail, then 1.9mi. down this trail back to SR 600.

Trail Description
Hannah Run Trail to Hazel Mtn. Trail

0.0-1.2 Junction with Hannah Run Trail 1.2mi. from Skyline Drive. Follow old roadbed, descending slightly. In 200 ft. reach another trail junction and turn right. (Catlett Mtn. Spur Trail leads straight ahead to Hazel Mtn. Trail.)

0.1-1.1 Bear right around a pit; remnants of old stone wall to right of trail. Climb gently.

0.3-0.9 Cross worn road. For some distance trail is level; summit of Catlett Mtn. is to right of trail.

0.7-0.5 Trail crosses shoulder of Catlett Mtn. From here it descends gradually through pine and abandoned orchard.

1.0-0.2 Cross stream and ascend.

1.2-0.0 Junction with Hazel Mtn. Trail 0.5mi. north of Hot-Short Mtn. Trail and 1.5mi. southwest of junction with Sams Ridge-Broad Hollow Trails.

CATLETT SPUR TRAIL

1.1 miles   blue-blazed
One end of this trail is on the Catlett Mtn. Trail a short distance from the Hannah Run Trail; the other is on the Hazel Mtn. Trail. Follow Hannah Run Trail from Skyline Drive; reach junction with Catlett Mtn. Trail in 1.2mi. (Hannah Run Trail turns right.) Follow Catlett Mtn. Trail straight ahead for about 200 ft. At trail junction, presently marked by metal post, Catlett Mtn. Trail turns right, whereas the Catlett Spur Trail goes straight ahead, following an old roadbed, passing stone walls and homesite clearings. It descends gently along one of the Hazel River tributaries, coming into the Hazel Mtn. Trail 2.2mi. east of Skyline Drive. This end of the Catlett Spur Trail is 1.4mi. nearer the Drive than the Catlett Mtn.-Hazel Mtn. Trail junction.

WHITE ROCKS TRAIL

2.4 miles   yellow-blazed
This horse/foot trail leads east from the Hazel Mtn. Trail. It is one of five routes down the mountain from the Hazel Mtn. Trail to the eastern Park boundary. *A circuit hike* can be made using this trail in combination with any one of the other four - Hazel River, Sams Ridge, Broad Hollow or Pine Hill Gap Trail.

Trail Description
Hazel Mtn. Trail to Hazel River Trail
  0.0-2.4 Follow old roadbed (former Old Hazel Rd.).
  0.9-1.5 Trail follows crest of White Rocks ridge.
  1.4-1.0 White Rocks to right of trail. Continue along crest then begin descent.
  2.1-0.3 In gap, turn right and descend to Hazel River.
  2.3-0.1 Cross Hazel River.
  2.3-0.0 End of trail on Hazel River Trail.

TRAILS IN THE SKYLAND-OLD RAG AREA

Skyland is situated almost in the center of Shenandoah National Park. The story of Skyland's early days, from about 1890 to the formation of SNP in the 1930s, and of its charismatic founder, George Freeman Pollock, has given the whole area around Skyland a romantic aura. Who can help smiling at the thought of Pollock's guests, elegant Washingtonians, rubbing elbows with rough mountain characters such as those who lived in the hollow once known as "Free State"? But what is Skyland today? A lodge, dining hall, cottages and dormitories, a recreation room, stables and much, much more.

At the northern entrance to Skyland, Skyline Drive reaches its highest elevation, 3,680 ft. Surrounding Skyland is as great a variety of fascinating places to explore as one could ask for. To start, listing them in clockwise order, there is that "Free State" Hollow (Nicholson Hollow), once home of the reputedly fierce and lawless Corbins and Nicholsons; then the unique Old Rag Mountain with its ragged top; next the magnificent Whiteoak Canyon with its series of cascades; Hawksbill Mtn. that towers over the rest of the Park; fearsome Kettle Canyon, immediately below Skyland; and lastly, Stony Man Mtn. whose "profile" is so visible when traveling south along the Drive. Small wonder that Shenandoah Park's most popular trails are here.

STONY MAN NATURE TRAIL
(and *AT* to Little Stony Man)

1.3 miles plus 0.4 mile loop   marked by signs and
                                            white blazes of *AT*
*(Attention: Dogs are not permitted on this trail except
with long distance AT hikers.)*
The Park Service has constructed a nature trail (self-guiding with leaflet) leading from the Stony Man Nature

Trail Parking Area to Stony Man Mtn. where the trail loops around the summit and offers a view from the top of the cliffs that form the Stony Man's profile. The Nature Trail and Appalachian Trail are coincident here.

The cliffs of Stony Man and Little Stony Man are the weathered remnants of ancient beds of lava. (See "Geology of SNP".) From 1845 to the turn of the century a copper mine operated near the top of Stony Man Mtn. Overgrown culm banks and tree-masked workings on the cliff-face, with green rock showing the presence of copper, mark the place. The ore was smelted at Furnace Spring, the site of which is on the Passamaquoddy Trail just north of Skyland. After operations were discontinued the mine was still a spot of much interest to visitors. The shaft, however, became a hazard and was filled in. There is now no trail to the spot.

A *circuit hike* can be made by starting at the Nature Trail Parking Area and following Nature Trail (also Appalachian Trail) to Stony Man. Continue on *AT* past Stony Man 0.6mi. to Little Stony Man. Descend and branch left onto Passamaquoddy Trail. After 1mi. turn left onto yellow-blazed horse trail leading back to Nature Trail Parking Area.

Access

Nature Trail Parking Area is on Skyline Drive, SDMP 41.7, at northern entrance to Skyland. Northern approach is from Little Stony Man Parking area, SDMP 39.1. Follow Appalachian Trail, white-blazed, 0.3mi. to start of Little Stony Man Trail.

Trail Description

Nature Trail Parking Area to Little Stony Man Parking Area (S to N)

0.0-1.3 Nature Trail Parking Area. Follow white blazes of Appalachian Trail.

0.4-0.9 Trail junction. Straight ahead Nature Trail continues and in 250 ft. starts 0.4mi. loop around summit of Stony Man Mtn. To left, a spur trail connects with Skyland-Stony Man Mtn. Horse Trail. Turn right here to continue on toward Little Stony Man, following white blazes..

0.8-0.5 Cliffs of Little Stony Man Mtn. Passamaquoddy Trail is directly below cliffs. From here trail descends steeply by switchbacks.

1.0-0.3 Junction with Passamaquoddy Trail. Follow white-blazed *AT* to parking area.

1.3-0.0 Little Stony Man Parking Area, SDMP 39.1.

PASSAMAQUODDY TRAIL

1.2 miles   blue-blazed

This is a slight relocation of the original Passamaquoddy Trail laid out by George Freeman Pollock in 1932. Until 1990 it was used as the route for the Appalachian Trail. (Passamaquoddy is a Maine Indian word meaning "abounding in pollock".)

The northern end is on the *AT*, 0.3mi. south of the Little Stony Man Parking Area, SDMP 39.1. The Passamaquoddy Trail takes the right fork at the concrete post then follows the base of the rocky cliffs and passes huge hemlock trees. Its southern end is at the end of the pavement behind Skyland Dining Room.

Trail Description
North to South

0.0-1.2 From intersection with *AT*, take right fork at concrete post. Follow ledge below Little Stony Man cliffs with excellent views and pass huge hemlock trees.

0.9-0.3 Pass Skyland powerline and housed Furnace Spring 25 ft. to left of trail. Enter hemlock grove and in 200 ft. turn left onto former Skyland Road.

1.0-0.2 Turn left off road at signpost. Ascend through woods.

1.1-0.1 Cross paved Skyland Road and continue through woods.

1.2-0.0 Follow paved path to left, uphill, to Skyland Dining Hall.

STONY MAN HORSE TRAIL

0.6 mile   yellow-blazed
This trail begins just beyond the Stony Man Nature Trail Parking Area, SDMP 41.7, at northern entrance to Skyland, and climbs to the top of Stony Man Mtn.

MILLERS HEAD TRAIL

0.8 mile   blue-blazed
This short but rewarding trail leads over Bushytop Mtn. and out the ridge to a lower peak known as Millers Head. The ridge forms the southern wall of the deep Kettle Canyon. A stone platform on Millers Head offers a superb view of the Shenandoah Valley, the Massanuttens and mountains farther west, Kettle Canyon, the buildings of Skyland, and, to the southwest, Buracher Hollow.

Access
Park at southern entrance to Skyland, SDMP 42.5 and walk up Skyland road toward stables (left fork) only a few feet to reach the *AT*. Follow *AT* to right until it crosses paved Skyland Road. Turn left along road for 200 ft. Sign indicates start of Millers Head Trail.

Trail Description
Skyland Road to Millers Head
0.0 Trail sign on paved Skyland Road. (Gravel road to left of trail rejoins trail on summit of Bushytop, where it ends.)
0.2 Summit of Bushytop. (Microwave installation here.) For excellent viewpoint to right, continue 100 ft. farther

along trail. Kettle Canyon is below and the Skyland buildings are quite visible above canyon.

0.8 Reach Millers Head.

OLD SKYLAND ROAD TRAIL

3.2 miles   yellow-blazed

As one walks this road it is fun to imagine what a trip to the "top of the mountain" was like in Pollock's day when it was barely usable for horse-drawn vehicles. The road climbs 2,200 ft., following up the ridge between Kettle Canyon and Dry Run Hollow. It is gated at the Park boundary and again just below Furnace Spring, located at the head of Dry Run.

Access

To reach the lower end from Luray, head south on US 340. Just south of town turn left onto SR 642. Follow SR 642 about 1.6mi., then turn right onto SR 689 and follow it another 2mi. Turn left onto SR 668 for 0.9mi. then right on SR 672. State maintenance ends in 0.6mi. and road continues as Skyland Road, soon entering the Park.

FURNACE SPRING TRAIL

0.5 mile   yellow-blazed

The upper end of the trail is on the Stony Man Horse Trail just north of the northern entrance to Skyland and west of the parking area for the Stony Man Nature Trail. The horse trail zigzags down toward the northwest, ending on Old Skyland Road Trail, just above where it is gated (and where the Passamaquoddy and Old Skyland Road Trail merge, a few feet from Furnace Spring.)

Hikers making the circuit using the Stony Man, *AT* and Passamaquoddy Trails may find this short trail a pleasant way to return to the parking area, rather than walking up the paved road.

WHITEOAK CANYON TRAIL

5.1 miles   blue-blazed

Whiteoak Canyon is one of the scenic gems of Shenandoah National Park. Whiteoak Run gathers waters from a number of streamlets gushing from as many springs located just below Skyline Drive in the Skyland area. The broad area where these headwaters gather is covered with a virgin hemlock forest and is still called the "Limberlost", the name given to it by Mr. Pollock as it reminded him of the locale of Gene Stratton Porter's novel, *Girl of the Limberlost.*

Below the Limberlost, Whiteoak Run has cut a deep canyon in its rush to Old Rag valley far below. There are six cascades, each more than 40 ft. high, along its route. (See Waterfall chart.) The falls occur between layers of the ancient lava beds, now tilted vertically, because the less resistant rock could withstand the creek's erosive powers much less than the basaltic rock. From the start of the Whiteoak Canyon Trail to the base of the sixth or lowest cascade there is a loss in elevation of 2,000 ft. The trail drops another 350 ft. before reaching the Berry Hollow Road (SR 600). The canyon is lined with towering trees - white oak, hemlock, tulip and ash.

A few miles to the south, Cedar Run forms a canyon paralleling Whiteoak Canyon. *A very popular circuit hike* includes a trip down one canyon and up the other. See Cedar Run Trail for description.

Access

Upper end of trail is at parking area east of Drive, almost directly across Skyline Drive from southern entrance to Skyland, SDMP 42.5.

To reach lower end by car, follow Va 231 to about 5mi. north of Madison and turn west onto SR 670 which passes through community of Criglersville. Five miles beyond Criglersville, at Syria, turn right onto SR 643. In 0.8mi. turn left onto SR 600. (One can also reach this point by turning west off Va 231 at Etlan onto SR 643 and reaching junction of SR 600 in about 4mi.) Follow SR 600 north, up the Robinson River, for 3.6mi. Just beyond fording of Cedar Run turn left into large parking area divided into two sections by Cedar Run but connected by a low-water bridge. Trailhead is at end of parking area most distant from SR 600.

Trail Description
Skyline Drive to SR 600

0.0-5.2 From parking area trail descends.

0.5-4.7 Cross branch of Whiteoak Run.

0.6-4.6 Cross Old Rag Fire Road. (To right road leads 0.2mi. to a parking area and 0.1mi. farther to Skyline Drive. To left it leads down mountain.) Trail soon enters Limberlost area.

0.8-4.4 Junction with Limberlost Trail. (To right it is 0.8mi. to parking area near beginning of Old Rag Fire Road. To left spur trail leads 0.1mi. to Old Rag Fire Road). Whiteoak Canyon Trail descends more and more steeply from here.

2.2-3.0 Turn sharp left and cross footbridge over Whiteoak Run. (Just below present bridge is location of Mr. Pollock's "Middle Bridge". This was the site of his famous barbecues in the old "Skyland Days" and a favorite spot of his Skyland guests.) A few feet farther trail intersects Skyland-Big Meadows Horse Trail. (Horses must ford the run. West of the run horse trail follows Whiteoak Fire Road up mountain to Skyline Drive, SDMP 45.0.

2.3-2.9 To right is excellent viewpoint over upper Whiteoak Falls, first of six cascades in canyon. From here trail descends very steeply.

2.4-2.8 Spur trail on right leads 250 ft. along Whiteoak Run to near base of upper falls. Canyon trail continues its steep descent, remaining on northeast side of run. Occasional views of various falls as trail switchbacks down canyon.

3.7-1.5 Cross side creek, Negro Run. (Falls on this creek visible from trail.) Trail now comes quite close to White-oak Run just below lowest cascade.

4.3-0.9 Junction with Cedar Run/Whiteoak Link Trail which leads right, fording Whiteoak Run, then continuing almost level until it reaches Cedar Run Trail in 0.8mi. (It is another 2.7mi. via Cedar Run Trail to Skyline Drive at Hawksbill Gap.)

4.8-0.4 Cross Whiteoak Run.

5.0-0.2 Cedar Run Trail leads right, soon crossing Cedar Run and climbing 3.1mi. to Skyline Drive, SDMP 45.6, at Hawksbill Gap.

5.1-0.1 Cross Cedar Run.

5.2-0.0 Parking area, just off SR 600.

CEDAR RUN TRAIL

3.1 miles   blue-blazed

Cedar Run flows southeast, paralleling Whiteoak Run which it joins near the Berry Hollow Road, SR 600. The two canyons are separated by a high ridge along which the former Halfmile Cliffs Trail extended. Cedar Run Canyon is deep and wild with tall trees. While the stream has a lesser flow of water than Whiteoak Run, it has several high falls, sheer cliffs and deep pools.

A circuit hike is often made using Cedar Run Trail and Whiteoak Canyon Trail. The full circuit, starting at Hawksbill Gap, would be to descend Cedar Run Trail, follow Cedar Run/Whiteoak Link Trail, ascend Whiteoak Canyon Trail all the way to the Drive, cross to *AT* and follow it back to Hawksbill Gap, a distance of 10.5mi.

A shorter circuit which would still include the deep canyon area of Whiteoak Canyon Trail would be to descend as before, then ascend Whiteoak Trail to just above Upper Falls; turn left across the Run and follow Whiteoak Fire Road up mountain to Drive; then walk along Drive 0.5mi. back to Hawksbill Gap, for total distance of 7.8mi. If starting the hike from SR 600 it is necessary to add 0.8mi. to distance.

Access

Upper end of Cedar Run Trail is on east side of Drive, directly across from Hawksbill Gap Parking Area, SDMP 45.6.

Lower end of trail is reached from Berry Hollow by following Whiteoak Canyon Trail from parking area near SR 600 for 0.2mi.

Trail Description

Hawksbill Gap to Berry Hollow

0.0-3.1 Hawksbill Gap Parking Area. Pass gate in 200 ft.

0.1-3.0 Cross Skyland-Big Meadows Horse Trail; trail soon descends along north side of Cedar Run.

1.1-2.0 To right is uppermost cascade of Cedar Run.

1.6-1.5 Cross to right of Cedar Run and swing away from it.

1.8-1.3 Trail again comes near Cedar Run near its highest falls. Sheer Halfmile Cliffs are across creek.

2.5-0.6 Trail turns left and fords the run immediately below a falls. (Old road which follows down right side of run passes through private property to reach SR 600.)

2.7-0.4 At trail fork, bear right. (To left is Cedar Run/Whiteoak Link Trail which leads 0.8mi. to Whiteoak Canyon Trail, joining it just below lowest falls.

3.1-0.0 Reach lower end on Whiteoak Canyon Road, about 0.2mi. west of parking area near SR 600.

CEDAR RUN-WHITEOAK LINK TRAIL

0.8 miles   blue-blazed

This trail connects the Whiteoak Canyon Trail and Cedar Run Trail near their lower ends. It is almost level. The northern terminus is on the Whiteoak Canyon Trail just below the lowest falls and about 0.9mi. from its lower end at the parking area near SR 600. The southern end is on the Cedar Run Trail 0.4mi. from its lower end.

This trail is part of the popular Cedar Run-Whiteoak Canyon circuit hike. See Cedar Run Trail.

WEAKLEY HOLLOW FIRE ROAD
2.5 miles   yellow-blazed
BERRY HOLLOW FIRE ROAD
0.8 mile   yellow-blazed

Prior to the establishment of Shenandoah National Park, Old Rag valley was an extensive mountain community. The state road that is now SR 600 went from the village of Nethers through this valley and out to Syria. A log building, the Old Rag Post Office, was located at the highest spot on this road, at its junction with a road coming down the Blue Ridge from Skyland. The section of the old highway now in the Park, that lies northeast of the junction, is now known as the Weakley Hollow Fire Road, whereas southwest of the junction it is called the Berry Hollow Fire Road. These two fire roads along with their extensions outside the Park (SR 600 in both directions) are very valuable for access purposes; both the Ridge Trail and Saddle Trail start from here, the lower termini of the Whiteoak Canyon Trail (and access to Cedar Run Trail) and Nicholson Hollow Trail are on this old route, as is the Old Rag Fire Road. The Robertson Mtn. Trail and the Corbin Hollow Trail also have their lower ends on the former state road.

The Weakley Hollow Fire Road is an important link for completing a circuit of Old Rag Mtn. The Park Service has constructed a parking area on this road just within the Park. There is also an "overflow" parking area 0.8mi. back on SR 600.

A *circuit hike* can be made using this road along with the Whiteoak Canyon Trail and the Old Rag Fire Road.

Access

To reach Weakley Hollow Fire Road turn west off Va 231 (south of Sperryville) onto SR 602 just south of bridge over Hughes River. Continue up river on SR 707 where SR 602 ends. About 4mi. from Va 231, where SR 707 turns right and crosses river, continue on paved SR 600, which follows up river. In 1mi. road turns sharply to left uphill and 0.3mi. farther reaches Park boundary with parking area just beyond.

To reach Berry Hollow Road, turn west off Va 231 onto SR 670 about 5mi. north of Madison. Continue on SR 670 through Criglersville and Syria, about 3.5mi., then turn right onto SR 643 and very shortly turn left onto SR 600. Follow SR 600 up Robinson River and Berry Hollow 4.8mi. to Park boundary. Parking space is very limited along road. Park at lower end of Whiteoak Canyon Trail.

Trail Description
Northeast to Southwest

0.0-3.3 Parking area just beyond end of SR 600. (Ridge Trail over Old Rag Mtn. leads south from here.)

1.2-2.1 Corbin Hollow Trail leads right, crossing Brokenback Run then following up creek.

1.3-2.0 Robertson Mtn. Trail leads to right up ridge.

2.5-0.8 Road junction. (To right Old Rag Fire Road leads to Skyline Drive, SDMP 43.0. To left, Saddle Trail leads 1.9mi. to summit of Old Rag Mtn., passing Old Rag Shelter in 0.4mi. and Byrds Nest #1 in 1.5mi.) Berry Hollow Fire Road continues straight ahead and descends.

3.3-0.0 Park boundary and SR 600. (Lower end of Whiteoak Canyon Trail is 0.9mi. farther down SR 600.)

OLD RAG FIRE ROAD

5.0 miles   yellow-blazed

In pre-Shenandoah Park days, a road led from Skyland down the east slope of the Blue Ridge to the Old Rag valley, coming into the road through the valley at its highest point. The Old Rag Post Office was located at this junction. Now the building that served as post office is gone, as is the community it served. But the lower 4mi. of the present fire road follows much the same route as the old road down the mountain. Above Comer's Deadening, the present road continues almost due west and reaches Skyline Drive about 1mi. southwest of spot where original road crossed the Drive.

From Skyline Drive the fire road is the shortest route to the start of the Saddle Trail up Old Rag Mtn. The fire road also serves as access to the Corbin Mtn. Trail, the Corbin Hollow Trail and the Robertson Mtn. Trail.

A *circuit hike* of about 11.5mi. can be made using this road in conjunction with the Whiteoak Canyon Trail and the Berry Hollow Fire Road.

Access

Skyline Drive, SDMP 43.0. Fire road leads east, with parking 0.1mi. on left.

From parking area at Park boundary at foot of Weakley Hollow Fire Road it is 2.5mi. to junction with Old Rag Fire Road; from parking area on Berry Hollow Fire Road it is 0.8mi. (See Weakley Hollow and Berry Hollow Fire Roads for travel directions.)

Trail Description

Skyline Drive to Weakley Hollow and Berry Hollow Fire Roads

0.0-5.0 Skyline Drive, 3,360 ft. Fire road leads eastward.

0.1-4.9 Parking area to left of road. (To right of road is upper end of Limberlost Trail leading 0.8mi. through virgin hemlocks to Whiteoak Canyon Trail.) Ahead fire road is gated. Just beyond gate Skyland-Big Meadows Horse Trail enters road from left and follows it.

0.3-4.7 Whiteoak Canyon Trail crosses fire road. (To left it is 0.6mi. to Skyline Drive at southern entrance to Skyland, SDMP 42.5. To right it is 0.2mi. to lower end of

Limberlost Trail, 1.6mi. to viewpoint above upper falls and 4.5mi. to SR 600 in Berry Hollow.)

0.5-4.5 Spur trail leads right 0.1mi. to junction of Whiteoak Canyon and Limberlost Trails.

0.7-4.3 Cross Whiteoak Run.

1.0-4.0 Area known as Comer's Deadening. (Skyland-Big Meadows Horse Trail turns right leaving fire road and reaching Whiteoak Run just above upper falls in 1.7mi. Along fire road 100 ft., horse trail, marked with concrete post, comes in from left and leads about 1mi. to Skyline Drive just opposite northern entrance to Skyland.)

1.1-3.9 Pass ranger cabin on right. Beyond here fire road descends steadily.

1.8-3.2 Corbin Mtn. Trail leads left 4.4mi. to Nicholson Hollow Trail.

2.3-2.7 Corbin Hollow Trail leads left 2mi. to Weakley Hollow Fire Road, 1.2mi. above parking area at SR 600.

2.4-2.6 Robertson Mtn. Trail leads left 2.4mi., climbing over Robertson Mtn., 3,296 ft., then descending to Weakley Hollow Fire Road.

5.0-0.0 Junction with Weakley Hollow and Berry Hollow Fire Roads, at top of gap between Old Rag Mtn. and the main Blue Ridge, 1,913 ft. Directly ahead is start of Saddle Trail.

LIMBERLOST TRAIL

0.8 miles   blue-blazed
  Attention: Dogs are not permitted on this trail.
  This trail leads through a very beautiful forest of virgin hemlock and some spruce, called by George Freeman Pollock the "Limberlost" because of its supposed similarity to the woods in the novel by Gene Stratton Porter entitled *Girl of the Limberlost*. There is little change in elevation on this trail.

For a short circuit hike, follow Limberlost trail down to Whiteoak Canyon Trail; turn left and follow Whiteoak Canyon Trail up for 0.2mi. to intersection with Old Rag Fire Road. Follow fire road left 0.2mi. back to parking area.

Another circuit, about 4mi. in length, includes upper 0.4mi. of Limberlost Trail, Crescent Rock Trail, *AT* back to Skyland, and short section of Skyland-Big Meadows Horse Trail between *AT* and Limberlost Parking area. See Crescent Rock Trail for slightly different circuit.

Access
Skyline Drive, SDMP 43.0. Follow Old Rag Fire Road 0.1mi. east to Limberlost Trail Parking Area.

Trail Description
Skyline Drive to Whiteoak Canyon Trail

0.0 From parking area trail leads gently down toward south.

0.4 Junction with Crescent Rock Trail which leads right 1.1mi. to Skyline Drive at Crescent Rock Overlook. Limberlost Trail swings east.

0.8 Trail ends at Whiteoak Canyon Trail.

CORBIN MOUNTAIN TRAIL

4.4 miles   blue-blazed

This trail has one terminus low on the Nicholson Hollow Trail; its other is on the Old Rag Fire Road. There is a change in elevation of over 1,800 ft. The trail route passes through a once-populated area and one can find house ruins and other indications of past human occupancy.

Good all-day circuit trips can be made utilizing this trail. Start from SR 600 (above Nethers) and hike up Nicholson Hollow Trail for 1.3mi. to reach this trail, then follow Corbin Mtn. Trail which ascends steadily.

One return route is via Indian Run and Nicholson Hollow Trails, about 11mi. A shorter return route is via Old Rag Fire Road, Corbin Hollow Trail and Weakley Hollow Fire Road, about 9.5mi.

Trail Description
Nicholson Hollow Trail to Old Rag Fire Road
   0.0-4.4 Trailhead marked with concrete post on Nicholson Hollow Trail 0.4mi. below Hot-Short Mtn. Trail junction and 1.3mi. northwest of SR 600. Cross Hughes River (be prepared to wade) and ascend along small tributary. (At first bend to right, faint trail leads left to very pretty waterfall.)
   1.2-3.2 Pass ruins of house. Trail crosses run just beyond ruins.
   3.8-0.6 In sag just below summit of Thorofare Mtn. trail turns sharply left. At turn, Indian Run Trail leads right, reaching Nicholson Hollow Trail 0.1mi. above Corbin Cabin in 1.7mi.
   4.4-0.0 Old Rag Fire Road. Skyline Drive is 1.8mi. right via fire road; upper end of Corbin Hollow Trail is 0.5mi. to left.

INDIAN RUN TRAIL

1.7 miles   blue-blazed
   This short trail connecting Nicholson Hollow Trail with the Corbin Mtn. Trail and, via the latter, with Old Rag Fire Road, widens the hiking opportunities for users of Corbin Cabin. Several circuit routes are possible using Indian Run Trail as a segment. From Skyline Drive, SDMP 43.0, follow Old Rag Fire Road 1.8mi. to reach upper end of Corbin Mtn. Trail. Follow latter 0.6mi. to sag where that trail makes sharp right turn. Here a post marks upper end of Indian Run Trail. Lower end is on Nicholson Hollow Trail 0.1mi. west of Corbin Cabin and 1.7mi. east of Skyline Drive (or 1.8mi. east of *AT*).

CORBIN HOLLOW TRAIL

2.0 miles   blue-blazed

Its upper end is on the Old Rag Fire Road, 2.3mi. from Skyline Drive, SDMP 43.0, and 2.7mi. on fire road from Weakley Hollow Fire Road. The lower end is on Weakley Hollow Fire Road, 1.3mi. on that road northeast of its junction with Old Rag Fire Road and 1.2mi. southwest of parking area at Park boundary. The trail follows Brokenback Run through Corbin Hollow. This area was formerly the location of a very primitive and poverty-stricken mountain community.

The upper terminus of this trail is 0.5mi. east of the upper end of the Corbin Mtn. Trail and 0.1mi. west of the upper end of Robertson Mtn. Trail. It can be used with either of these for *a circuit route.*

ROBERTSON MOUNTAIN TRAIL

2.4 miles   blue-blazed

This trail offers some excellent views of Corbin Hollow and Old Rag Mtn. Its upper end is on Old Rag Fire Road 2.4mi. east of Skyline Drive, SDMP 43.0, via the fire road, and 2.6mi. northwest of Weakley Hollow Fire Road.

The lower end is on Weakley Hollow Fire Road 1.3mi. up road from SR 600 at Park boundary (and parking area) and 1.2mi. down road from its junction with Old Rag Fire Road. The upper and lower ends of Robertson Mtn. Trail and Corbin Hollow Trail are each about 0.1mi. apart.

From Old Rag Fire Road the trail, starting at an elevation of about 2,800 ft., climbs for 0.8mi. with many switchbacks, to top of Robertson Mtn., 3,296 ft. From the summit it descends eastward, again with many switchbacks. Where it joins Weakley Hollow Road the elevation is only 1,532 ft.

WHITEOAK FIRE ROAD

1.8 miles   yellow-blazed
  The chief use of this road, for hikers, is as a link to
complete the circuit when descending Cedar Run Trail
and ascending Whiteoak Canyon as far as the upper
falls. The Skyland-Big Meadows Horse Trail also utilizes
this road, following it from Whiteoak Run to just short
of Skyline Drive. The lower end of this road is at Whiteoak Run, just above the upper falls at site of G.F.
Pollock's Middle Bridge. The upper end is on Skyline
Drive, SDMP 45.0, about 0.6mi. "north" of Hawksbill
Gap and the upper end of Cedar Run Trail.

OLD RAG MOUNTAIN CIRCUIT

7.1 miles
  Ridge Trail, 2.7mi.
  Saddle Trail, 1.9mi.   blue-blazed
  Weakley Hollow Fire Road, 2.5mi.   blue-blazed
                                                yellow-blazed

*Attention: dogs are not permitted on either the Ridge
Trail or the Saddle Trail.*
  To hikers Old Rag Mountain has a very special character. The only other mountains in the east that can
compete with it are Katahdin in Maine and Grandfather
Mountain in North Carolina. Of the three, Old Rag has
the advantage, or disadvantage, of being the most
accessible. Old Rag is the favorite hike of many youth
organizations of the Washington area, so that every
weekend finds one or more large groups of youngsters
camping or hiking on the mountain, as well as family
groups, novice hikers, and veteran walkers. Those who
survive the steep climb up the Ridge Trail are rewarded
by the fascinating walk over and around the tremendous
rocks and by the outstanding views, first one direction,
then another.

Old Rag stands apart from the main Blue Ridge, separated from it by the narrow Old Rag valley. It consists of a long, rocky ridge composed primarily of granite. However, long ago, lava welled up in cracks in the granite and formed a series of basaltic dykes, varying in thickness from a few feet to fifty. This basaltic material has weathered more rapidly than the surrounding granite, creating some of the rock features that give the mountain its ragged appearance. At one place on the Ridge Trail there is a regular staircase, with high vertical walls of granite and "steps" formed by the characteristic weathering of columnar basalt in blocks.

In wintertime, when snow and ice make the trails on Old Rag too difficult and dangerous for most hikers, there is still a special breed of walker who enjoys the challenge this mountain has to offer He or she comes equipped with proper clothing for exposure to cold and wind, and uses crampons when traveling over icy spots.

It is advisable to carry water when hiking up Old Rag. There is no water at Byrds Nest #1 (picnic shelter) which is situated in the saddle, about 0.4mi. from the summit, along the Saddle Trail. The other picnic shelter, Old Rag Shelter, is much lower down on the Saddle Trail and water is available there. (*No camping is allowed on Old Rag above the 2,500 ft. elevation.*)

Access

From Va 231 south of Sperryville, turn west onto SR 602 just south of bridge over Hughes River. Stay on south side of river, first on SR 602, then SR 707, then SR 600 for about 5mi. Weakley Hollow Fire Road is continuation of SR 600 within the Park. Parking lot is just inside Park boundary. If it should be filled, there is some parking space 0.3mi. down SR 600, where road makes sharp turn; also there is an "overflow" parking area 0.5mi. farther down.

The Ridge Trail starts at parking area on Weakley Hollow Fire Road. To reach lower end of Saddle Trail, walk 2.5mi. up Weakley Hollow Fire Road to its junction with Berry Hollow Fire Road and Old Rag Fire Road.

Trail Description
Circuit described in clockwise direction, starting with Ridge Trail.

0.0-7.1 From Old Rag Parking Area on Weakley Hollow Fire Road, just inside Park boundary (1,080 ft.), Ridge Trail heads due south.

0.5-6.6 Spring is 100 ft. to right of trail, under walnut trees. This is last sure water on Ridge Trail.

1.3-5.8 Pass wet weather spring, to right of trail, close under steep side of ridge.

1.4-5.7 Crest of ridge in broad wooded saddle; turn sharply right.

1.6-5.5 Emerge from woods onto rocks.

2.7-4.4 End of Ridge Trail. To right are projecting rocks forming summit of Old Rag, 3,291 ft. The trail, now Saddle Trail, descends south along ridge crest.

2.8-4.3 Path leads right 300 ft. to site of former fire tower.

2.9-4.2 Spur trail leads right 300 ft. to cave formed by huge sloping rocks. Saddle Trail descends.

3.1-4.0 Reach the "Saddle" and Byrds Nest #1. *No camping; day use only.* There are inside and outside fireplaces but no water. (Beyond shelter, Ragged Run Road descends to south. Road is *closed to hikers* outside Park boundary.) Trail turns sharply right, leaving ridge, and descends steadily by switchbacks along northwest slopes of mountain.

4.2-2.9 Old Rag Picnic Shelter *(no camping; day use only)* is 100 ft. ahead. Trail turns right onto blue-blazed dirt road and continues to descend.

4.6-2.5 Junction of 3 fire roads, all yellow-blazed - Weakley Hollow, Berry Hollow and Old Rag - at site of former Old Rag Post Office. Turn right on Weakley Hollow Fire Road and descend. (From fire road junction it is 5mi. to Skyline Drive, SDMP 43.0, via Old Rag Fire

Road and 1.6mi. left via Berry Hollow Fire Road to foot
of Whiteoak Canyon Trail.)
  7.1-0.0 Old Rag Parking Area and SR 600 just beyond.

SKYLAND-BIG MEADOWS HORSE TRAIL

11.0 miles   yellow-blazed
  From the east side of Skyline Drive this trail leads to
Old Rag Fire Road which it follows down to Comer's
Deadening. Here it turns right and enters Whiteoak
Canyon. It crosses Whiteoak Run just above the upper
falls, then follows the Whiteoak Fire Road almost to its
junction with Skyline Drive, SDMP 45.0. From here it
parallels the Drive until beyond the Upper Hawksbill
Parking Area; it then descends along the southwest slope
of Spitler Hill and circles the head of Rose River Canyon.
It again crosses the Drive just south of Fishers Gap and
then parallels the Drive to reach Big Meadows stables.
The trail has posts marking the half miles.
  The section of horse trail between Whiteoak Canyon
Trail and Fishers Gap gets very little horse traffic so is
pleasant walking. The part near Rose River is quite
scenic. Hikers should remember to yield right-of-way to
a horse party should they meet.

Access
  Northern end of trail is on Skyline Drive, SDMP 41.7,
across from northern entrance to Skyland; southern end
is at Big Meadows, SDMP 51.2.

Trail Description
Skyland to Big Meadows
  0.0-11.0 East side of Skyline Drive. Trail parallels
Drive.
  0.4-10.6 Come to Old Rag Fire Road and follow it to
left. (A parking area is 200 ft. to right along road.
Skyline Drive is 0.1mi. farther.)

1.3-9.7 Horse trail turns sharply right away from fire road at signpost and heads toward Whiteoak Canyon. This area is known as Comer's Deadening. Horse trail follows old road.

2.5-8.5 Ford Whiteoak Run just above upper falls. From here horse trail follows Whiteoak Fire Road.

4.1-6.9 About 0.1mi. from Skyline Drive, horse trail turns left and parallels Drive.

4.6-6.4 Intersection with Cedar Run Trail. (To right it is few feet to Skyline Drive at Hawksbill Gap.)

6.0-5.0 Horse trail comes into old farm road near summit of Spitler Hill and follows road to left. (To right road leads to Skyline Drive just south of Upper Hawksbill Parking Area, SDMP 46.7.) Ladies'-tresses, a type of orchid, may be found here, blooming in Sept. and Oct. For over 0.5mi. trail passes through old fields, now quite overgrown. Old road gradually narrows into trail.

7.8-3.2 Cross stream, branch of Rose River.

8.3-2.7 Cross second branch of Rose River.

8.9-2.1 Dark Hollow Falls-Rose River Loop Trail enters from left and follows horse trail.

9.4-1.6 Cross Rose River Fire Road just east of Fishers Gap, SDMP 49.3. In 0.1mi. cross to right(west) of Skyline Drive. Horse trail swings out of sight of Drive, then turns to parallel it.

10.8-0.2 Intersection with Story of Forest Nature Trail.

11.0-0.0 Big Meadows stables, SDMP 51.2.

CRESCENT ROCK TRAIL

1.1 miles   blue-blazed

This short trail runs from Skyline Drive, SDMP 44.4, across from the Crescent Rock Overlook (look for concrete post just south of north entrance) down to Limberlost Trail, with a gentle downgrade all the way.

A pleasant half-day circuit hike, 4.5mi.,can be made by following this trail from the overlook, turning right onto

Limberlost Trail and following it 0.4mi., then ascending Whiteoak Canyon Trail to Skyline Drive. Cross Drive and, a few yards up road toward Skyland stables, turn left onto *AT* and follow it for 2mi. A short spur trail, marked with concrete post, leads to north end of Crescent Rock Overlook.

BETTYS ROCK TRAIL

0.3 mile   blue-blazed

From Crescent Rock Parking Overlook, SDMP 44.4, this short trail leads due north to a rocky outcrop known as Bettys Rock which affords excellent views west. A short trail, 0.1mi., leads downhill from Bettys Rock Trail (just north of overlook) to *AT*.

HAWKSBILL MOUNTAIN TRAIL

1.8 miles   blue-blazed

Hawksbill Mtn. is the highest mountain in Shenandoah National Park. Native spruce and balsam are found on its upper slopes. An observation platform at the summit, 4,050 ft., provides excellent views of Timber Hollow to the north and Page Valley and the Massanuttens to the west.

Byrds Nest #2, an open-faced picnic shelter, is situated just below summit of Hawksbill. *No camping permitted.* Water is available from spring 0.8mi. downhill.

This trail begins at Upper Hawksbill Parking Area, SDMP 46.7, and ascends to the Hawksbill Service Road in 0.6mi. It turns right and follows service road 0.3mi. to summit of Hawksbill, then descends northeastward 0.9mi. to end in Hawksbill Gap, SDMP 45.6, where there is another parking area.

A circuit hike over Hawksbill could include the Hawksbill Trail from Hawksbill Gap to the summit, 0.9mi., the

Nakedtop Trail down to the *AT*, 0.7mi., and the *AT* back
to Hawksbill Gap.

NAKEDTOP TRAIL

0.7 miles   blue-blazed
   The Nakedtop Trail leaves the *AT* just north of Rock
Spring Hut and leads east to the top of Hawksbill. It can
be reached via the *AT* by hiking north from Rock Spring
Cabin Parking/Spitler Knoll Overlook, SDMP 48.0. In
1mi. Nakedtop Trail (no name on sign) leads right 0.8mi.
to summit of Hawksbill. It can also be approached via
the *AT* from Hawksbill Gap.

SERVICE ROAD TO BYRDS NEST #2

0.9 miles   not blazed
   This service road leaves Skyline Drive at SDMP 47.1
and climbs to Byrds Nest #2 near the summit of Hawksbill. There is little or no parking at its beginning on
Skyline Drive.

TRAILS IN THE BIG MEADOWS-CAMP HOOVER
AREA

   The Big Meadows developed area includes the Byrd
Visitor Center, a wayside, lodge, cabins, restaurant,
camp store, stables (wagon rides only), gift shop, picnic
area and the largest campground in the Park.
   Big Meadows is located on a very broad, flat area of the
Blue Ridge. Many geologists believe that this area is the
remnant of an old, high peneplain. Because of its surpris-
ing flatness water does not run off easily and some of the
area is quite boggy. There are several uncommon, in

Virginia, plants growing here; Canadian burnet (Sanguisorba canadensis) is one. A network of trails and fire roads provides the camper with many miles of good walking. There are a number of circuit hikes possible in the area, some quite short, others which can provide a full day of hiking. Hikers using trails maintained primarily for horses should yield the right-of-way.

Camp Hoover, situated within the Park on the Rapidan River, was originally built for a presidential hide-away by Herbert Hoover while he was in office. Later he donated the camp to the U.S. Government for use by future presidents and their guests. The Park Service administers the property and welcomes visitors - hikers and horseback riders - on the grounds of the camp. Only three of the original buildings - the President's Cabin, the Prime Minister's Cabin and "The Creel" - remain today. However, historical markers have been placed at the sites of the former buildings explaining how and by whom they were used.

Access to Camp Hoover from the east is via the Rapidan Fire Road and SR 649. Refer to write-up for this road. From Skyline Drive one can (1) follow the Rapidan Fire Road from Big Meadows, SDMP 51.3, (2) descend the Mill Prong Trail from Milam Gap, SDMP 52.8, or (3) follow the AT north from Bootens Gap, SDMP 55.1, to reach the Laurel Prong Trail and descend the latter.

RED GATE FIRE ROAD

4.8 miles   yellow-blazed

This road, gated at both ends, leads from the base of the mountains 4mi. east of Stanley to Skyline Drive at Fishers Gap, SDMP 49.3. (This road is the western portion of the old Gordonsville Pike. It continues on the east slope of the Blue Ridge as the Rose River Fire Road.) The Red Gate Fire Road climbs with a gentle grade and has many switchbacks to gain 1,500 ft. of elevation. It offers a pleasant walk except that one does have to beware of cars as Park and concessionaire personnel use this road to reach Big Meadows.

To reach the lower end of the Red Gate Fire Road, turn east from US 340 in Stanley onto either SR 624 or SR 689. Beyond junction of these roads, follow SR 689 eastward for about 1mi. then continue straight on SR 611 where SR 689 turns sharply left. Continue on SR 611 to the Park boundary where road becomes the Red Gate Fire Road and is gated.

STORY OF THE FOREST NATURE TRAIL

1.8 miles   not blazed
   Attention: Dogs are not permitted on this trail.
   This self-guiding trail describes the natural succession of the forest in the area of Big Meadows. A map may be obtained at the Byrd Visitor Center, SDMP 51.0, where trail begins.

Trail Description
   0.0 From visitor center head east and cross lovely stone bridge.
   0.3 Spur trail on right leads down 300 ft. to Skyline Drive directly opposite Dark Hollow Falls Trail.
   0.8 Trail turns sharply left. (Straight ahead leads to campground.)
   0.9 Paved road leading to picnic and camping areas of Big Meadows. Nature trail turns left here and follows paved path along road back to visitor center. To reach Amphitheater Parking Area and *AT*, turn right on paved path as far as campground registration office, then walk along road to picnic area, keeping left at road fork (wrong way for cars). Look for trail, just left of parking area, that leads on to *AT*.
   1.8 Big Meadows Wayside and Byrd Visitor Center.

LEWIS SPRING FALLS TRAIL

1.8 miles   blue-blazed

This trail leads from the *AT* immediately below Big Meadows Lodge, SDMP 51.0, to Lewis Spring Falls and ends on the *AT* at Lewis Spring. To reach start of trail find path between Amphitheater Parking Area and lodge. Follow it north about 0.1mi. to *AT* intersection, marked by signpost. (*AT* leads south to Lewis Spring and north to Big Meadows Campground.) Lewis Spring Falls Trail is directly across from here.

For a circuit hike of 2.7mi., follow this trail, then turn left onto *AT* for return to Big Meadows.

Trail Description
Big Meadows Lodge to Lewis Spring
   0.0 Trail descends.
   1.1 Spur trail leads right steeply downhill for 0.2mi. to base of falls.
   1.2 Trail leads right 150 ft. to overlook at head of falls. Trail now ascends steeply.
   1.7 Lewis Spring service road.
   1.8 End at *AT*.

DARK HOLLOW FALLS-
ROSE RIVER LOOP TRAIL

3.5 miles   first 2.6mi. blue-blazed
                                                 last 0.9mi. yellow-blazed

The Dark Hollow Falls Trail, 0.8mi. in length, is the most popular one in the Park. It leads to a very lovely cascading waterfall on the Hogcamp Branch of the Rose River. For a very short trip park at Dark Hollow Falls Parking Area on Skyline Drive, SDMP 50.7.

For a somewhat longer trip park at the Amphitheater Parking Area of Big Meadows (follow road signs). On foot follow the exit road as far as campground registration office. Then walk, going to right, along paved path which follows road. In 0.1mi., at concrete post, turn left onto Story of the Forest Nature Trail and continue on it for about 0.6mi. At an intersection marked by a concrete post continue straight ahead (Nature Trail bears right) and in 300 ft. reach Skyline Drive directly across from Dark Hollow Falls Trail Parking Area.

A *circuit hike* of about 6mi. can be made by starting at the Amphitheater Parking Area. Proceed to Dark Hollow Falls Trail as described above and descend; continue along Rose River Loop Trail (which is very scenic and passes a falls on Rose River) to Fishers Gap. Cross Drive and follow Red Gate Fire Road few feet to *AT*. Turn left and return to Big Meadows via the *AT*.

Access

The northern end of trail is in Fishers Gap, SDMP 49.3; the southern end is at Dark Hollow Falls Parking Area, SDMP 50.7.

Trail Description

Dark Hollow Falls Parking Area to Fishers Gap

0.0-3.5 From northern end of parking area trail descends steadily with stream on right.

0.6-2.9 Top of Dark Hollow Falls, a series of terraced cascades. From here trail descends very steeply.

0.8-2.7 Rose River Fire Road. (This is a portion of old Gordonsville Pike. To left it is 1.1mi. to Fishers Gap.) Turn right onto road and cross bridge over Hogcamp Branch. Fifty feet beyond bridge, at sign, turn left off road and follow Rose River Loop Trail down creek.

1.7-1.8 At junction marked with concrete post turn sharply left and cross Hogcamp Branch. (Trail right leads 0.3mi. to Rose River Fire Road.) In 250 ft. cross small stream. In 50 ft. pass site of old copper mine to left of trail. Trail soon approaches main branch of Rose River, turns left at sign pointing to Rose River Falls and climbs along west bank of river.

2.3-1.2 Pass waterfall.

2.6-0.9 Turn left, uphill, onto old road, now route of Big Meadows-Skyland Horse Trail (yellow-blazed).

3.5-0.0 Turn right onto Rose River Fire Road and in few feet reach Skyline Drive, SDMP 49.3, at Fishers Gap.

ROSE RIVER FIRE ROAD

6.5 miles   yellow-blazed

From Fishers Gap, SDMP 49.3, this old road winds its way down to SR 670 west of Syria. In pre-Park days it was known as the Gordonsville Pike and many hikers still refer to it by that name. (West of Skyline Drive the road continues as the Red Gate Fire Road.)

A *circuit hike* can be made using the lower portion. It involves ascending the Rose River either by scrambling over the rocks or following a "fisherman's trail" upcreek along the southwest bank, then following Rose River Loop Trail left to fire road. Descend the latter to starting point. Refer to Dark Hollow Falls Trail for circuit using that trail.

Access

From Va 231 about 16mi. south of US 522 near Sperryville and 5mi. north of Madison, turn west onto SR 670. Follow SR 670 through Criglersville and Syria to Park boundary. Parking space near end of SR 670 is very limited. From boundary continue up road on foot, with river to right of road in deep gorge. (At spot where road bends left away from river (1.3mi. from lower gate) a path leads right to river and up southwest bank. If you miss this path and come to concrete post with metal band on left, marking Upper Dark Hollow Trail, backtrack about 0.1mi.)

Trail Description
Fishers Gap to SR 670
0.0-6.5 Skyline Drive at Fishers Gap, SDMP 49.3.

1.1-5.4 Dark Hollow Trail, marked by post, leads to right 0.8mi. uphill to Skyline Drive. Just beyond junction, road crosses Hogcamp Branch. In 50 ft. post marks Rose River Loop Trail which leads left down Hogcamp Branch.

2.0-4.5 Stony Mtn. Trail leads right 1.1mi. to Rapidan Fire Road.

2.5-4.0 To left spur trail leads 0.3mi. to Rose River Loop Trail.

5.2-1.3 Post on right marks Upper Dark Hollow Trail which leads 2.2mi. to Rapidan Road at Broyles Gap.

6.5-0.0 Park boundary where road becomes SR 670.

STONY MOUNTAIN TRAIL

1.1 miles   yellow-blazed

This trail may be weedy in summer. It follows an old road which connects the Rose River Fire Road (Gordonsville Pike) and the Rapidan Fire Road. Its northern end is 2mi. down the Rose River Fire Road from Skyline Drive. The southern end is 2.9mi. down the Rapidan Fire Road from the Drive.

UPPER DARK HOLLOW TRAIL

2.2 miles   yellow-blazed

This trail route connects the Rose River Fire Road and the Rapidan Fire Road. Its lower end is about 1.3mi. up the Rose River Fire Road from the Park boundary (at end of SR 670). The trail route involves a climb of about 1,250 ft. to reach its upper end on the Rapidan Fire Road at Broyles Gap. The lower portion of the trail passes through a beautiful hemlock forest. For the upper half of its route the trail utilizes an old roadbed so it offers easy walking.

For a circuit hike of about 9mi., start at lower end of Rose River Fire Road, walk up road for about 4mi. to Stony Mtn. Trail. Follow this trail about 1mi. to Rapidan Fire Road. Descend the Rapidan Road for about 1mi. to Broyles Gap, then descend Upper Dark Hollow Trail back to Rose River Fire Road and descend to car.

TANNERS RIDGE HORSE TRAIL

2.5 miles   yellow-blazed
This is a loop trail that leads from the Big Meadows stables out along Tanners Ridge and back, crossing the *AT* twice.

TANNERS RIDGE ROAD

1.4 miles within SNP   yellow-blazed
This road, gated at the Drive and at Park boundary, leads west from Skyline Drive, SDMP 51.6, for 1.4mi. to Park boundary where it becomes SR 682 (about 6mi. from Stanley). There is a cemetery, still being used for burials, at junction of this road with the *AT*, about 0.3mi. from the Drive.

RAPIDAN FIRE ROAD-SR 649

9.8 miles   yellow-blazed
This fire road is gated at Skyline Drive (Big Meadows) and at the "first" Park boundary, just below the junction with Camp Hoover Road. The upper portion of this road is used as a horse trail and also by hikers. The road continues east of the gate through a Virginia Wildlife Area and descends along the Rapidan River. It then reenters SNP. After another mile along the river the road climbs to the top of Chapman Mountain ridge before

reaching the easternmost Park boundary. Although there is some traffic on this part of the road it is light and the road is not unpleasant for walking. There is a good swimming hole on the river at the junction of this road and the Graves Mill-Lower Rapidan Road.

A *circuit hike* can be made using this trail in conjunction with the Mill Prong Trail and the *AT*.

Access

The upper end is on Skyline Drive, SDMP 51.3, across from the Big Meadows Wayside where there is ample parking.

To reach the road from the east, turn west off Va 231 onto SR 670 about 16mi. south of US 522 near Sperryville and 5mi. north of Madison. Follow SR 670 for about 1mi. beyond Criglersville. Turn left onto SR 649, crossing the Rose River and following up a side stream toward Chapman Mountain. Road is narrow but drivable over Chapman Mtn. and on beyond junction with SR 662 on the Rapidan River to just below Camp Hoover access road where it reenters SNP. Here it is gated.

Trail Description

Skyline Drive to easternmost Park boundary. (Mileages estimated.)

0.0-10.0 Junction with Skyline Drive, SDMP 51.3, across from Big Meadows Wayside.

1.2-2.8 Mill Prong Horse Spur Trail leads right 1.8mi. to Camp Hoover.

2.9-7.1 Stony Mtn. Trail leads left to Rose River Fire Road.

3.8-6.2 Upper Dark Hollow Trail leads left to Rose River Fire Road.

5.4-4.6 At road junction, fire road continues straight ahead. Road to right leads up Rapidan River for about 0.8mi. to Camp Hoover.

5.8-4.2 Reach Park boundary where road is gated and enter Virginia Wildlife Area where road becomes SR 649 and is open to automobile traffic.

7.5-2.5 At road fork, SR 649 continues straight ahead descending along Rapidan River. (Fork Mtn. Road, gated, goes right to radio tower on Fork Mtn.)

7.6-2.4 Reenter SNP.

8.8-1.2 At road junction take left fork and climb, leaving river. (Right fork is Graves Mill-Lower Rapidan Road which follows down Rapidan River to Park boundary in 1.7mi.)

9.4-0.6 At road junction on top of Chapman Mtn. ridge, continue straight ahead. (To right a Virginia forest road leads out Blakey Ridge past Utz Hightop Lookout Tower. Gated road to left is access road to private land.)

10.0-0.0 Road leaves Park. (From here it is 3mi. to SR 670.)

MILL PRONG TRAIL

1.0 mile   blue-blazed

This trail leads from the *AT* in Milam Gap east to the Mill Prong Horse Spur Trail. *A good circuit hike* of 7mi. can be made using these two trails along with the Laurel Prong Trail and the *AT*. *A longer circuit,* 12mi., includes the Mill Prong Trail, Mill Prong Horse Spur Trail, Rapidan Fire Road, Camp Hoover Road and *AT*.

Trail Description
Milam Gap to Mill Prong Horse Spur Trail

0.0-1.0 Junction with *AT*, a few feet south of Skyline Drive crossing at Milam Gap, SDMP 52.8. Trail descends gently through old field and orchard, now overgrown.

0.6-0.4 Cross main branch of Mill Prong. Trail now descends through tall trees and fern-covered forest floor.

1.0-0.0 Cross another branch of Mill Prong and bear right, reaching junction with Mill Prong Horse Spur Trail which comes in from left. (Via Spur Trail it is 1mi. north to Rapidan Fire Road and 1.2mi. farther along fire road to Skyline Drive at Big Meadows Wayside.)

MILL PRONG HORSE SPUR TRAIL

1.8 miles   yellow-blazed
   A circuit hike to Camp Hoover can be made using this
trail along with the Mill Prong Trail and *AT;* distance
about 8mi.

Access
   The upper end of this trail is on the Rapidan Fire Road,
1.2mi. from Skyline Drive at Big Meadows, SDMP 51.3.
   The lower end is at Camp Hoover just west of road
bridge over Mill Prong Trail.

Trail Description
Rapidan Fire Road to Camp Hoover Road
   0.0-1.8 Rapidan Fire Road. Horse trail heads south.
   1.0-0.8 Mill Prong Trail leads right for 1mi. to *AT* in
Milam Gap. Trail now descends along creek.
   1.5-0.3 Cross to right of creek just below Big Rock
Falls. Crossing is easy to miss.
   1.8-0.0 Junction with Camp Hoover Road 100 ft. west
of bridge over Mill Prong. It is 1.2mi. to Mill Prong Trail
and another 0.8mi. to Camp Hoover.

LAUREL PRONG TRAIL

2.8 miles   blue-blazed
   This trail starts from the *AT* near Bootens Gap,
descends very gently along the southern slope of Hazeltop Mtn. to Laurel Gap, then descends more steeply
through an area of much mountain laurel (kalmia). For
the final mile it leads through the valley of Laurel
Prong. To the right of the trail, in several locations along
the creek, one can find the great laurel or rosebay
rhododendron which blooms here in late June or early
July. Near its end at Camp Hoover the trail passes
through much large hemlock. In some places a carpet of

false lily-of-the-valley, blooming in late May, carpets the ground; in other places running cedar, a type of club moss, acts as a ground cover.

Access

From Bootens Gap, SDMP 55.1, follow *AT* north for 0.6mi. Concrete post marks trailhead.

To reach lower end, follow directions for getting to Camp Hoover from the east (Rapidan Fire Road). The Laurel Prong trailhead is near end of access road to Camp Hoover, about 300 ft. west of bridge over Mill Prong.

Trail Description

AT to Camp Hoover

0.0-2.8 Junction with *AT*.

1.0-1.8 Laurel Gap. (Concrete post marks start of Cat Knob Trail leading right to Jones Mtn. Trail.) Turn left and continue to descend.

2.2-0.6 Concrete post marks Fork Mtn. Trail which leads right 1.5mi. to "The Sag" and Fork Mtn. Fire Rd. (Upper end of Fork Mtn. Trail also connects with Staunton River Trail and Jones Mtn. Trail.)

2.8-0.0 Camp Hoover. To reach Mill Prong Horse Spur Trail follow access road left for 250 ft.

CAT KNOB TRAIL

0.5 mile　　　　　　　　　　　　　　　blue-blazed

This is a short trail which connects Laurel Prong and Jones Mtn. Trails. The shortest route to Jones Mtn. Cabin from Skyline Drive, 5.7mi., would use this "short cut", along with the *AT*, Laurel Prong Trail, Jones Mtn. Trail and Jones Mtn. Cabin Trail.

GRAVES MILL-LOWER RAPIDAN ROAD

2.2 miles   yellow-blazed
  The Graves Mill-Lower Rapidan Road is the continuation of SR 662 within the Park, entering SNP about 1.3mi. north of Graves Mill. (Graves Mill is about 5.5mi. north on SR 662 from Wolftown on Va 230.) Within the Park the road continues up the Rapidan River to its junction with the Rapidan Fire Road. It is open to automobile traffic its entire length but is very rough; it serves as an access road to the Camp Hoover area and to the Staunton River Trail. The Rapidan River along this road offers a number of spots suitable for swimming.

FORK MOUNTAIN ROAD

4.5 miles (approx.)   blue-blazed
  This road is gated. It leads from the Rapidan Fire Road about 2mi. southeast of Camp Hoover up the eastern and southern slopes of Fork Mtn., winding in and out of SNP. It reaches "The Sag", the divide between the Staunton River drainage area and that of Laurel Prong, then climbs to the tower on top of Fork Mtn., 3,840 ft. Where the road crosses the upper reaches of the Staunton River the Staunton River Trail enters from the left. At "The Sag" the Fork Mtn. Trail leads west 1.3mi. to Laurel Prong Trail and the Jones Mtn. Trail leads south to Cat Knob and then descends the Jones Mtn. ridge.

STAUNTON RIVER TRAIL

4.3 miles (approx.)   blue-blazed
  This trail follows up the Staunton River from SR 662 at the junction of the Staunton and Rapidan Rivers all the way to its source and continues on to "The Sag" where it connects with the upper ends of the Jones Mtn. Trail and the Fork Mtn. Trail. The last 0.8mi. of the trail is

along the Fork Mtn. Fire Road which continues beyond "The Sag" to the summit of Fork Mtn.

A *circuit hike* can be made from Jones Mtn. Cabin by ascending the Jones Mtn. Trail and returning via the Staunton River Trail (and including the McDaniel Hollow Trail if so desired) for a distance of 7.5mi.

Access

To reach lower end of this trail follow Va 230 west from US 29 south of Madison for 4mi. to Wolftown (or follow Va 230 northeast from US 33 in Stanardsville). Turn north onto SR 662 and continue on paved road as far as Graves Mill, 5.5mi. At road junction, take right fork, still SR 662, which crosses Kinsey Run and follows up Rapidan River, soon entering SNP as the Graves Mill-Lower Rapidan Road. Junction of Staunton and Rapidan Rivers is 2mi. beyond Graves Mill. Room for a few cars on fire road and also a few feet up Staunton River Trail. One small parking area is reserved for cabin users. Do not block either road.

Trail Description

SR 662 to "The Sag"

0.0-4.3 SR 662 at junction of Staunton and Rapidan Rivers. Trail follows old road along southwest side of Staunton River.

2.0-2.3 Jones Mtn. Trail leads left, uphill, passing Bear Church Rock. It passes side trail to Jones Mtn. Cabin in 0.8mi.

2.4-1.9 McDaniel Hollow Trail leads southeast to join Jones Mtn. Trail in 0.5mi.

3.5-0.8 Turn left onto Fork Mtn. Fire Road and continue to climb.

4.3-0.0 Reach "The Sag". Here Staunton River Trail, Fork Mtn. Trail and upper end of Jones Mtn. Trail meet.

FORK MOUNTAIN TRAIL

1.4 miles (approx.)   yellow-blazed

This very lovely trail has its lower end on the Laurel Prong Trail 0.6mi. from Camp Hoover. The Fork Mtn. Trail crosses Laurel Prong in an area with much rosebay rhododendron, R. maximum, and hemlock. As it gradually climbs Fork Mtn. the rhododendron is replaced by mountain laurel. The route of the trail follows an old farm road as it switchbacks up the mountain to reach "The Sag" where is meets the Fork Mtn. Fire Road, Jones Mtn. Trail and Staunton River Trail.

JONES MOUNTAIN TRAIL

4.8 miles (approx.)   blue-blazed

The Jones Mountain Trail passes over Bear Church Rock which offers an excellent view of Staunton River Valley and eastward. This is also the access route to PATC Jones Mtn. Cabin. See "Accommodations and Facilities".

Access

The lower end of this trail is on the Staunton River Trail 2mi. from its junction with Graves Mill-Lower Rapidan Road, the extension of SR 662 within the Park. The trail's upper end is at "The Sag" on Fork Mtn.

Trail Description

Staunton River Trail to "The Sag"

0.0-4.8 Junction with Staunton River Trail 2mi. west of SR 662.

0.5-4.3 McDaniel Hollow Trail leads right 0.5mi. to Staunton River Trail.

0.7-4.1 Jones Mtn. Cabin Trail leads left(east) 0.2mi. to cabin.

1.2-3.6 Bear Church Rock; excellent view north and east.

1.3-3.5 Reach highest point. Trail now follows ridge of Jones Mtn.

2.2-2.6 Trail turns northwestward where ridge from Bear Church Rock and Bluff Mtn. join.

3.4-1.4 Slight sag between Jones Mtn. and Cat Knob.

4.0-0.8 Summit of Cat Knob. Trail swings sharply to northeast. (Cat Knob Trail leads left to end on Laurel Prong Trail in 0.5mi.)

4.8-0.0 Reach "The Sag" and junction with Fork Mtn. Fire Road and upper ends of Fork Mtn. Trail and Staunton River Trail.

McDANIEL HOLLOW TRAIL

0.5 mile   blue-blazed

This short trail has one end on the Jones Mtn. Trail and the other on the Staunton River Trail. It follows the route of an old mountain road across McDaniel Hollow and affords a short cut for hikers making a circuit using the Staunton River and Jones Mtn. Trails.

POWELL MOUNTAIN TRAIL

3.0 miles   blue-blazed

This trail leads from Skyline Drive at the Hazeltop Ridge Overlook, SDMP 54.4, to the summit of Powell Mtn. in 1.2mi. It descends westward to the Park boundary and on to SR 759.

A circuit hike of under 10mi. uses this trail, the upper stretch of SR 759, the Meadow School Trail and the *AT*.

WEST BRANCH NAKED CREEK TRAIL

1.8 miles   yellow-blazed
The southern end is in Harris Cove/Jollet, where SR
607 comes to an end at the Park boundary. The trail cuts
across a long westward-reaching side arm of the Park
then ends at the Park boundary.

MEADOW SCHOOL TRAIL

1.5 miles (approx.)   yellow-blazed
This former fire road, now maintained as a horse/foot
trail, is gated at Skyline Drive and at the Park boundary. Its upper end is on Skyline Drive, SDMP 56.8,
directly opposite the Slaughter Trail. From here it
descends the western slope of the Blue Ridge. Outside
the Park the Meadow School Trail becomes SR 759.

LEWIS MOUNTAIN EAST TRAIL

1.0 mile   blue-blazed
One end of this trail is on the *AT* at the southern edge
of the Lewis Mountain Campground. The first 1mi. over
the highest peak of the mountain can be followed with
no difficulty but beyond there it may be impossible.

CONWAY RIVER FIRE ROAD

1.4 miles within Park   yellow-blazed
This road, gated at the top and at the Park boundary,
leads from Skyline Drive, SDMP 55.1, to the edge of the
Park, about 1.4mi., then continues for another 2.8mi.
through land set aside as a Virginia Wildlife Area. From
here it continues as SR 615 down the valley to Graves
Mill on the Rapidan River.

BEARFENCE MOUNTAIN LOOPS

0.3 mile   blue-blazed
A very short but very scenic trail leads from the *AT* up over the rocky ridgetop of Bearfence Mtn., then back down to the *AT*. In addition, a very rough trail - more rock scramble than a real trail - continues north along the ridgetop for another 0.2mi., then swings downhill, crossing the *AT* and continuing on for another 0.1mi. to Bearfence Mtn. Parking Area on Skyline Drive, SDMP 56.4. The Park Service conducts nature hikes here during the summer.

A *circuit hike* can be made using the Bearfence Mtn. loops and the *AT*. The southernmost junction of the loop trail with the *AT* is 0.6mi. north of access road to Bearfence Mtn. Hut via the *AT*. The northernmost junction is 0.4mi. farther north along the *AT*.

SLAUGHTER TRAIL

4.0 miles   yellow-blazed
From the Drive the trail first follows the service road to Bearfence Mtn. Hut for 0.1mi., crossing the *AT* a few feet from the Drive. The first 1.5mi. is pleasant walking and should be particularly lovely in early June as there is much mountain laurel along the trail as it descends along the Devils Ditch.

A *long circuit hike* can be made by descending the Pocosin Fire Road and Pocosin Hollow Trail, continuing outside the Park to SR 667, then following up SR 667 and Slaughter Trail, finally following the *AT* south to Pocosin Fire Road; total distance about 13mi.

Access
The upper end of this former fire road is on Skyline Drive, SDMP 56.8, and is just across the Drive from the Meadow School Trail.

Its lower end is near the Conway River on SR 667 roughly 7.5mi. north of Va 230 (and an additional 3mi. from Stanardsville).

POCOSIN FIRE ROAD

2.5 miles   yellow-blazed

From Skyline Drive, SDMP 59.5, this road leads southeastward passing Pocosin Cabin, a locked structure available for use with advance reservations. See "Accommodations and Facilities". It becomes SR 637 outside the Park and is gated at both Skyline Drive and the Park boundary.

A *circuit hike* of 7.5mi. can be made using this road, Pocosin Horse Trail, South River Fire Road and the *AT*.

A *longer circuit* would also include the South River Falls Trail.

Trail Description

Skyline Drive to Park boundary

0.0-2.5 Skyline Drive, SDMP 59.5.

0.2-2.3 Intersection with *AT*. (Via *AT* it is 2.8mi. south to South River Fire Road and 0.5mi. farther to South River Falls Trail.)

0.3-2.2 Pocosin Cabin to right of road.

1.1-1.4 Pocosin Horse Trail leads right 1.3mi. to South River Fire Road. (Via fire road it is 1.2mi. to South River Falls Trail and 0.8mi. farther to *AT*.) Just beyond junction and to right of road are interesting ruins of former Upper Pocosin Mission.

1.3-1.2 To left, Pocosin Hollow Trail leads north.

2.5-0.0 Park boundary. Road continues outside Park and becomes SR 637 farther east.

POCOSIN TRAIL

1.3 miles   yellow-blazed

This trail connects the Pocosin Fire Road and the South River Fire Road and can be used with them for *a good circuit hike*. At the junction of the trail with the Pocosin Fire Road one can examine the ruins of the old Upper Pocosin Mission. On the trail about 0.1mi. from its end on the South River Fire Road a side road leads east passing the interesting, periwinkle-covered South River Cemetery in 0.1mi.

POCOSIN HOLLOW TRAIL

2.8 miles   blue-blazed

Pocosin Hollow, like Nicholson Hollow and "Hazel Country" farther north, was once well populated. When bushwhacking one sees remnants of old farm roads, rock walls and chestnut log fences, old homesites and at least one quite large cemetery with fieldstone grave markers.

The Pocosin Hollow Trail has its upper end on the Pocosin Fire Road, 1.3mi. from Skyline Drive, SDMP 59.5. The trail heads north, then swings eastward descending along the run. (Most of the old homesites are up the hollow from the spot where the trail reaches the run.) After the first crossing of the run, hollow narrows considerably, revealing numerous waterfalls and pools along the boulder-choked streambed. At Park boundary the trail ends on a private road (not posted) which leads 0.7mi. to SR 667. (This point is about 6mi. from Va 230 and 3mi. farther from Stanardsville.)

SOUTH RIVER FALLS TRAIL

1.9 miles   blue-blazed
This scenic trail leads from the South River Picnic
Area, SDMP 62.8, down into the deep wooded gorge of
South River. It continues as far as the foot of the very
lovely South River Falls. From top to bottom the trail
loses 1,000 ft. of elevation. The cascading falls are about
70 ft. high.

For a circuit hike, follow South River Falls Trail to base
of falls then backtrack 0.7mi. to point where South River
Falls Trail turns left off road. Continue straight ahead
here for another 0.4mi. to South River Fire Road. Follow
fire road uphill about 0.8mi. to *AT.* Turn left onto *AT*
and follow it 0.5mi. to South River Falls Trail.

Trail Description
Skyline Drive to base of falls
   0.0 Trailhead is on road that loops through South River
Picnic Area at point where road is farthest to east.
   0.1 Intersection with *AT.* (Via *AT* it is 3mi. south to
Swift Run Gap and 3.3mi. north to Pocosin Cabin.)
   1.0 Pass observation point near top of falls.
   1.2 Old road leads left to South River Fire Road. Stay
right.
   1.8 Reach South River about 500 ft. below falls. Go
upstream on foot-trail.
   1.9 Base of falls.

SOUTH RIVER FIRE ROAD

2.3 miles described   yellow-blazed
This road leads east from Skyline Drive, SDMP 62.7,
just north of South River Overlook. It eventually becomes SR 642 which becomes paved SR 637 about 5mi.
north of Stanardsville. The road is gated at the Drive
and at the Park boundary.

Several circuit hikes are made possible by this road in conjunction with South River Falls Trail, the *AT*, Pocosin Trail and the Pocosin Fire Road.

Trail Description
Skyline Drive to Pocosin Trail
  0.0 Skyline Drive, SDMP 62.7, just north of South River Overlook.
  0.3 Intersection with *AT*. (Via *AT* it is 0.5mi. south to South River Falls Trail and 2.8mi. north to Pocosin Cabin.)
  1.1 Junction with old road, branch of South River Falls Trail.
  1.5 Cross gate.
  2.0 Old road leads uphill on left.
  2.3 Junction with Pocosin Horse Trail. Fire road continues down into valley, becoming SR 642.

SADDLEBACK MOUNTAIN TRAIL

1.4 miles   blue-blazed
  This trail runs from the *AT* to the *AT* passing the South River Maintenance Bldg. (no camping). To reach the northern trailhead park in South River Picnic Area and follow South River Falls Trail 0.1mi. to the *AT*. Follow the *AT* south(right) for 0.5mi. The southern trailhead is 1.1mi. farther south along the *AT*. Total distance for *circuit hike* is 3.5mi. There are no hard climbs making this walk ideal for families with small children.

DRY RUN FALLS FIRE ROAD

2.8 miles   yellow-blazed
  This fire road, gated at Skyline Drive and near the Park boundary, leads from the Drive, SDMP 62.6, down the west side of the Blue Ridge. Near the lower end a

faint trace of an old road leads left to Dry Run, a few hundred feet upcreek from Dry Run Falls. These falls are well worth seeing after a period of wet weather.

The lower end of the fire road is on SR 625, 3.1mi. from SR 759 and 2.6mi. farther from Elkton on US 340. To right it is 1.1mi. to Hensley Church.

SHENANDOAH NATIONAL PARK
SOUTHERN DISTRICT

HIGHTOP HUT ROAD

0.7 miles   blue-blazed

This road leads from the Smith Roach Gap Fire Road, 0.8mi. from Skyline Drive, SDMP 68.6, and continues to Hightop Hut, crossing the AT 0.2mi. before reaching hut.

For a short circuit one can follow the *AT* from Smith Roach Gap to the summit of Hightop, then descend by backtracking as far as Hightop Hut, following Hightop Hut Road to Smith Roach Gap Fire Road and the fire road back to Smith Roach Gap.

SMITH ROACH GAP FIRE ROAD/HORSE TRAIL

1.0 miles within Park   yellow-blazed

This road leads southeastward from Skyline Drive at Smith Roach Gap, SDMP 68.6, to the Park boundary. The access road to Hightop Hut leads left from the fire road about 0.8mi. from the Drive. Beyond this point and also at the Park boundary, the road is blocked to vehicular traffic as well as at the Park boundary. A short way beyond the Park boundary the road divides. The left fork, SR 626, descends gradually, skirting the head of Whiteoak Spring Branch, then descending a ridge extending from Hightop Mtn. and finally coming into SR 630 very near SR 810. The right fork leads south over private land, following a long ridge toward Slaters Mountain, eventually coming into SR 631. Both road branches are of interest to hikers.

SIMMONS GAP FIRE ROAD

1.0 miles east of Skyline Drive   yellow-blazed
1.5 miles west of Skyline Drive,
    within Park   yellow-blazed
  This road leads from the western Park boundary in
Beldor Hollow as a continuation of SR 628, crosses
Skyline Drive at Simmons Gap, SDMP 73.2, then
descends to the eastern Park boundary where it becomes
SR 628 again. The road is gated at both boundaries and
on both sides of the Drive. The western portion is also
known as Beldor Road.

ROCKY MOUNT TRAIL

5.4 miles   blue-blazed
  In the Southern District of the Park there is a Rocky
Mount, a Rocky Mountain and a Rockytop. Rocky Mount
is the most northern of these. The Rocky Mount Trail
starts at Skyline Drive, SDMP 76.1, and is marked by a
concrete post. It leads along a northward-bearing side
ridge reaching the peak of Rocky Mount, 2,741 ft., in
3.4mi. From the peak it descends steeply to Gap Run.
  A circuit hike of 10mi. begins by descending the Rocky
Mount Trail, turning right, following the Gap Run Trail
to its upper end on the Rocky Mount Trail and returning
to start via Rocky Mount Trail.

Trail Description
Skyline Drive to Gap Run
  0.0-5.4 Skyline Drive, SDMP 76.1. Follow ridge which
extends northward. Many good views.
  2.2-3.2 Gap Run Trail leads down Gap Run to rejoin
Rocky Mount Trail at its lower end.
  3.4-2.0 Summit of Rocky Mount, 2,741 ft. From here
trail descends rather steeply. In about 1mi. trail turns
right off ridge, descends to creek and follows it down.

5.4-0.0 End of Rocky Mount Trail. Gap Run Trail leads right, rejoining Rocky Mount Trail in 2.3mi.

GAP RUN TRAIL

2.3 miles   blue-blazed
This trail starts from the Rocky Mount Trail 2.2mi. from Skyline Drive and leads down along Gap Run to rejoin the Rocky Mount Trail at its lower end in the gap. The Gap Run Trail is often used along with the Rocky Mount Trail for a *circuit hike.*

ONEMILE RUN TRAIL

4.5 miles   blue-blazed
This trail leads north from Skyline Drive and follows the narrow Twomile Ridge which separates Twomile Run and Onemile Run. In 1mi. it turns off the ridge and descends to Onemile Run, continuing down the run for nearly 2mi. It swings north, crosses over to Twomile Run and ends on a private road just north of the run.

Access
To reach start of this trail, park at Twomile Run Overlook, SDMP 76.2, and walk south along Drive for about 0.1mi. Trailhead is marked. (*AT* comes within 100 ft. of east side of Drive just south of here. Look for unmarked path.)

Trail Description
Skyline Drive to Park boundary
0.0 From Skyline Drive, SDMP 76.3, trail heads northwest along Twomile Ridge.
1.0 In sag, trail leaves ridge and descends westward.
1.4 Reach Onemile Run and descend along run.
2.9 Trail leaves Onemile Run and heads north.
3.7 Park boundary. Although faint blazes may continue

outside Park, some of land through which trail passes is now posted denying public access. It is advisable to turn back here. Posted closures must be respected.

IVY CREEK MAINTENANCE BUILDING ROAD

0.4 miles   not blazed

This short road, which runs from Skyline Drive, SDMP 79.4, to the Ivy Creek Maintenance Building (no camping) can be used by hikers as part of a *short circuit hike* which would include a climb up to Loft Mtn. ridge via the Deadening Nature Trail, SDMP 79.5, then the *AT* between the Nature Trail and Ivy Creek Maintenance Bldg., return to Skyline Drive via service road, and a 0.1mi. walk along the Drive for total distance of 2.1mi.

DEADENING NATURE TRAIL

1.3 mile circuit   not blazed

Attention: Dogs are not permitted on this trail.

This is a short but very interesting Park Service self-guiding trail. It involves a fairly steep climb of 0.6mi. from Skyline Drive to the *AT* on Loft Mtn., turns left on *AT* for 0.1mi., then makes an equally steep descent. The trail starts on the east side of the Drive, at the entrance to Loft Mtn. developed area, SDMP 79.5.

DOYLES RIVER TRAIL-JONES RUN TRAIL

4.7 miles   blue-blazed

These lovely trails, formerly know as Doyles River Trail for entire length, leave Skyline Drive and involve steep descents of 1,500 ft. along Doyles River and Jones Run, passing beautiful waterfalls and enormous trees growing near the creeks. They come together midway, at the junction of the two creeks. The graded trails were constructed by the CCC in 1936-37. PATC Doyles River Cabin, a locked structure for use of hikers with advance reservations. (See "Accommodations and Facilities".) is near the Doyles River Trail, 0.4mi. from Skyline Drive.

A *circuit hike* of 8mi. includes these two trails and a section of *AT*. For *a shorter circuit* of 6.5mi., descend along Jones Run, ascend along Doyles River past upper falls, then follow Browns Gap Fire Road to *AT*. Complete circuit by proceeding south along *AT* to Jones Run Parking Area.

Access

The Doyles River Trail has its upper end at Doyles River Cabin Parking Area on Skyline Drive, SDMP 81.1.

The Jones Run Trail has its upper end at the Jones Run Parking Area, SDMP 83.8. Both trails have their lower ends at the junction of Doyles River and Jones Run.

Trail Description

South (Jones Run) to North (Doyles River)

0.0-4.7 Jones Run Parking Area, Skyline Drive, 2,700 ft. Jones Run Trail crosses *AT* in 100 ft. then continues eastward, descending.

0.6-4.1 Trail crosses Jones Run.

1.5-3.2 Trail returns to run and follows south bank.

1.6-3.1 Base of sloping falls.

1.7-3.0 Top of upper falls. Short side trail affords good view of falls.

1.9-2.7 Top of lower falls.

2.5-2.2 Half-way point, junction of Jones Run and Doyles River. Jones Run Trail ends. Ascend on Doyles River Trail.

3.2-1.5 Top of lower falls of Doyles River, a two-step cascade between high rock cliffs.

3.5-1.2 Top of upper falls. This is a three-step cascade in lovely canyon.

3.8-0.9 Cross Browns Gap Fire Road. (Road leads west uphill 1.7mi. to *AT* at Browns Gap. To east it leads to Browns Cove.)

4.4-0.3 Pass spring on right of trail. Spur trail leads right 0.1mi. steeply up to Doyles River Cabin.

4.7-0.0 Cross *AT*. (To north it is 10mi. to Simmons Gap, to south 2.2mi. to Browns Gap and 3.4mi. to Jones Run Trail.) In 200 ft. reach Skyline Drive at Doyles River Cabin Parking Area, 2,800 ft.

BROWNS GAP FIRE ROAD

3.5 miles in Park   yellow blazed

This old road, the eastern extension of the Madison Run Road, leads from Skyline Drive at Browns Gap, SDMP 82.9, down the east slopes of the Blue Ridge to Browns Cove, crossing the Doyles River Trail and the Doyles River in 1.8mi. The old road continues beyond the Park boundary for another 1mi. where it becomes SR 629. The start of SR 629 is 0.8mi. above the highway bridge over the Doyles River and 1.2mi. from SR 810. One should park along or near SR 810 as SR 629 is only a one-track road above the bridge and there is almost no place to pull off road. (*Attention:* Lower access from SR 629 may be posted. Please respect "No Trespassing" signs on private land.)

The Browns Gap Road was used by Stonewall Jackson and his men during the Civil War. About 0.4mi. down from Skyline Drive, to the left of road, a short footpath leads to the grave of William H. Howard, Co. F, 44 Va. Inf., C.S.A. Farther down the road but above the Doyles River is a tulip tree of tremendous girth. The stretch of old road between the Doyles River Trail intersection and the Park boundary is quite lovely. There are many large trees including hemlock, and the road itself clings along the edge of a steep hillside with the river far below.

TRAILS IN THE BIG RUN AREA

Big Run and its tributaries comprise the largest watershed in the Park. This area is contained in the largest of the Park's wilderness areas and is separated from the one just south of it only by the Madison Run Fire Road. The ten trails included in the Big Run Area are for the most part rugged but scenic. There are many circuit hikes that can be made; some are quite long so are ideal for backpackers.

A serious fire, the worst Shenandoah National Park has experienced since the 1930s, burned over 4,300 acres of the watershed in May, 1986. It will undoubtedly be some time before the area regains much of its vegetation and wildlife. *Be alert* for deadened trees along the trail.

BIG RUN PORTAL TRAIL

4.4 miles   yellow-blazed

This is the valley route through the canyon of Big Run, which flows from south to north. The grade of the trail is very gentle all the way from the Park boundary to its upper end on the Big Run Loop Trail. It is a very pleasant walk. The cliffs, talus slopes and gorge at "The Portal" just below the Big Run Portal Trail's bridge over Big Run are spectacular.

A *circuit hike* can be made using this trail in conjunction with either the Rockytop Trail or the Rocky Mtn.-Brown Mtn. Trail.

Access

The upper end can be reached from the Big Run Loop Trail, following it "south" from Big Run Parking Overlook, SDMP 81.2, for 2.2mi. to its lowest elevation, or by following the Big Run Loop Trail north from its intersection with the *AT* 0.6mi. north of Browns Gap, SDMP 82.9. No access across private land at Park boundary.

Trail Description
Big Run Loop Tr. to Park boundary
   0.0-4.4 Intersection with Big Run Loop Trail.
   0.7-3.7 Ford side creek. While descending run, there are nine fords, seven of Big Run, the other two of side streams. When run is full fording may be difficult.
   0.9-3.5 Trail crosses to west bank, then recrosses again in 0.2mi. and again in 0.3mi.
   2.3-2.1 Patterson Ridge Trail enters from right. In 250 yds. cross Rocky Mtn. Run, immediately come to fork and continue straight ahead. (To right is Rocky Mtn. Run Trail which connects with Rocky Mtn.-Brown Mtn. Trail in 2.7mi.)
   2.7-1.7 After two more fords, reach deep pool. To right area is flat and shrubby where once there was a field.
   3.7-0.7 Cross bridge over Rocky Run. Rocky Mtn.-Brown Mtn. Trail comes in on right at far end of bridge.
   4.2-0.2 Junction with Rockytop Trail which enters from left. (To right one can bushwhack down to Big Run at "The Portal".)
   4.4-0.0 Gate at Park boundary.

ROCKY MOUNTAIN RUN TRAIL

2.7 miles   blue-blazed
   This trail runs from the Big Run Portal Trail up to Rocky Mtn.-Brown Mtn. Trail and is used with them for a circuit hike.

PATTERSON RIDGE TRAIL

3.1 miles   yellow-blazed
   This trail leads from Skyline Drive, SDMP 79.4, opposite the service road leading to Ivy Creek Maintenance Bldg., descending westward along Patterson Ridge. It comes into the Big Run Portal Trail 0.1mi. above the lower end of the Rocky Mtn. Run Trail and 1.5mi. above the lower end of the Rocky Mtn.-Brown Mtn. Trail. It can be used for circuit hikes.

BIG RUN LOOP TRAIL

4.2 miles   blue and yellow-blazed

This trail affords access to the upper end of Big Run. The Big Run Loop Trail together with the Big Run Portal Trail affords access to the lower ends of the Rockytop Trail and the Rocky Mtn.-Brown Mtn. Trail as well as the Rocky Mtn. Run Trail and the Patterson Ridge Trail. The Big Run Loop Trail, at its southern end, links the *AT* with the Rockytop Trail.

An excellent circuit hike of 5.8mi. can be made by using the *AT* in one direction and the Big Run Loop Trail in the other.

Access

The northern end of this trail is at the Big Run Parking Overlook on Skyline Drive, SDMP 81.2.

The southern end is on the *AT* 0.6mi. north of Browns Gap, SDMP 82.9.

Trail Description

North to South

0.0-4.2 Big Run Parking Overlook. Trail (blue-blazed here) descends steeply by switchbacks.

0.7-3.5 Trail follows crest of ridge between branches of Big Run, then swings left down into main hollow.

2.2-2.0 Junction with Big Run Portal Trail (yellow-blazed). Turn left. This 1.3mi. section is dual-blazed blue and yellow. Trail ascends steadily following above branch of Big Run.

3.0-1.2 Turn sharply right, away from ravine.

3.5-0.7 At trail junction in sag Big Run Loop Trail (blue-blazed) turns left. (Rockytop Trail goes right, blue-blazed, and leads along ridge 5.7mi. to Big Run Portal Trail. Madison Run Spur Trail, yellow-blazed, goes straight ahead to descend to Madison Run Road.)

4.2-0.0 Junction with *AT*. It is 0.3mi. north to Skyline Drive, SDMP 82.2, and 0.6mi. south to Browns Gap, SDMP 82.9.

MADISON RUN SPUR TRAIL

0.3 mile   yellow-blazed
   This short trail runs from the junction of the Rockytop
Trail with the Big Run Loop Trail down to Madison Fire
Road, entering it 0.8mi. west of Skyline Drive at Browns
Gap.

ROCKY MOUNTAIN-BROWN MOUNTAIN TRAIL

5.3 miles   blue-blazed
   Rocky Mtn. and Brown Mtn. comprise the ridge extending west from the main Blue Ridge along the north side
of Big Run. To the north of this ridge is the lower
Twomile Ridge with Rocky Mount in the background. To
the south is the high, imposing ridge along which the
Rockytop Trail runs. From Skyline Drive the trail leads
west along the ridge, first crossing the twin summits of
Rocky Mountain, then over Brown Mtn. before dropping
steeply to the Big Run Portal Trail.
   A circuit hike can be made by descending this trail and
ascending the Big Run Portal Trail, then turning left
onto the Big Run Loop Trail to Big Run Overlook. Walk
north a few feet, cross the Drive and descend to the *AT*.
Turn left(north) and follow *AT* to Ivy Creek Overlook.
Walk north along Drive remaining distance to Brown
Mtn. Overlook. Complete circuit is 18mi. *For a shorter
loop hike,* 11mi., descend on Rocky Mtn.-Brown Mtn.
Trail, ascend on Big Run Portal Trail, and turn left onto
Big Run Loop Trail to Big Run Overlook.
   A shorter circuit, 9.3mi. can be made by descending the
Rocky Mtn.-Brown Mtn. Trail, ascending the Big Run
Portal Trail for 1.3mi., then turning onto the Rocky Mtn.
Run Trail and climbing along this trail for 2.7mi. to its
junction with the Rocky Mtn.-Brown Mtn. Trail. Turn
right to return to Brown Mtn. Overlook.

Access
The upper end of this trail begins at the Brown Mtn. Parking Overlook on Skyline Drive, SDMP 76.9.
The lower access is from the Big Run Portal Trail.

Trail Description
Skyline Drive to Big Run Portal
0.0-5.3 Brown Mtn. Parking Overlook, Skyline Drive, SDMP 76.9.
0.7-4.6 Rocky Mtn. Run Trail leads left down to Big Run Portal Trail.
1.6-3.7 Reach crest of peak of Rocky Mtn., 2,800 ft. Striking views of Massanutten range. Footing is rough beyond this point.
2.2-3.1 Pass to right of second peak of Rocky Mtn., 2,864 ft. Along trail from here to summit of Brown Mtn. there is much turkeybeard, a grass-like member of the lily family blooming in early June. Turkeybeard is a close relative of western beargrass.
3.1-2.2 Summit of Brown Mtn., 2,560 ft. (The Brown Mtn. ridge, like Rockytop to the southwest, consists of a sandstone streaked with fossil wormholes.) Descend along a ridge crest with magnificent views of Rockytop, Shenandoah Valley and southern end of Massanutten Range. Descend steeply toward Big Run.
5.3-0.0 Junction with Big Run Portal Trail at east end of bridge over Big Run. "The Portal" of Big Run is a short distance down creek from here. Upstream it is 1.4mi. to lower end of Rocky Mtn. Run Trail and 3.7mi. to Big Run Loop Trail. To right on Big Run Portal Trail it is 0.5mi. to lower end of Rockytop Trail and 0.2mi. farther to gate at Park boundary. There is no access at this boundary. Posted closures must be respected.

ROCKYTOP TRAIL
5.7 miles   blue-blazed

This trail extends along the crest of the ridge which forms the sheer southwest wall of Big Run Canyon. It takes its name from its outstanding feature, Rockytop. (Hikers prefer to call the more northern peak, 2,856 ft., the "real" Rockytop, rather than the one marked on USGS maps.) Where the trail skirts the western face of this highest peak it offers a superb view of the peaks to the southwest and of the Shenandoah Valley. In addition, the rocks of this part of the ridge are quite fascinating. An examination of them will show they contain long, slender cylindrical markings, perhaps an eighth inch in diameter. It is believed that these are fossils of wormholes now 500 million years old! (See "Geology of Shenandoah National Park".) For wildflower enthusiasts the Rockytop Trail also offers an abundance of Turkey-beard, our eastern version of the west's beargrass. You'll find it in bloom in early June.

This trail has a rather narrow footway and is rough underfoot. However, its advantages far outweigh its disadvantages. It offers excellent views, and access to the Austin Mtn. Trail and the Lewis Peak Trail. *A circuit hike* can be made using the Rockytop Trail along with either of these trails.

Access

The upper end of the Rockytop Trail is on the Big Run Loop Trail. From Skyline Drive follow *AT* north from Browns Gap, SDMP 82.9, for 0.6mi., turn left onto the Big Run Loop Trail and follow it for 0.7mi. Rockytop-Big Run Loop Trail junction is marked by concrete post.

The lower end of the Rockytop Trail is on the Big Run Portal Trail, 0.2mi. east of gate at Park boundary.

Trail Description
Big Run Loop Trail to Big Run Portal Trail

0.0-5.7 From junction with Big Run Loop Trail, marked by concrete post, Rockytop Trail ascends.

0.4-5.3 Take right fork here. (Left fork is Austin Mtn. Trail.) Trail now skirts right side of ridge for 0.6mi. then swings to left side, crossing a talus slope with views of Austin and Lewis Mtns.

2.2-3.5 Junction with Lewis Peak Trail, marked by concrete post. Rockytop Trail is right fork.

3.0-2.7 Sag at base of hikers' "Rockytop", highest peak of ridge. Ascend along its left side.

3.5-2.2 Cross talus slope with outstanding views of Austin Mtn., Lewis Mtn. and Lewis Peak to southwest and Shenandoah Valley and Massanutten range farther north. Many of rocks here and on smaller rock slopes beyond are full of "wormhole" fossils giving rocks a striated appearance.

3.6-2.1 Bear right and ascend by switchbacks over crest of ridge bearing northwest. Descend along northbearing ridge. (Hangman Run splits main ridge here.)

5.7-0.0 Big Run Portal Trail, marked with concrete post. To left on Big Run Portal Trail it is 0.2mi. to Park boundary where it is gated. No access at this boundary.

AUSTIN MOUNTAIN TRAIL

3.2 miles   blue-blazed

This trail runs from Rockytop Trail across Austin Mtn. and down to Madison Run Fire Road. The Austin Mtn. Trail is the more southern of the parallel routes that lead westward from the high ridge of the Rockytop Trail to outlying conical peaks. The upper (eastern) end of the Austin Mtn. Trail begins on the Rockytop Trail near the upper end of the latter. It follows a side ridge between Deep Run and Madison Run to just short of the top of Austin Mtn. The trail slabs the south side of the mountain, then descends steeply to Madison Run Fire Road. Sections of this trail are rocky, steep and poorly graded. Heavy-duty foot gear is recommended.

A circuit hike of 9.5mi. can be made from Browns Gap using the *AT*, Big Run Loop Trail, Rockytop Trail, Austin Mtn. Trail and Madison Run Fire Road.

Access

To reach upper end of this trail follow *AT* for 0.6mi. north from Browns Gap, SDMP 82.9. Turn left onto Big Run Loop Trail and follow it for 0.7mi. to its junction with Rockytop Trail. Follow Rockytop Trail (straight ahead at junction) for 0.4mi. to Austin Mtn. Trail trailhead.

Lower end of Austin Mtn. Trail is on Madison Run Fire Road 4.4mi. from Skyline Drive at Browns Gap, SDMP 82.9. To reach trail from US 340 follow SR 663 from Grottoes (or SR 659 from just north of Grottoes) and continue on SR 663 beyond junction with SR 659 passing SR 708 on left and parking at junction of a second road, also entering from left. From here (about 2.5mi. from US 340) continue up SR 663 on foot another 0.2mi. to gate, then continue up fire road for 0.7mi. to trailhead marked by concrete post.

Trail Description

Rockytop Trail to Madison Run Road

0.0-3.2 Junction with Rockytop Trail.

2.1-1.1 Trail descends steeply across rock slopes and under cliffs.

2.7-0.5 Sharp turn in trail. Steep descent continues.

3.2-0.0 Madison Run Road. To left it is 4.4mi. to Skyline Drive at Browns Gap. To right it is 0.6mi. to lower end of Furnace Mtn. Trail and 0.1mi. farther to gate where road becomes SR 663.

LEWIS PEAK TRAIL

2.6 miles   blue-blazed

This trail is the more northern of the parallel routes leading west from the Rockytop Trail. It continues beyond Lewis Peak, descending to the Park boundary and on a short distance farther to a dirt road in the valley. Lewis Peak itself is reached by a 0.3mi. side trail. From the peak there is a panoramic view of the Shenandoah Valley and the Massanutten range to the northwest and west and the surrounding peaks of the Blue Ridge on the north, east and south.

Access

The upper end is reached via the Rockytop Trail. The trailhead is 2.3mi. from the Rockytop Trail-Big Run Loop Trail junction and 3.4mi. from the Rockytop Trail-Big Run Portal Trail junction.

The lower end of this trail is posted at the Park boundary. There is no access here.

Trail Description

Rockytop Trail to Shenandoah Valley

0.0-2.6 Junction with Rockytop Trail. Follow crest of ridge extending west between branches of Lewis Run.

0.7-1.9 Reach sag.

0.9-1.7 At junction, main trail goes left. (Right fork is 0.3mi. spur trail leading to summit of Lewis Peak, 2,760 ft. Panoramic view of Shenandoah Valley, Massanutten range and surrounding peaks.) Main trail descends toward west and northwest along ridge paralleling Upper Lewis Run.

2.4-0.2 Cross Upper Lewis Run. In 50 ft. turn right onto well-worn road, passing a cabin.

2.6-0.0 Come into private road where trail ends. Posted closures must be respected.

MADISON RUN FIRE ROAD

5.1 miles   yellow-blazed

This road, gated at each end, runs from Browns Gap down west side of Blue Ridge, becoming SR 663 outside

Park. It can be used with either Austin Mtn. Trail or Furnace Mtn. Trail for *a circuit hike.* The upper end of this road starts at Browns Gap, SDMP 82.9 (2,599 ft.). The lower end can be reached by following SR 663 east until it becomes fire road, about 2.8mi. from US 340 in Grottoes. Elevation at Park boundary is 1,360 ft. Madison Run Spur Trail, 0.3mi., connects fire road with Big Run Loop Trail.

STULL RUN FIRE ROAD

yellow-blazed in Park

Starting near the junction of SR 663 and SR 629 east of Grottoes, the Stull Run Fire Road leads south. In about 2mi. it runs out of the Park and continues as a private road. A bit farther south a short section of the road, where it follows Stull Run, lies within the Park but this portion is being abandoned and closed to vehicles. No trails connect with the fire road but it offers bushwhackers access to the wilderness area that includes Abbott Ridge and Hall Mountain.

CRIMORA FIRE ROAD

yellow-blazed in Park

The Crimora Fire Road runs from SR 614 near Paine Run south to SR 612 east of Crimora. Only 2 small segments of this road lie within the Park, but the southern stretch from SR 612 north serves as access to Riprap Trail.

TRAYFOOT MOUNTAIN TRAIL

5.4 miles   blue-blazed

This trail leads from Skyline Drive to the top of Trayfoot Mountain, 3,374 ft., then descends along a narrow ridge leading southwest and forming the divide between Paine Run and Stull Run. Along the route are some rock formations offering outstanding views. The trail's lower end on the Paine Run Trail is at an elevation of 1,440 ft.

A *circuit hike* of 10mi. would include the Paine Run Trail and the stretch of *AT* between Blackrock Gap and the Trayfoot Mtn. Trail.

The Trayfoot Mtn. Trail offers the shortest route (about 0.5mi.) to Blackrock from the Drive. There is parking space for several cars on the trail a few hundred feet from the Drive.

Access

Upper end is on Skyline Drive, SDMP 84.7, about 2mi. south of Browns Gap.

To reach the lower terminus, turn east from US 340 just south of Grottoes onto SR 661. Park at "turnaround" at end of state maintenance. Continue up private road on foot to Paine Run. Paine Run Trail, blocked to vehicles at its lower end by large rocks, is just north of the run. Follow it up the run for 0.3mi. to start of Trayfoot Mtn. Trail. Please help keep road and parking area free of trash. Access across private land at Park boundary is by goodwill of landowners. Posted closures must be respected.

Trail Description

Skyline Drive to Paine Run Trail

0.0-5.4 Trailhead on Skyline Drive, SDMP 84.7. Trail leads west, soon almost touching but not crossing *AT*. Trails run parallel for about 0.1mi. Then Trayfoot Mtn. Trail passes to south of Blackrock whereas *AT* circles through Blackrock area.

0.4-5.0 Intersection with *AT* just south of Blackrock.

0.5-4.9 Old road to left leads down southwestward ridge paralleling *AT*. (Road used as service road to Blackrock Hut.) Trayfoot Mtn. Trail continues straight ahead and enters largest wilderness area in Park.

0.9-4.5 Where trail reaches ridge crest, Blackrock Spur Trail leads right and back along ridge crest for 0.1mi. to *AT* at Blackrock.

1.4-4.0 Where trail turns sharply to left climbing Trayfoot Mtn., Furnace Mtn. Trail leads north (straight ahead) to Madison Run Fire Road in 3.4mi.

1.6-3.8 Just short of summit of Trayfoot Mtn. trail leaves old fire road and bears right, heading southwest along crest of long Trayfoot Mtn. ridge. Descend gradually, crossing numerous knobs. Views on both sides of trail.

4.8-0.6 Turn sharply left(east). Excellent view of Buzzard Rock peak across Paine Run.

5.1-0.3 Turn sharply right.

5.4-0.0 Junction with Paine Run Trail. (To left it leads to Skyline Drive in 3.4mi. To right leads to Park boundary and SR 614.)

BLACKROCK SPUR TRAIL

0.1 mile   blue-blazed

From the *AT* at Blackrock this trail follows the ridge crest toward Trayfoot Mtn., coming into the Trayfoot Mtn. Trail where the latter reaches the ridge crest. This is a very short but useful connector trail.

FURNACE MOUNTAIN TRAIL

3.4 miles   blue-blazed

This trail, which has its upper end on the Trayfoot Mtn. Trail, leads down the long northwest-bearing ridge of Trayfoot Mtn. toward the peak of Furnace Mtn. From a sag at the base of this peak the main trail descends along the west slopes of the mountain while a spur trail leads right 0.5mi. over the summit to an excellent viewpoint. Almost the entire trail lies within a wilderness area and is in one of the remoter sections of the

Park. The lower end of the trail is on the Madison Run
Fire Road.

Access

  To reach lower end of trail, follow SR 663 east from US
340 in Grottoes (or from US 340 north of Grottoes turn
onto SR 659 and follow it to SR 663) and continue up
road to Park boundary where road is gated. Continue up
road (Madison Run Fire Road) on foot 0.1mi. to concrete
post marking start of Furnace Mtn. Trail on south side.
It crosses Madison Run, then heads *downstream* for a
hundred feet or so before starting to climb.

  To reach upper end follow Trayfoot Mtn. Trail from
Drive, SDMP 84.7, for 1.4mi. to point where latter makes
sharp bend to left before ascending toward summit of
Trayfoot Mtn. Trailhead is right at the bend, to right of
road. One may also reach trailhead by following *AT*
1.1mi. from its crossing of Skyline Drive, SDMP 84.3, to
Blackrock, then Blackrock Spur Trail 0.1mi. to Trayfoot
Mtn. Trail. Continue out ridge for 0.6mi. to sharp bend
described above.

Trail Description

Trayfoot Mtn. Trail to Madison Run Fire Road

  0.0-3.4 Junction with Trayfoot Mtn. Trail. Follow ridge
leading north-northwest.

  0.7-2.7 Trail turns sharply right. Caution is needed
because former trails (one to Hall Mtn. and one that
leads out Abbott Ridge) may still be visible.

  1.8-1.6 Take left fork at junction. (To right leads 0.5mi.
to beyond summit of Furnace Mtn., ending on ledge with
excellent view over Madison Run.)

  3.4-0.0 Madison Run Fire Road. (To right is lower end
of Austin Mtn. Trail in 0.6mi. To left is Park boundary
where road is gated and becomes SR 663 leading to US
340.)

PAINE RUN TRAIL

3.7 miles   yellow-blazed
   This trail, formerly a fire road, leads west from Skyline
Drive at Blackrock Gap, SDMP 87.4. In about 1mi. it
passes near Blackrock Springs, site of a former hotel.
Below the springs the trail descends along Paine Run,
finally passing through a narrow gorge between the
southeast end of the Trayfoot Mtn. ridge and a sharp
peak, Buzzard Rock. About 0.3mi. before its lower end,
the Trayfoot Mtn. Trail branches to the north to Skyline
Drive in 5.4mi.
   A *circuit hike* of 9.5mi. can be made from Blackrock
Gap by following the *AT* north to Blackrock, the Blackrock Spur Trail to Trayfoot Mtn. Trail, west and south
on Trayfoot Mtn. Trail to Paine Run Trail and ascending
the latter back to Blackrock Gap.

RIPRAP TRAIL

4.5 miles   blue-blazed
   This is a very picturesque route. From its northern
trailhead on the *AT* it swings west and climbs along
Calvary Rocks with excellent views, then continues on to
Chimney Rocks with more views. It descends Cold Spring
Hollow and on to Riprap Hollow. This is one of the few
areas of the Park where one can find the Catawba
rhododendron (a very common shrub farther south), also
mountain laurel, fly poison, turkeybeard, starflower and
wild bleeding heart, all blooming in late May.
   A *circuit hike* of 9.5mi. makes use of the Wildcat Ridge
Trail, most of the Riprap Trail and the section of *AT*
between them.

Access
   To reach northern end of Riprap Trail, park at Riprap
Trail Parking Area, SDMP 90.0, take short spur trail to

AT and turn right. Follow *AT* north 0.4mi. to start of Riprap Trail.

To reach southern terminus, turn east from US 340 onto SR 612 at Crimora and drive about 1.7mi., nearly to end of state maintenance. Follow Crimora Fire Road left for 1mi. Large boulders at trailhead block trail to vehicles.

Trail Description
Skyline Drive to Crimora Fire Road

0.0-4.5 Junction with *AT* at a point on *AT* 0.4mi. north of short spur trail leading to Riprap Trail Parking Area, SDMP 90.0 (and 2.9mi. south of Blackrock Gap via *AT*).

1.0-3.5 Path leads right 15 ft. to cliffs, good overlook, near Calvary Rocks.

1.2-3.3 Trail turns sharply left. Spur trail leads right 75 ft. to edge of cliffs, Chimney Rock, with fine views north.

1.8-2.7 Turn sharply left from ridge down into Cold Spring Hollow.

2.8-1.7 Trail descends steeply through a rocky chasm. Route here is very spectacular.

3.0-1.5 Cross to east of stream.

3.1-1.4 Recross stream. Deep pool at base of sloping falls makes excellent swimming hole. Considerable amount of pink Catawba rhododendron near run.

3.6-0.9 Junction with Wildcat Ridge Trail which goes east(left), climbing 2.7mi. to Skyline Drive, SDMP, 92.1.

4.5-0.0 Crimora Fire Road at Park boundary.

WILDCAT RIDGE TRAIL

2.7 miles   blue-blazed

This lovely trail starts at the Wildcat Ridge Parking Area on Skyline Drive, SDMP 92.1. It crosses the *AT* in 0.1mi., continues west following Wildcat Ridge, then descends into Riprap Hollow to end on the Riprap Trail. It is used along with the Riprap Trail and the *AT* for an exceptionally beautiful *circuit hike* of about 9.5mi.

Trail Description
Skyline Drive to Riprap Trail

0.0-2.7 Junction with Skyline Drive at Wildcat Ridge Parking Area, SDMP 92.1.

0.1-2.6 Intersection with *AT*. (To right, via *AT*, it is 2.8mi. to Riprap Trail Parking Area and 3.1mi. to northern end of Riprap Trail. To left it is 0.3mi. to next *AT* crossing of Drive and 2.3mi. to Turk Gap.) From here trail descends gradually along Wildcat Ridge.

1.0-1.7 Cross over knob, 2,514 ft., then continue descent along ridge. Occasional good views south. In winter one may be able to glimpse Crimora Lake in Dorsey Hanger Hollow below the trail.

1.5-1.2 Come into sag.

1.8-0.9 In another sag trail turns sharply to right, leaves ridge crest and descends steeply.

2.1-0.6 Cross a run, then turn sharply left descending along it and recrossing it farther down.

2.6-0.1 To right, across run, short spur trail leads to a conspicuous cave at base of cliffs.

2.7-0.0 Junction with Riprap Trail. (To left it is 0.9mi. to Park boundary and Crimora Fire Road. To right it is 3.6mi. to *AT*.)

TURK GAP TRAIL

1.6 miles   yellow-blazed

This former fire road, blocked to vehicles, runs from Turk Gap on Skyline Drive, SDMP 94.1, down the west side of the Blue Ridge, reaching the Park boundary just above the muddy ponds of the old Crimora mine.

The Crimora Manganese Mine was one of the largest manganese mining operations in the Blue Ridge. The operations commenced in 1867 and extended, through various mining methods, periodically to 1947; operations resumed in 1949, but the mines are now closed. The manganese was mined out of clay deposits in a syncline of Cambrian quartzite. Crimora Lake, an artificial lake, furnished water power for mining operations. Visitors will find this area more interesting if they have read the detailed history of the mines, "The Crimora Manganese Mine" by Samuel V. Moore, in the October 1947 PATC bulletin.

TURK MOUNTAIN TRAIL

0.9 miles   blue-blazed
   This short trail is highly recommended. It starts from the *AT* 0.2mi. south of Turk Gap and heads west, following a ridge. In about 0.4mi., where the Sawmill Ridge goes off to left, the Turk Mtn. Trail continues straight ahead and begins to climb Turk Mtn., 2,981 ft. The view from the summit is outstanding. As on several of the other peaks of the Park which are west of the main Blue Ridge crest, the rock is a type of sandstone full of fossil wormholes, giving it a distinctive striated appearance. In early June turkeybeard, a member of the lily family, can be found blooming here.

MOORMANS RIVER FIRE ROAD

9.5 miles   yellow-blazed
   This was the original route of the Appalachian Trail between Blackrock Gap and Jarman Gap. From Blackrock Gap the road leads southeast, then south, following down the North Fork of the Moormans River to SR 614. From here the fire road fords the North Fork a short distance above the Charlottesville Reservoir. It then climbs southwestward to Jarman Gap following up the South Fork of the Moormans River. The fire road is gated at both ends and at the Park boundaries.
   A long circuit hike can be made by following the fire road in one direction and the *AT* in the other. *For shorter circuits* a portion of the fire road can be used

along with the Turk Branch Trail and *AT*. From Black-rock Gap a circuit using the fire road, Turk Branch Trail and the *AT* is about 18mi.; from Jarman Gap a circuit using the southern portion of the fire road, the Turk Gap Trail and the *AT* is only 8mi. in length.

Access

The northern end of the fire road is on Skyline Drive, SDMP 87.4, at Blackrock Gap. The southern end is at Jarman Gap, SDMP 96.7.

To reach the fire road from the valley follow SR 810 from Crozet to White Hall (about 4.5mi.). Follow SR 614 west 5.8mi. to its end just beyond Charlottesville Reservoir. Junction with fire road is here.

Trail Description

Blackrock Gap to Jarman Gap

0.0-9.5 From Skyline Drive at Blackrock Gap, SDMP 87.4 (2,321 ft.), road leads southeast, immediately crossing *AT*.

1.4-8.1 Take right fork and cross stream. (Old road to left leads up valley through overgrown fields to Via Gap.) Continue downstream, heading almost due south.

1.6-7.9 To left an old road leads uphill to Pasture Fence Mtn.

3.7-5.8 To right a side trail leads 0.1mi. up Big Branch to series of cascades, highest of which has a free fall of about 50 ft.

5.5-4.0 Cross SR 614 at end of that road. In 0.1mi. ford North Fork of Moormans River. The ford, elevation 1,000 ft., is a few hundred feet below the former highway bridge, the foundations of which are still visible, and a few hundred feet upriver from Charlottesville Reservoir. Fire road continues south to South Fork of Moormans River, then climbs along it, crossing stream several times.

7.6-1.9 Turk Branch Trail leads right up mountain 2.1mi. to Skyline Drive, joining it at Turk Gap, SDMP 94.1.

9.3-0.2 Intersection with *AT* 0.2mi. north of Bucks Elbow Mtn. Fire Road.

9.5-0.0 Junction with Skyline Drive and Bucks Elbow Mtn. Fire Road at Jarman Gap, SDMP 96.7 (2,173 ft.)

TURK BRANCH TRAIL

2.1 miles   yellow-blazed

This is a pretty trail and not a difficult one to follow. From Skyline Drive and *AT* at Turk Gap, SDMP 94.1 (2,600 ft.), the trail follows an old road down the east side of the Blue Ridge. Its lower end is on the Moormans River Fire Road, 1,440 ft., at a point on fire road 1.9mi. north of Jarman Gap.

A *circuit hike* of 7.5mi. can be made by descending the Turk Branch Trail to Moormans River Fire Road, following up the fire road (south) to the *AT* just below Jarman Gap, and then taking the *AT* north to Turk Gap. (Starting the circuit at Jarman Gap the hike would be 0.3mi. longer as one would first have to hike down the Moormans River Fire Road to its intersection with the *AT*.) A *longer circuit*, 18mi., can be made by following the fire road north to Blackrock Gap and returning to Turk Gap via the *AT*.

BUCKS ELBOW MOUNTAIN FIRE ROAD

0.6 mile in Park   not blazed

From Skyline Drive and its junction with the Moormans River Fire Road at Jarman Gap, SDMP 96.7, the Bucks Elbow Mtn. Fire Road leads east, uphill, winding its way up to the top of Bucks Elbow Mtn. (outside Park) to an FAA installation. Road is gated near Skyline Drive. It intersects the *AT* 0.1mi. from the Drive.

GASLINE ROAD

2.0 miles   yellow-blazed

From Skyline Drive, SDMP 96.2, the Gasline Road leads down the west slopes of the Blue Ridge to the Park boundary. It was constructed to give access to the gas pipeline and is of little interest to hikers. Like the fire roads, it is gated at Skyline Drive.

ACCOMMODATIONS AND FACILITIES

Picnic Shelters

Of the open-faced shelters in the Shenandoah Park, five are for day use only, Old Rag Shelter and the four Byrds Nests. Water is available during the warmer months at all but Byrds Nest #1, situated on a shoulder of Old Rag Mountain and Byrds Nest #2 on the summit of Hawksbill Mtn. Byrds #3 is on the *AT* between Marys Rock and Pinnacle Overlook; Byrds Nest #4 is near the *AT* (0.3mi.) a short distance north of Beahms Gap. Shelters are provided with a picnic table and fire place.

Huts

Huts are the open-faced shelters in the Park which have been designated for camping by long distance Appalachian Trail backpackers. Park camping permits are required here as for other backcountry camping. There are seven huts in the park - Gravel Springs and Pass Mtn. Huts in the Northern District, Rock Spring and Bearfence Mtn. Huts in the Central District and Hightop, Pinefield and Blackrock Huts in the Southern District. During the summer The Potomac Appalachian Trail Club (PATC) employs knowledgeable individuals to serve as hutkeepers and *AT* monitors to prevent overuse and misuse of the huts and to educate hikers on trail etiquette. Users of these huts are asked to pay a small fee ($1.00 in 1991) to help cover the expenses of the hut managers. One night's stay is permitted per hut, except in an emergency.

In addition to the Park huts, a covered shelter is available for backpackers at the Tom Floyd Wayside just north of the Park. A new shelter for hikers was constructed in 1984 just south of the Park on Calf Mtn. It is on land recently purchased by the Park Service for the Trail corridor. These two facilities are not to be confused with the day-use shelters and huts within the Park.

AT distances between huts and shelters, listed north to south: (Parentheses indicate distance off trail.)

From US 522 to Tom Floyd Wayside	3.1
Tom Floyd Wayside to Gravel Springs Hut (0.2mi.)	9.9
Gravel Springs Hut (0.2mi.) to Pass Mtn. Hut (0.2mi.)	13.3
Pass Mtn. Hut (0.2mi.) to Rock Spring Hut (0.2mi.)	15.0
Rock Spring Hut (0.2mi.) to Bearfence Hut (0.2mi.)	11.4
Bearfence Hut (0.2mi.) to Hightop Hut (0.1mi.)	12.5
Hightop Hut (0.1mi.) to Pinefield Hut (0.1mi.)	8.3
Pinefield Hut (0.1mi.) to Blackrock Hut (0.2m)	13.1
Blackrock Hut (0.2mi.) to Calf Mtn. Shelter (0.3mi.)	13.2
Calf Mtn. Shelter (0.3mi.) to US 250 at Rockfish Gap	6.9

Cabins

The PATC operates six locked cabins in the SNP. These cabins are the property of the National Park Service and are operated by the PATC under permit. Each cabin is attractively located in the center of good hiking country. Four of them are near both the AT and Skyline Drive.

The cabins are designed for either overnight or longer use and make excellent bases for stays of several days while exploring the surrounding country.

A moderate fee is charged for use of the cabins. Details are available from the Potomac Appalachian Trail Club

Headquarters, 118 Park St., S. E., Vienna, Virginia 22180, open from 7pm to 10pm Monday through Friday, closed Saturday, Sunday and holidays. Cabin reservations must be made in advance; keys are obtained at PATC Headquarters. The cabins are available both to members and to responsible non-members. Reservations may be made not more than three weeks in advance. (Members may make a reservation one month in advance once per year.) Non-members making a reservation for the first time must be properly identified and will be required to fill out a responsibility statement.

The cabins are equipped with all necessary items except food, personal bedding, lights and firewood. There is an inside wood stove and/or fireplace for cooking, plus all necessary pots, pans, plates, cutlery, cups, saucers, glasses, etc. Also provided are bunks, mattresses and blankets (one per occupant) up to stated capacity of the cabin. It is advisable to bring one's own sleeping bag, lanterns and fuel. Broom, ax, saw, first-aid kit and other items necessary for good housekeeping are provided.

The number of occupants may not exceed the stated capacity of the cabin. The maximum stay by one party at one or a succession of cabins is 10 days, including only one weekend. Because of the popularity of the cabins, only one reservation may be in process at one time. The cabin reservation period runs from 4pm of the first date to 4pm of the day succeeding the last date. If a reservation is to be canceled it must be canceled for the entire period and a new application filed if reservation for a shorter period is desired.

Range View is located in the Northern District; Corbin, Rock Spring, Pocosin and Jones Mtn. Cabins are in the Central District; Doyles River Cabin is in the Southern District. All are shown, along with their trail and road approaches, on the appropriate PATC maps.

For a small fee a book may be purchased from PATC Headquarters giving a detailed description and a photo of each cabin.

Description of Cabins

Range View Cabin

This is a one-room stone cabin built in 1933 by members of the PATC. It is equipped with four double-decked, single-width bunks, an inside cooking stove and an outside fireplace under eaves of the cabin. The cabin looks out across an area cleared of trees and tall brush toward farms in the valley below. Campers from Mathews Arm Campground and hikers along the *AT* often visit the cabin area, especially on weekends, so it is somewhat lacking in privacy.

Hike-in distance from Skyline Drive, SDMP 21.9, is 0.9mi.

Distance from the *AT* is 0.1mi.

Corbin Cabin

This is an old mountaineer's cabin, restored by PATC volunteers in the early 1950's. (See Alvin Peterson's article in July-September 1954 PATC Bulletin.) It is a solidly built, two story cabin with sleeping quarters on both floors, accommodating 12 persons. There is a fireplace in the living room, wood stove in the kitchen and an outside fireplace. It is included in the National Register of Historic Places.

The cabin is located in Nicholson (Free State) Hollow beside the Hughes River, a pleasant mountain stream. Water is obtained from this stream.

Hike-in distance from Skyline Drive, SDMP 37.8, is 1.4mi.; from SDMP 38.6 it is 1.9mi.; from the eastern side in the Piedmont it is 4mi.

Distance from the *AT* is 1.5mi.

Rock Spring Cabin

This cabin, built of squared logs, looks out across the valley to the Massanutten range. The view from the cabin is excellent during the day but at night the twinkling lights of Stanley and Luray add a magical touch to the landscape. The cabin is equipped with enough bunks to sleep 12 persons, an inside wood stove and outside fireplace. It can be kept cozily warm in winter. There is a spring 50 yds. north of the cabin.

Warning: There is an extremely sharp drop-off in front of the cabin which can be dangerous for small children.

Hike-in distance from Skyline Drive, SDMP 48.1, is 0.8mi.

Distance from the *AT* is 0.2mi.

Jones Mountain Cabin

This cabin was originally the home of mountaineer moonshiner Harvey Nicholson. It was unoccupied from the 1930s when the SNP was established until recently and was falling into ruins. Members of PATC, with the Park Service Administration's permission, restored the cabin, making every effort to retain those parts of the original structure that were still serviceable and to replace damaged material with handcrafted replacements. In 1975 the restored cabin, which now presents a fine example of early cabin workmanship, became available for campers. For some history of this area read *Lost Trails and Forgotten People* by Tom Floyd (a PATC publication). A person may not reserve the Jones Mountain Cabin, however, unless he has previously reserved and used cabins elsewhere and cared for them properly.

The cabin is equipped with mattresses to sleep 10, a wood stove for heating, and both inside and outside fireplaces. There is a spring about 75 ft. from the cabin. There is a large front porch high above the ground. *Warning*: While double railings have been built along the edges of the front porch and inside the cabin along the edge of the open-ended loft used for sleeping quarters, *this cabin is not recommended for families with small children*. The long hike in may be difficult for families.

Hike-in distance from Skyline Drive is 5mi.; from the Piedmont it is 3mi.

Distance from *AT* is 5.4 to 5.9mi.

Pocosin Cabin

This cabin is a one-room squared log structure located in a pleasant area with a good view toward the Piedmont. There are a number of excellent hiking possibilities in the area for both the experienced and novice hiker. The cabin is furnished with three double-deck double-width bunks with foam mattress. A wood stove is provided for cooking and heating inside and there is also a fireplace outside under the cabin eaves. This cabin is recommended for families with small children as there are no hazards nearby.

Hike-in distance from Skyline Drive is 0.2mi.

Distance from the *AT* is 0.1mi.

Doyles River Cabin

This cabin, constructed of squared logs, sits above a cliff near the head of the Doyles River. It overlooks a picturesque valley with views of Cedar Mtn. and Via Gap. Sunsets are often spectacular as viewed from the cabin. There are bunks enough to sleep 12 persons, an inside wood stove and an outside fireplace. The spring is 350 ft. downhill from the cabin. *Warning:* Because of the cliff face in front of the cabin, it is *not recommended for families with small children.*

Hike-in distance from Skyline Drive, SDMP 81.1, is 0.4mi.

Distance from the *AT* is 0.3mi.

OTHER FACILITIES

Two **visitor centers** provide publications, displays, audio-visual programs, and ranger-naturalists to answer questions. Dickey Ridge Visitor Center is located on Skyline Driver at SDMP 4.6 and Byrd Visitor Center at SDMP 51.0 (Big Meadows). The latter is close to the Appalachian Trail.

The **waysides, lodges and restaurants** at Elkwallow, Big Meadows, Skyland and Lewis Mtn. and Loft Mtn. are operated by a concessioner, ARA Virginia Sky-line Co., Inc. Reservations for the lodges may be made by writing this firm at P.O. Box 191, Luray, VA 22835. Phone 1-800-999-4714.

Campgrounds are located at Mathews Arm (closed 1991 season), Big Meadows, Lewis Mountain and Loft Mountain. See adjoining chart. In summer and fall campsites at Big Meadows may be reserved through Ticketron or by calling 1-800-452-1111 and using a Visa or MasterCard.

ACCOMMODATIONS IN SHENANDOAH NATIONAL PARK
(excluding shelters, huts, and cabins)

Facility	Northern District	Central District	Southern District
Picnic Areas	Dickey Ridge Elkwallow	Pinnacle Big Meadows Lewis Mountain South River	Loft Mountain Dundo (winter only)
Campgrounds	Mathews Arm (summer)	Big Meadows (closed Jan. & Feb.) Lewis Mountain (summer)	Loft Mountain Dundo (group camping, summer)
Waysides[1]	Elkwallow (mid-May—Oct. 31) Dickey Ridge (May thru Nov.)	Big Meadows (closed Jan. & Feb.)	Loft Mountain (April thru Oct.)
Visitor Centers	—	Big Meadows (open all year)	—
Lodges (hotel-cottage)		Skyland (400) (April thru Oct.) Big Meadows (250) (mid-May thru Oct.) Lewis Mountain (24) (mid-May thru Oct.)	—
Restaurants[2]	—	Panorama (April thru early Nov.)	

[1] Provide refreshments and limited food supplies: Loft Mountain and Lewis Mountain have campers stores.
[2] In addition to seasonal food facilities at waysides and lodges. Located between Northern and Central Districts.

SUMMARY OF CABIN INFORMATION

Cabin	Capacity	Recommended for families with small children	Driving distance from D.C. to parking area (mi.)	Hike-in distance from parking area (mi.)	Hike-in distance from AT (mi.)	SDMP at or near parking area	PATC map
Range View	8	Yes	93	0.8	0.1	21.9	9
Corbin	12	No	93	1.4	1.5	37.9	10
Rock Spring	12	No	103	0.8	0.2	48.1	10
Jones Mtn.	10	No	106	3.0	-	-	10
Pocosin	12	Yes	114	0.2	0.1	59.5	10
Doyles River	12	No	129	0.3	0.3	81.1	11

List of Photos

INDEX
of Place Names
(Detailed trail description is indicated by boldface print.)

NOTES